T H White

Books by or about Sylvia Townsend Warner published by
Handheld Press

Kingdoms of Elfin, by Sylvia Townsend Warner

Of Cats and Elfins. Short Tales and Fantasies, by Sylvia Townsend Warner

*The Akeing Heart: Letters between Sylvia Townsend Warner,
   Valentine Ackland and Elizabeth Wade White*, by Peter Haring Judd

Valentine Ackland: A Transgressive Life, by Frances Bingham

T H White

A Biography

by Sylvia Townsend Warner

with an Introduction by Gill Davies

Handheld Press

Handheld Classic 31

Contents

Note on this edition

The text for this edition was non-destructively scanned from the first edition and proofread. In a few instances a line of explanation has been added in square brackets to make the authorship of letters clearer. The Italian version of White's lobster poem has not been included. The index has been expanded slightly from the original.

Warner's footnotes have been retained in the main text, as they indicate what she felt needed to be explained to her original readers; her single word remarks have been added to the main text in square brackets. Additional explanatory notes are given at the end of the book. Since *The Book of Merlyn* had not yet been published when Warner was writing (she would write the Preface to it a decade later), her styling of its title in Roman within inverted commas as an unpublished MS has been retained, while references to the book in the Davies Introduction style the title in italics, as a published work.

The publishers are grateful to Gloria Glover of David Higham Associates for permission to reproduce the quotations from White's works and letters that were selected by Sylvia Townsend Warner in her biography. Thanks are also due to Janet Montefiore and Luke Seaber for supplying missing references.

Gill Davies taught English Literature and was an academic manager in higher education. Now retired, her most recent post was at Edge Hill University in north-west England. She has written on nineteenth- and twentieth-century literature and edited and contributed to *Critical Essays on Sylvia Townsend Warner* (2006) and *Critical Essays on T H White* (2008), both published by The Edwin Mellen Press.

Introduction

BY GILL DAVIES

In 1964, at the age of seventy, Sylvia Townsend Warner was asked to write the biography of T H White who had recently died at the height of his literary fame. They had never met but their careers had developed in parallel and White had admired her work. An earlier candidate to write the biography had been proposed by White's agent but had been considered unsuitable by White's publisher and friends. Warner's name had been put forward by the artist John Verney, who had known White for some time. Over the winter of 1962, when White had been staying in Florence where Verney and his wife were then living, the two men had discussed

> most aspects of contemporary writing ... He was generous in his admiration of other authors ... inveighing against the neglect of older writers or of certain of their works which, he thought, had not been given their due ... Of these the name that recurred by far the most frequently was that of Sylvia Townsend Warner, all of whose books he much admired and whose *Mr Fortune's Maggot* he called the greatest and tenderest novel of this half-century. When, after his death, the question arose of a biographer, I suggested to his publisher the person I knew he would have wished, above all others, to write his life. (8)

After completing the biography Warner said that she 'did partly undertake it as a dare; seventy is rather an advanced age to begin an entirely different technique.' And she relished the challenge 'because I wanted to do something that would take a long time and involve some sort of research' (Maxwell 1982, 226). What resulted, according to the *New York Times*, was 'a small masterpiece which may well be read long after the writings of its subject have been forgotten' (Allen 1968). The *Times Literary Supplement* said 'by the highest standards this is a fine biography' (Anon 1967). Robert Nye in the *Guardian* called it 'a splendidly intuitive appreciation' (Nye 1967). The *New Yorker* said Warner was 'White's perfect biographer ... the portrait she draws ...

is not only unmistakeably right, but one of the finest portraits of an artist in many years' (Anon 1968). A later critic has called it 'one of the classics of English biography, written by a major artist of narrative with a lifetime of experience and achievement behind her ... yet still at the height of her powers.' (Montefiore 2002, 143)

T H White, known to his friends (and Warner) as 'Tim', was a challenging subject. The *Sunday Times* said 'From the contradictions in his nature came Arthur, Merlyn, Mordred, Lancelot, and King Pellinore' (Toomey 1967). His publisher had no doubt wanted to capitalise on White's recent successes, and his friends were keen that his life and talents should be more widely known. However, his literary career had been uneven and his personal life contained secrets. When he died aged fifty seven he had published more than twenty books of fiction, non-fiction and poetry over a period of thirty years. But he was best known, then and now, for the novels which he collected together as *The Once and Future King*, a re-telling of the Arthurian legends.

The biography opens as White experienced his first major success (literary and financial) when his novel *The Sword in the Stone* was chosen for the American Book of the Month Club in 1938: 'He would have dollars, he would have readers' (10). Despite this success, the progress of his career continued to be uneven and his reputation mixed. This unevenness was just one of the challenges that Warner faced. White was many – often contradictory – things; throughout his life he tried out roles and relationships, as well as literary genres. He was briefly a school-master; he experimented with the life of a hunting, shooting and fishing country gentleman; he learned to fly an aeroplane; for a while, he lived a hermit-like existence trying to train a hawk in the medieval way; and despite being conservative in his politics, his opposition to the Second World War led to his move from England to Ireland for its duration. He was at different times a serious scholar (he translated a medieval Latin bestiary, *The Book of Beasts*, 1954); a children's writer (including *The Sword in the Stone*, which has never gone out of print); the author of a classic of nature writing (*The Goshawk*, 1951); a historical novelist, a satirist and an accomplished detective story/thriller writer. His best-known work, *The Once and Future King,* re-imagined Malory and became the source of his fame and fortune as the stage musical and film, *Camelot*. He was a diverse writer whose output included poetry, short stories, novels and non-fiction. Much of this is now unread, with the exception of the Arthurian books and *The Goshawk*. Faced with such a various output, Warner wrote that 'White was a single talent inattentively employed; I could not pretend that he had a purpose or a star to steer by' (Maxwell 1982, 230). Nevertheless, one of the great merits of Warner's biography is that she recognised White's complexity and produced a compelling portrait of the man who was as odd as his writing.

The project came at a good time for Warner. She had to immerse herself in a new kind of writing and research at a point in her own career when she was fearful that her creativity was flagging. There were already some connections. In 1963 White had sent her a book of his poems, inscribed 'from an unknown worshipper', with no address except an Alderney postmark. Warner liked them, 'some of them I liked very much: partly no doubt because they are of my own way of writing' (Warner 1994, 284). A few months later she read that White had died and wrote in her diary 'T H White is dead, alas! – a friend I never managed to have' (Warner 1994, 290). White's closest male friend had probably been David Garnett, with whom Warner had been friends and a regular correspondent since 1922. When White's publisher wrote to her to propose that she should write White's life she replied 'I very much incline to the project. I would not hesitate at all if it were not for the thought that David Garnett would be a better choice' (Garnett ed. 1994, 72).

In accepting the commission Warner finally *discovered* White – the man as well as the writer – and found him fascinating. She went to Alderney to look at his house and see what material might be available, and felt his vivid presence:

> His suitcases were at the foot of the stairs, as though he had just come back. The grander furniture had gone to the sale room, but the part of the house he mainly inhabited he still inhabited. His clothes were on hangers. His sewing-basket with an unfinished hawk-hood; his litter of fishing-flies, his books, his *awful* ornaments presented by his hoi polloi friends, his vulgar

toys bought at the Cherbourg Fairs, his neat rows of books about flagellation – everything was there, defenceless as a corpse. And so was he; morose, suspicious, intensely watchful and determined to despair. I have never felt such an *imminent* haunt. (Maxwell 1982, 226)

Soon afterwards, Michael Howard, White's publisher, arrived at Warner's house in Dorset with a car full of books, diaries, and letters. She would immerse herself for the next three years in White's own account of himself, reading material much of which no-one else had ever seen. Indeed, some of it was so private, and potentially scandalous, that it was two years before she saw it. He had bequeathed some of his diaries to Michael Howard with strict instructions that they should remain in his possession. They found a way round this obstacle by arranging for Warner to consult them in the library of the Dorset County Museum, before they were returned. It was a disturbing experience, like being 'at home in hell … White's raving, despairing soliloquy whispering on and on in my ear' (Maxwell 1982, 227).

It was not all pain. She wrote to William Maxwell, her American friend and editor at the *New Yorker,* about the sheer pleasure of being 'fastened on' by White:

> I get up at 6.30 and work till 8.30, drinking black coffee and from time to time eating a little more bread & honey; and it is delightful. Not a bell, not a bore, not a telephone; and a sense of virtue that keeps me in a good temper all day. There is about five hundred weight of him disposed about the house. It is like trying to write the biography of a large and animated octopus. (Maxwell 1982, 213)

Throughout the biography, as well as in her letters and other comments, Warner has a strong sense of the multitudes of White. In 1974 she was interviewed by a young scholar, François Gallix, who was doing research on White. She described meeting people who knew him or had made his acquaintance and 'every single person who talked to me about White had known a different White. I had a thousand incompatible Whites to put together.' She concluded that 'the real White was a kind of mirror – he mirrored the people he was talking to. He fell in with them' (Gallix 2017, 58). She thought that this may have applied to her too. After three years of being immersed in his life and writing she said that sometimes 'I feel I know him very well indeed, but then I remember all I know is my own White, I am just another of the people who have their own White ... I never felt that I had come to the end of him' (Gallix 2017, 68).

Because White had few close friends there was no pre-existing image for Warner to draw on and she was very reliant on the autobiographical materials, White's own account of himself. And he speaks in this biography to an extraordinary extent and with great effect. However, though much of Warner's research concentrated on documentary materials, she also tried to meet as many people as possible who knew him. David Garnett and she were working on White at the same time (Garnett was editing his own edition of letters to and from White, eventually published in 1968). His son Richard Garnett notes that in his later edition of his father and Warner's letters to each other he had omitted a 'mass of letters about the obscurer details of T H White's life' (Garnett 1994, vii–viii). Thus the elder Garnett's views, and the material he was turning up at the same time, would have contributed significantly to Warner's research for the biography.

Warner corresponded with White's friends, acquaintances, former colleagues and pupils from Stowe school, university friends and tutors, and talked with Mrs Herivel the charwoman for his Alderney house about his last days there. She also went to many of the places where he had lived. When she visited Belmullet in Ireland in 1965 she found that White was vividly present in the reminiscences of people he met there. Their anecdotes were still fresh, and she brought them to life by astute summary and quotation. She enjoyed the new experiences and the odd encounters that working on the biography produced. It was a source of delight and frustration:

> I am getting involved in the queerest correspondences. There is a correspondence still *in petto* with a gentleman 'in the Persian Gulf' as Siegfried Sassoon expresses it, whose address has to be got from a nun in a convent in Worcestershire. And beside me is a letter from the man who stage-managed *Camelot* ... But ... there are the most agonising gaps and deficits. White dementedly left

a quantity of his notebooks and files in a coal shed in bleakest Yorkshire; and the celebrated winter of 47 melted through the roof. Among the lost was a long run of letters from a man called L J Potts, who taught him at Cambridge. Potts is dead; the few of his letters to White that have survived show that he was one of the best English letter-writers. Potts, I discovered from one of these, knew, loved, had been taught by my father. I am inconsolable. (Maxwell 1982, 213)

The biographer and her subject came from the same sector of the English ruling class, but his background was imperial and military, hers educated and humane. Within that social stratum is hard to imagine two more different people than Sylvia Townsend Warner and T H White. She was a woman confident in her social and literary identity, at ease with a wide range of friends and cultural interests. Her politics were radical, she was a life-long fighter against injustice and inequality. White's political instincts were right-wing and individualistic. He aspired at various times to be part of the English gentry but he never fitted in. It was perhaps his position as an outsider that called up Warner's sympathy, her 'heart was with the hunted, always' (Maxwell 1982, vii). His deracinated upbringing explained much for her, as did the active cruelty and neglect he had suffered. By contrast, she was raised in a stimulating, socially secure and culturally rich family. There are also superficial similarities and some commentators have noted that both lived an unconventional sexual and personal life. But there are important differences.

In her love for her partner Valentine Ackland, Warner was untroubled by the views of others or the prejudice of society, while White was unsettled all his life by his sexuality (homosexual acts were illegal in Britain for all White's life, whereas lesbian acts were not). White tried for a time to force his identity into a heterosexual channel but failed. He may have been a suppressed homosexual but he was also a self-confessed – if not practising – sadist, flagellant and fantasist about boys. Warner noted that his tormented private life was partly a consequence of a very honourable decision not to act upon his desires. She read and was disturbed by his private outpourings but was still able to show compassion for the man. It tells us much about the reasoned and critical empathy she employs throughout the book. Janet Montefiore suggests that while the similarities between Warner and White are limited, she may have felt some 'indirect' correspondence between White and Ackland. Both 'were solitaries, lovers and killers of animals ... both were lifelong homosexuals burdened with neurotic, demanding mothers; both were insecure self-tormentors with loving hearts who struggled ... against alcoholism' (Montefiore 2002, 144). This would have been a powerful force behind the biography, especially given the troubles that haunted Warner's relationship until Ackland's death two years after the book was published.

In the biography Tim White is first introduced to the reader in his own words, a poem from his diary of 1938, mourning his unhappy childhood and his dreadful parents. Warner waits to fill in the details (who his parents were, his birth-place, childhood, and so on) letting his words evoke his life. Then, rather like the opening of a novel *in medias res,* she reports that four months earlier, after his first big success, he had celebrated by taking off for Wales and Wiltshire in a new car with Brownie his dog, two merlins and four 'human friends' (10). The trip was not a success – he lost the merlins, the bitch came on heat, and he started drinking too much. Thus, Warner gives us White: the formative misery of his early years, his devotion to animals, his difficulty in forming regular relationships. She continues this startlingly abrupt immersion into White's life to say that it was the year of the Munich crisis and White was in turmoil about how he would react to another war breaking out. As we begin to wonder who this man was, she lets him speak for himself in a long quotation from a lecture given in America in 1964. Only then, with Chapter One, does she revert to biographical convention to outline his early life. The slightly perplexing juxtapositions of the Introduction are key to Warner's method. Its aim is to create a powerful sense of White's presence, his verbal fluency and his complicated character.

Subsequent chapters have a more traditional chronology and structure, though she compresses some stages of her subject's life while pausing for lengthy contemplation in others. She does not give equal attention to each decade of his life, always preferring to concentrate on key moments, especially literary ones. Warner draws on White's harrowing account of his early life, noting that his parents regretted their unsuitable marriage and neglected the child. She goes further than him in concluding that the neglect was also a product of their social position, saying a 'ruling race has other things to attend to' than a child (13). Her critique continues with the physical brutality at his public school being equalled by his mother's brutal indifference. Her access to White's private diaries underpins the intensity of Warner's account but she also has a novelist's perception of what to quote, what to summarise, and how to develop what her source material suggests. She selects the most apposite passages from White to illustrate his pain, for example 'It was my love that she extracted, not hers that she gave' (16).

Rescued by a sympathetic teacher and escaping from his family, White spent a year earning money so that he could go to read English at Cambridge. He began to write fiction, journalism and poetry, went on to teach at a prep school and then at Stowe School. Throughout this chronological account of White's first jobs and his exploration of what he wanted for the future, Warner interweaves details of his writing. She sees him making and re-making himself, trying out roles and identities. Her summary is concise and perceptive:

> White collected techniques – it was part of his theory about the Renaissance or polytechnic man who could shoot and gut a hare in the morning, fell a tree in the afternoon and write a sonnet in the evening. If he saw an implement – plough or paintbrush – he wanted to use it; if he watched a skill, to practise it; and having got what he wanted, went on to something else. (58)

Having to sift through a mountain of raw material, and never having met White, she made astute choices about what to include, how much to quote, what would show him most clearly. For example, she discovered he had written a 'Biography of Brownie', his dog, for his godson William Potts (78) and she saw that a lengthy quotation from this would be powerful and revealing. It is also one of the book's most moving sections. It describes his emotional crisis treating Brownie's near-terminal attack of distemper. She then contrasts this with his behaviour towards a barmaid he had used to try to discover (or perhaps 'normalise') his sexual and emotional preferences. Warner concludes that 'The trick of withholding his heart, which shows so odiously in the courtship of the barmaid, was gone, abolished by the shock of finding himself essential to a living creature' (79).

In 1977, she was asked to write the Prologue to the last book in White's Arthurian sequence, *The Book of Merlyn,* that was finally to be published. Warner summarises his life up to the point when, living alone in a gamekeeper's cottage, White re-read Malory's *Morte D'Arthur* – the moment when he began to develop his ideas for *The Once and Future King.* Warner's elegant Prologue, 'The Story of the Book', demonstrates some of the ways in which biography interprets a life and the ways the life can in turn interpret the writer's work. She shows how re-making Malory led to White's best work and at last fulfilled his life. After writing a handful of potboilers in different genres, 'he had a subject into which he could unloose his frustrated capacity for hero worship, his accumulated miscellany of scholarship, his love of living, his admiration of Malory' (Warner 1978, 14). The difficult political situation added the final stimulus to creation.

White was writing the first volumes of his Arthurian epic in the late 1930s, during the years of the build-up to war and appeasement. *The Sword in the Stone* was published in 1938, *The Queen of Air and Darkness/The Witch in the Wood* in 1939 and *The Ill-Made Knight* in 1940. He was a product of the inter-war years, and his strong opposition to war underpins *Merlyn*, written while in self-imposed exile in Ireland. Here, his contempt for the belligerence of human beings is only partly countered by his sense of the wisdom of animals. He sent *The Book of Merlyn* to his publishers in 1941, demanding that it be republished as the final volume in his Arthurian pentalogy with revised versions of the first three books and a new, fourth, book, *The Candle in the Wind.* Somehow, and it is not clear how, *The Book of Merlyn* evaded publication as part of *The Once and Future King* in 1958 and was only rediscovered in White's papers after his death (Warner 1978, 25).

While her personality and views were very different from her subject's, some of Warner's sympathy for White arose from their shared empathy with animals. She understood how intense a life with animals could be, recognising the significance of White's engagement with falconry, the importance of animals in the Arthurian novels, and his love for his dog Brownie. However, Warner's relationship with animals was different from White's, in part because she also had deep relationships with people. She shared her life with cats and treated them as equals, respecting their individuality, always attentive to their presence. In her diary, during a troubled period she describes her cat Niou 'waiting for me with concern' (Warner 1994, 230). She frequently makes acute observations of cat behaviour as when Valentine dropped a catnip mouse between the sleeping Niou and Kit: 'It was like dropping a new idea into the Athenaeum. They became conscious of, while still not stirring, a joint growing consciousness. Then Kit seized it, rolled and rolled in an ecstasy, lay stretched out with wild glazed eyes, not like the Athenaeum any longer' (Warner 1994, 271). Her love of and delight in the cats' behaviour is tempered by an ironic detachment, her acknowledgement of the separation of cat and human.

Such boundaries were not so clear with White. His attempts at control were alien to Warner, though she found them consistent with his psycho-sexual personality. And she was critical of his occasional carelessness and arrogance towards the animals in his care: 'Unlike the frayed twine and the strawberry netting [which led to the loss of two goshawks] and Killie's rape, this calamity [ruined notebooks] was not really his fault' (208). She tried to understand the specific nature of White's engagement with animals, which for him often replaced human fellowship: 'He did not treat animals as pets, or as a pastime or a hobby. He turned to them for a renewal and enlargement of his being' (117).

As Janet Montefiore noted, above, perhaps Warner understood White's needs better after reflecting on the similarities with her lover Valentine Ackland. She was powerfully drawn to animals, often depending on them for comfort. In 1954 Valentine wanted a poodle – for consolation, Warner thought, 'medicine against her melancholy' and 'alas, her woe, her void, can't be stuffed up with a poodle' (Warner 1994, 212). This understanding is present in her reading of White. Considering the impact on him of Brownie's death, she enters his feelings about the creature that began as a pet but became the beloved:

> With her death, he lost the only being he dared to love, the only being who found security in his insecurity. The trust she fixed

on the handsome, rather showy, not very attentive young man with a beautiful top hat, who accepted her dependence as an embellishment – like a rich tassel – had become the thing he depended on. (185)

White's private diaries revealed what even many of his friends did not suspect. They became for Warner the key to his personality and his unhappiness, revealing dark and repressed desires. They explained, for example, how a man devoted to animals could nevertheless be fascinated by cruelty. In his diary, he wrote that in Ireland calves as old as eighteen months are de-horned with a saw and 'stand in the field, bloody and bedimmed'. Warner sees this horrifying scene as one to which White was strangely drawn. She concludes that he 'had a sadist's acute intelligence for pain (when he hooked a salmon he was so conscious in himself of the steel lodged in the living flesh that he could not "play" it till it was safely exhausted but dragged it in to the bank)' (100). Getting pleasure from inflicting pain was something he had experienced and observed at public school – punishment, caning, and bullying had, he said, turned him into 'a flagellant' (18). Warner (whose father had been a master at Harrow) recognised it as a familiar phenomenon, stating in her matter of fact way that White was 'a sadist ... and a flagellant ... the ordinary English public school things' (Gallix 2017, 60). The consequence for White was that he was incapable of forming close adult relationships.

His self-scrutiny was intense and his diaries revealed a man struggling to understand himself, speculating that he was homosexual and (quite apart from its then illegality) unable to see a personal future there. Despite his self-knowledge, he was unable to accept his sexuality, longing for a stable and monogamous relationship but believing that it was impossible for a homosexual. His struggles led him to briefly try psychoanalysis, and to make some attempts at a 'normal' sexual life with women but all these failed. Warner astutely observes that he had difficulties with the female character, Morgause, because 'Constance White inhabits her and invalidates the book by being hated as an actual person. The real incest theme of the story is the maternal rape on the child' (109). His attitude to women must have disturbed Warner but she deftly concludes that 'The woman of his dreams, if a woman figured there at all, was a Nannie – the ghost of the ayah he had loved and whom his mother had sent away' (131). Sympathy does not, of course, exclude criticism or even dislike. Both feature at times in the sections where Warner deals with these topics. In a later interview, she described his mother as 'a frightful, vulgarised weakened version of White because she was an intense egoist ... very romantic, self-romanticising, bore the most awful grudges ... she was an amalgam of all that was worst in White' (Gallix 2017, 64–5).

In her Prologue to *The Book of Merlyn*, Warner argued that White was tormented by a generalised and constant 'fear':

> fear of being afraid, of being a failure, of being trapped. He was afraid of death, afraid of the dark. He was afraid of his own proclivities which might be called vices: drink, boys, a latent sadism. Notably free from fearing God, he was basically afraid of the human race. His life was a running battle with these fears, which he fought with courage, levity, sardonic wit, and industry. (Warner 1978, 11)

White had to be very careful about his attraction to boys and to one boy in particular, called Zed in his diary, with whom he fell in love towards the end of his life. He knew he could not act upon it and confided his anguish to his private diary. The extracts Warner quotes were risky to publish at the time and may still undermine the reader's sympathy for him. Nevertheless, she handles a difficult topic with detachment and compassion, and without moralising. But she had to tread carefully. She expressed her difficulty in a letter to David Garnett: 'If I could use his lust and rage and frenzy and defeat over the -- boy I could make a real dragon's tail ending. But everybody's bloody feelings are in the way, and if I observe them I shall be reduced to the portrait of a frustrated Scout-Master' (Garnett 1994, 83).

While she was writing, the trial of the sadistic child murderers Brady and Hindley was taking place. She feared that 'exactly this sort of thing ... waited round every corner for White. This I must both grasp and STATE' (Warner 1994, 303). That White appears neither as a frustrated scout-master nor a monster is a tribute to Warner's skill. It is a deft and subtle handling of a very difficult topic that would probably now dominate any biography. It is one of the great strengths of her book that Warner does not make White's psycho-sexual character its central focus; his identity is not contained by his sadism or his paedophilic urges. His writing is always for Warner the central fact of his life. In the interview with François Gallix she was compassionate about how these desires crippled White but also suggested that 'fear is a very good companion to writers: they often do very well. Baudelaire would not have written half as well as he did if he had not been a frightened man' (Gallix 2017, 64).

Biography is a genre that enmeshes its author in a unique way with the life of another person, different from a living relationship but nonetheless powerful. Warner often comments on the way in which her life is invaded by White's presence. For example, working at home in Dorset, it overpowers the scents from her garden:

> My room is full of the smell of roses and new cut hay and of elder blossom; and coiled up in all this like the snake in Eden, is the smell of long wet winters in Ireland; Tim White's Irish diaries, written twenty years ago and more, but still exuding a smell of damp and melancholy and a very faint smell of paraffin. I see I shall be leading two lives at once, rather as I did when I was translating *Contre Sainte-Beuve*. (Maxwell 1982, 212–3)

Warner knew she was not writing a conventional biography. She did, of course, base her book on his diaries and letters, and she drew on the expected sources, his friends, the people he worked with, visits to the places where he had lived, and so on. But several months into her task, she realised that she was in fact *creating* T H White – much as a novelist might. In a diary entry for February 1966 she describes writing the section about White's life in Yorkshire: 'Scribble-scrabble round Duke Mary's – but writing *too well* for a biographer – as though I were creating it' (Warner 1994, 301). She was imagining his life and bringing it alive with all her customary skills. She sent the section about White's time in Ireland to her *New Yorker* editor and friend William Maxwell, saying 'it is a narrative, not a biography. He was interesting enough for a narrative but not important enough for a biography. I realised this at first with alarm, then with delight, since it allowed me to use the narrator's devices of binds: references back and intimations forward' (Maxwell 1982, 219). I think this explains why her biography is so unconventional, covering some parts of the life in great detail while skipping over others. The chronology is fairly loose and she never attempts to make White's published writing explicate his life. It is a portrait, and she had the pleasure of arriving at *her* Tim. It is perhaps similar to an earlier, much briefer biography, *The Portrait of a Tortoise* (1946) in which she wrote about the parson and naturalist Gilbert White, drawing on selections from his journals and letters in which he in turn described the life and times of a tortoise called Timothy. (The coincidence of the names is a small pleasure.) That biography, like this one, is a delight and a revelation – observant, funny, bizarre, compassionate, clever.

There is humour and a lightness of touch in much of what Warner writes. Her witty summary of *The Sword in the Stone* acknowledges its role for White as the wish-fulfilment of a happy boyhood, but she also gently mocks it for the fantasy adult it contains: 'He gave himself a dauntless, motherless boyhood; he also gave himself an ideal old age, free from care and the contradiction of circumstances, practising an enlightened system of education on a chosen pupil, embellished with an enchanter's hat, omniscient, unconstrainable and with a sink where the crockery washed itself up' (81).

That this is a biography written by a novelist and poet is apparent throughout. There is the expressive control in the way she sets a scene, as in the description of Doolistown:

> A straight causeway, ditched and hedged on either side, turns off the road between stone gate-posts and is the avenue to Doolistown House, though it appears to lead only to a group of farm buildings. The house stands to one side of these. Derelict, now, and falling to ruin, it asserts its eighteenth-century dignity and composure among its shambling appurtenances like some fine turn of phrase persisting in a dialect. (152)

Then there is the manner in which she creates the character of T H White, relying on significant quotation so that he speaks and thus reveals himself. But she also goes beyond White's own words as in this passage which follows a rather technical description of a day's shooting on the Lincolnshire Wash which he ended with 'It was a lovely morning'. She adds:

It was his state of mind that made it lovely – as he walked out beyond the frontier of the sea-bank, so outstandingly a moving shape on the expanse of the marsh that the geese in the dark sky saw him before his pricked ears heard them; as he knelt, an early morning worshipper, on the frozen saline mud; as he kept in mind the controlling sea and how when you saw the tidal water turn in the creeks you could still take your time, unless a high tide flooded over the marsh, when you must hurry before it. (94)

This is a remarkable passage. White says nothing like this; the quoted diary entry is rather dull and factual. Perhaps Warner was trying to discover why White chose to spend tedious (for Warner) time just waiting to shoot geese. It certainly elevates White's account and makes him seem more sensitive to the surrounding landscape than he admits. Its lyricism may also be in part autobiographical, as when Warner was reminded of her discovery of the Essex marshes many years before. She wrote that

I knew that mysterious sensation of being where I wanted to be and as I wanted to be, socketted in the universe, and passionately quiescent ... Refreshed all night by the mist, and now penetrated by the warmth of the sun, the marsh was exhaling its particular smell, pure, fertile, sweet with vegetation, and yet slightly salt. (Warner 2012, 32)

This is, of course, a biography, not a novel. Warner embarked on it with her writer's enthusiasm for the challenge of a new or little-practised form. Despite not being considered a 'biographer', she had a lot of experience of life-writing before she took on T H White. Some of the lives she had written about during her career included Rosa Luxemburg, Nancy Cunard, John Craske, Countess Markiewicz, George Eliot, Thomas Hardy, Arthur Machen, A J Munby and many more. (For a full list see Montefiore 2020 and several examples in *With the Hunted*.) What she had not done was to research a full-length biography and this was a welcome challenge. She had considered many of the issues raised by biography and had reflected on her own life in her constant letter- and diary-writing. She had also published a number of autobiographical short stories. We know from the books in her library that she and Valentine Ackland read a large number of biographies and autobiographies (Swaab) and they both ensured that their own lives would be recorded and commented on for posterity (Warner 1998).

For Warner, writing the biography had been a great opportunity. It helped refresh her writing, stimulated her interest in her own archival work and gave her confidence to continue to experiment with short fiction, like her *New Yorker* stories published as *Kingdoms of Elfin* in 1977. Living with White for so long was an experience very different from writing fiction. He had become a companion to her everyday life and the focus of almost all her attention. She wrote that 'as I handle these mss, note-books, letters the sense of his existence – that he handled them, knew the look of them – almost overwhelms me, and I think, I shall die when these are withdrawn: *they are mine, he bequeathed them to me*' (Warner 1994, 303). For two years her life had been a 'long *solitude à deux*' (Steinman 2001, 169) and she felt bereft. She wrote in her diary that 'The lights are going out all over Sylvia ... It has been a strange love-story between an old woman and a dead man' (Warner 1994, 308).

This is not to say that Warner is uncritical. When in 1938 White was worrying about the personal impact of war, she did not have very much time for his ignorance of the wider political world, his 'suspended mind'. She disliked his solipsism 'like a man in the lightning-slashed darkness of a midnight storm, attentively studying what lay within the beam of a small electric torch' (91). Towards the end of his life his personality seems to have shrunk to that of the golf club bore. Wealthy, lonely, and drinking too much, the English colony in Florence 'came to dread' his conversation, full of old stories and jokes (283). From a position on the Left, she is critical of his hostility to personal taxation, his flight to one of the 'sanctuaries where British subjects can retire from the taxes of real life' (209) when he moved to Alderney after the financial success of *Camelot*. Recording her disapproval of White's 'tax-diddling' she recognised their fundamental political differences but was able to mock herself for 'writing this book from the standpoint of an Aunt' (Maxwell 1982, 215). She was not very enthusiastic about a number of White's books, saying in a letter to David Garnett 'I often dislike his writing to the point of embarrassment' (Garnett ed. 1994, 93). She quotes Noel Coward's tactful rejection of White's play *The Candle in the Wind* but then goes on to demolish it herself:

> Not only are the speeches long; they are lifeless. Past events are related in order to give the action a shove on; coming events are summarised beforehand. When the dialogue escapes from the speeches it is affectedly simple: Arthur, dragging his doom after him, seems to have come in for a cup of tea after tinkering unsuccessfully with the lawn-mower. (152)

Warner is an honest biographer who does not let her sympathy obscure her critical understanding. This is perhaps most apparent in her account of White's last years which though financially secure, were rather sad. He was unable to write, grieving for his separation from Zed, aimlessly wandering around Europe or seeking affirmation from the American lecture circuit. But she found a powerful summation, writing that throughout his life he 'had been unlucky with his happinesses' (339). They came at the wrong time or were too short-lived; circumstances intervened to disrupt his contentment, and in his last attempts at human kindness and sociability he never found the love he had sought. He died alone in his cabin on a ship moored in Piraeus harbour, aged only fifty seven. As so often, when she wants to make a powerful point, Warner uses White's own voice to conclude her book: 'I expect to make rather a good death. The essence of death is loneliness, and I have had plenty of practice at this' (306).

Works cited

Walter Allen, 'Lucky In Art Unlucky In Life', *The New York Times*, 21 April 1968, 123.

Anon, 'The Metamorphoses of a Merlin', *Times Literary Supplement*, 7 December 1967, 3432, 1186.

—, 'General', *The New Yorker*, 2 November 1968, 202–203.

François Gallix, 'François Gallix interviews Sylvia Townsend Warner about T H White' (1974), *The Journal of the Sylvia Townsend Warner Society*, 17:2 (2017) 56–70.

Richard Garnett, 'Introduction' in Richard Garnett (ed.) *Sylvia and David – The Townsend Warner/Garnett Letters* (Sinclair-Stevenson, 1994), vii–x.

— (ed), *Sylvia and David – The Townsend Warner/Garnett Letters* (Sinclair-Stevenson, 1994).

William Maxwell (ed.), *Letters of Sylvia Townsend Warner* (Chatto & Windus, 1982).

Janet Montefiore, 'Sylvia Townsend Warner and the biographer's 'moral sense'' (1993) in *Arguments of Heart and Mind: Selected Essays 1977–2000* (Manchester University Press, 2002), 143–164.

—, *Sylvia Townsend Warner: A bibliography* 2020, http://townsendwarner.com/bibliography/selected-bibliography (accessed 18 February 2022).

Robert Nye, 'A mad black wind', *The Guardian*, 10 November 1967, 7.

Michael Steinman (ed.), *The Element of Lavishness: Letters of Sylvia Townsend Warner and William Maxwell 1938–1978* (Counterpoint, 2001).

Peter Swaab, 'A Lot of Lives: Biographical Books from Warner's and Ackland's Library', Sylvia Townsend Warner Society *Newsletter* no. 41, nd, np.

Philippa Toomey, 'Out of Air and Darkness', *The Sunday Times*, 11 November 1967, 20.

Sylvia Townsend Warner, *The Diaries of Sylvia Townsend Warner*, (ed.) Claire Harman (Random House, 1994).

—, *I'll Stand By You. The Letters of Sylvia Townsend Warner & Valentine Ackland*, (ed.) Susanna Pinney (Pimlico, 1998).

—, 'The Story of the Book', in T H White, *The Book of Merlyn* (1977, Collins 1978), 11–25.

Further reading

Frances Bingham, *Valentine Ackland. A Transgressive Life* (Handheld Press, 2021).

Claire Harman, *Sylvia Townsend Warner: A Biography* (Chatto & Windus, 1990).

Peter Haring Judd, *The Akeing Heart. Letters Between Sylvia Townsend Warner, Valentine Ackland and Elizabeth Wade White* (Handheld Press, 2018).

Helen Macdonald, *H is for Hawk* (Vintage Books, 2014).

Wendy Mulford, *This Narrow Place: Sylvia Townsend Warner & Valentine Ackland: Life, Letters and Politics 1930–1951* (Pandora Press, 1988).

Sylvia Townsend Warner, *With the Hunted. Selected Writings*, (ed) Peter Tolhurst (Black Dog Books, 2012).

T H White

A Biography

Acknowledgments

These pages will indicate the extent of my indebtedness to
T H White's friends. Their ready help is a proof of how well, and
with what interest, affection and curiosity they remember him,
'It's twenty years since I saw him,' one of them said to me. 'And
I'm still puzzling about him.'

In particular I must record my gratitude to Mrs L J Potts for
White's letters to her husband – letters supplying a portrait of
White as a young man which would otherwise be lacking; to the
Executors of the late Sir Sydney Cockerell and to Mr Wilfrid
Blunt for the use of the White-Cockerell letters; to David
Garnett who has allowed me to draw on the correspondence
between White and himself which he is now editing for
publication; and to Michael Howard for encouraging me to
undertake this book, providing much material for it, preparing
the illustrations and allowing me to read the intimate diaries
which White left to his guardianship.

I gratefully acknowledge the assistance given me by the
Executor and Trustee Departments of Lloyds Bank, both in
Jersey and Threadneedle Street, London.

I must also record my gratitude to Mrs Ralph White, Mrs
Michael Howard, Lady Sherwill, Mrs Charles Lane, the late
John Moore, Sir John Verney and Lt-Cdr Harry Griffiths
whose recollections and loans of letters have been of essential
value; to David Higham who allowed me to consult his files for
the many years during which he was White's literary agent; to
Dr R Snow, T R Henn, Ian Parsons, Professor George Rudé,
J C Saunders, H Heckstall Smith, Lord Annan, Colonel J M
Ashton, the Rev P T Ashton, Peter Hughesdon, John da Silva,
Nigel Clive, John Vickers, Anthony Ireland, Nigel Henderson,
Tommy Rose and F T Smith for their recollections of White at
Cambridge and at Stowe, and to the late Miss Rosemary Hill
who supplied the addresses of his friends and pupils at Stowe and
copied extracts from the Stowe files for me; to Jack McLaughlin
and Henry Cronin who told me about White's life at Belmullet;
to J G Mavrogordato, Mrs Maurice McGrath, Henry Wheeler,

3

Maurice Craig, G Wren Howard, John Betjeman, John Wyllie, Mrs Herivel, Miss Florence Collier, Mrs Maisie Allen, John Gloag, Bob Downing, Peter and Tim Lane, Sabrina, Juliet and Angelica Verney, L H F Walton, and Alan Warren, all of whom have helped me to a clearer understanding of my subject. I am grateful to Messrs Cassell for permission to quote from *Dead Mr Nixon*, to William Collins & Sons for permission to quote from *Earth Stopped* and *The Once and Future King*, to Chatto & Windus for permission to quote from David Garnett's *The Familiar Faces*, to Hutchinson & Co. for permission to quote from L J Potts's *Comedy* and to John Murray for permission to quote from C Northcote Parkinson's *A Law Unto Themselves*. Finally I must express my affectionate gratitude to Carol Walton (Mrs Rex Stallings) who besides supplying letters, reminiscences and passages from her diary has typed this book and watched over it from start to finish, and whose Catalogue of White's MSS has been my standby.

For much of his life White used roman numerals for dating the month and year. Later he turned to the ordinary usage and I have taken this as sanction for applying the better-known form throughout. Similarly, though with regret, I have tamed his spelling. In order to include as many extracts from his diaries and letters as possible I have made occasional omissions in the text, cutting details of falconry, much shooting and fishing, theorizings about Irish politics and examinations of conscience over his position as a non-combatant. He was a man of so many interests and could be so interesting about any of them that I cannot hope to avoid complaints from sportsmen, patriots, and casuists that I have left out what I ought to have left in. If I could have made the book twice as long I might have better pleased them and would have been better pleased myself. Apart from these cuts and the customary substitutions for proper names where feelings might be hurt, I have tried throughout to let him speak for himself, contradict himself, even misrepresent himself – since it was part of his character that he was not always a very good judge of it.

August 1967
STW

Erratum slip pasted in the first edition

= JERSEY = 12.41 = 9.10.67
FORTHCOMING BIOGRAPHY TH WHITE STATES PAGE 52
WAS FELLOW MASTER STOP HAVE NEVER BEEN
A SCHOOLMASTER IN MY LIFE PLEASE DELETE STOP
WROTE BOOK WITH WHITE AND ARRANGED PUBLISHER
SO HE COULD BUY ONE OF MY CARS SECONDHAND
WITH ROYALTIES = R MCNAIR-SCOTT MFH JP +

Foreword

BY JOHN VERNEY

One like's one's friends for their virtues; one loves them for their faults. Tim White's were on the same generous scale as the rest of him. After reading Sylvia Townsend Warner's beautifully just and perceptive study I love him for them the more, and wish, more than ever, that I had known him in his prime rather than at the end of his life.

We'd met a few times with Michael Howard, and I suppose made a casual suggestion, in a letter, that he might come to Florence where my wife and I were spending a year. At any rate he wrote back:

> Why Florence? Isn't it just as damp and cold as anywhere else? As a matter of fact I am getting fed up myself wintering in Alderney and I once spoke Italian pretty well and used to live about the Sorrentine peninsula …

He turned up in November 1962 and rang me on arrival from the most luxurious hotel. We had booked a room for him in a charming and inexpensive *pensione* in the Piazza Santo Spirito next door to us but, over the phone, he rejected the idea,

> I've got some money at last from *Camelot*. Being rich is a new *experience*. Staying at the best hotel is *fun*. I have a private bath and telly. The sheets and towels are pale mauve and scented with lavender. A nice barber comes and shaves me in bed …

He sounded quite miserable.

When I went to fetch him for dinner he was sitting alone in the resplendent lounge, looking conspicuously distinguished in a black cape lined with scarlet; looking, too, as if the fun had already worn pretty thin. The food had upset his digestion. An American lady had just asked him if he was Ernest Hemingway. 'Madam,' he replied, when his own name failed to register, 'don't you realize that I'm the best-known man in the United States after President Kennedy?' – or he claimed to have replied, for he was soon entertaining us with the incident and the rest of his experience of living among the rich. I moved him and his luggage to the Pensione Bandini the next morning. It was the start of a memorable winter.

With strangers he could be quite odious; rude and suspicious if he thought they were lionizing him, still more so if he thought they weren't; shouting down anyone who disagreed with his more preposterous assertions or even ventured to interrupt. One heard some of his stock anecdotes rather too often for comfort – 'Shut up, Marlene, and listen to *me*!' was the theme of one about Hollywood. One also learnt to dread the appearance of certain hobby-horses: the 'Farewell State'; the iniquity of the 1945 Labour Government whose only identifiable policy had been to rob T H White of his few earnings; the contemptible trickery of all Modern Art, led by its most famous exponent whose name he took a schoolboyish pleasure in mispronouncing. But that side to him did not really matter. It was the drizzle of an English summer which one accepted as the price for the unforgettable sunshine, for the sudden flashes of true sympathy and affection, for the feeling that here was someone who, when he did care for a thing, cared for it with every ounce of his being.

He was at his best with animals and children, or with one or two companions when he could feel sure of being liked simply for himself. I recall the attempt to tame a wild squirrel for one of my daughters – a sort of miniature Goshawk episode, ending in similar failure – or his patience rehearsing my daughters to recite Christina Rossetti's 'In the bleak midwinter' for an International Christmas Festival at which they had been invited to represent England. On the Day he and I sat together at the back of the crowded church, so nervous about the result that we were biting our knuckles, and with the tears rolling down our cheeks when they did England, and him, much credit.

But the happiest evenings of all were spent getting him to talk about poetry and books. He had mastered, or tried to master, many skills, and the eagerness with which he tackled any unfamiliar technique that cropped up was a great part of his charm. But, after all, literature was his life. He read about ten books a day, or through the night, and would often bring round an armful to our flat with the injunction that we must read them all, *at once!* By the time he had finished describing their merits I felt I knew them – some still wait reproachfully by my bed. He was assembling notes for a lecture tour in the States the following summer and we served, willingly enough, is a preliminary audience.

In the course of that winter we covered most aspects of contemporary writing – detective stories, science fiction, novels, biography … He was generous in his admiration of other authors, shouting the praises of younger men such as Salinger or Ray Bradbury, envying, with complete sincerity, the skill of contemporaries such as Waugh, Greene, and Ackerley, inveighing against the neglect of older writers or of certain of their works which, he thought, had not been given their due. He intended to make this neglect the subject of a lecture in itself. Inevitably names recurred – of books like Masefield's *The Midnight Folk* or John Collier's *His Monkey Wife*; and of authors who, though well known, were not well known enough. Of these the name that recurred by far the most frequently was that of Sylvia Townsend Warner, all of whose books he much admired and whose *Mr Fortune's Maggot* he called the greatest and tenderest novel of this half-century.

When, after his death, the question arose of a biographer, I suggested to his publisher the person I knew he would have wished, above all others, to write his life. And I shall boast of that suggestion to my grandchildren.

T H White

To return once more to Titania and Bottom. I suggested that
in their love scene Shakespeare was symbolizing one aspect
of the curious love of eternity for the productions of time: we have
fairy minds, but they are tied to the distracting, inconvenient,
and sometimes grotesque behaviour of our bodies.

L J Potts, *Comedy*

Introduction

> Of hapless father hapless son
> My birth was brutally begun,
> And all my childhood o'er the pram
> The father and the maniac dam
> Struggled and leaned to pierce the knife
> Into each other's bitter life.
> Thus bred without security
> Whom dared I love, whom did not flee?

These lines with their period overtones of Housman and Blake were written by Terence Hanbury White in his diary on December 1st, 1938. He was then thirty-two.

Four months earlier, he had heard that the American Book of the Month Club had chosen his Morte d'Arthur romance, *The Sword in the Stone*, for one of its 1939 publications. He would have dollars, he would have readers. Instantly buying a Jaguar car, he set off for Radnorshire next day, taking Brownie (his red setter bitch), two merlins, and four human friends. From Wales he went on to Wiltshire, where he met Siegfried Sassoon, Major Allen, 'the greatest falconer alive', and at Sassoon's house another eminent person, Sir Sydney Cockerell. But while being flown at larks his merlin Balin died of heart failure; he left Wiltshire on the morrow and loosed Balan, the second merlin, a week later. After a brief visit to Norfolk, where the setter bitch came on heat and where he was drinking too much, he drove back to his five-shillings-a-week cottage in Buckinghamshire, where he was fitted with a gas mask. It was the year of the Munich crisis; war was still a year away, but he did not know this. War was inevitable, and he could not bring his mind and his heart to the same decision: his mind abjured any part in it, his heart was bruised by a sense of obligation to the simple and dutiful who would fight without questioning. On October 9th he wrote in his diary:

> Last night David Garnett and Ray stayed with me at the
> Wheatley Bridge Hotel, and we talked a great deal about the

crisis, and what we were to do about it. Ray, who is one of the people who only speaks about a dozen times a day because she will not speak unless she has something to say, said we must spend our time writing, while there is still a chance of peace. She said almost anybody could be taught to stick bayonets into people but it took much longer to teach the rules of grammar. So we decided that we would try to help with our pens, while there was still time, because we had to do something, however little it was.

Still at the Wheatley Bridge Hotel, during the last week-end in November he entertained Sir Sydney Cockerell, Humbert Wolfe and Pamela Frankau. At this party, conversation was livelier and more general. Sydney Cockerell recalled burying Wilfred Scawen Blunt, uncoffined in unconsecrated ground, and Thomas Hardy, coffined but minus his heart, in Westminster Abbey; Pamela Frankau recited the authentic text of the Abdication lampoon on Archbishop Lang; Humbert Wolfe (at some point conversation must have veered towards Munich) told of a friend who, volunteering eight times for the 1914–18 war and always rejected on medical grounds, had been assailed with a white feather by a patriotic young lady to whom, accepting the feather, he said mildly, 'Have you a pin? And when they were gone, the gifted, high-spirited, fortunate, admired young writer, with his foot on a golden ladder and no one feeling sorry for him, dashed off – for a quick invention was another of his good fortunes – that sad, residual self-summary.

Twenty-five years later, in the last year of his life, White went on a lecture tour through the United States. He was asked, this gifted, stimulating, wild-bearded man of letters, to say something about himself. In a lecture called 'The Pleasures of Learning' he did so:

My parents loathed each other and were separated; divorced, when I was about fourteen or so. This meant that my home and education collapsed about my ears; and ever since I have been arming myself against disaster. This is why I learn. Now, believe it or not, I can shoot with a bow and arrow, so when the next atomic bomb is dropped poor old White will be hopping about in a suit of skins shooting caribou or something with a bow and arrow. I have made a list of some of the things which my compulsive sense of disaster has made me excel at. I won a prize for flying aeroplanes about thirty years ago. I can plough with horses. I used to ride show jumpers; I have taught myself to be a falconer. One of the odder things I have done is to learn to go down in diving suits – the old brass hat diving suit. I have had to learn to sail. I swim fairly well. I was a good shot before I took to spectacles – clay pigeons and geese and things of that sort. Fishing. I was a very good fisherman. I used to drive fast cars – God knows why. I had to be good at games. I had to be able to win at darts (in English public houses you throw darts against a board for drinks). I had to teach myself not to be clumsy. Compensating for my sense of inferiority, my sense of danger, my sense of disaster, I had to learn to paint even, and not only to paint – oils, art, and all that sort of thing – but to build and mix concrete and to be a carpenter and to saw and screw and put in a nail without bending it. Not only did I have to be physically good at things, I had to excel with my head as well as with my body and hands. I had to get first-class honours with distinction at the University. I had to be a scholar. I had to learn medieval Latin shorthand so as to translate bestiaries.

It is a fine brag, and a respectable one – since, as with the little figure drawn to scale which shows the height of the monument, the formidability of this accumulation of achievements depended on the boy whose home and education collapsed about his ears. If those applauding it remembered that earlier in the lecture White had quoted from *The Sword in the Stone* the passage beginning "'The best thing for being sad", replied Merlyn, "is to learn something'", it may have occurred to them that so much learning presupposed a good deal of sadness.

I India, Cheltenham 1906–24

Terence Hanbury White, born in Bombay on May 29th, 1906, was an only child. His father, Garrick White, was a District Superintendent of Police. His mother, Constance, born Constance Aston, was the daughter of an Indian Judge. Garrick White was Irish-born and considered himself Irish; in fact, he was Irish by the maternal line only. Constance was Scottish, with a strain of French blood. She was handsome and had many suitors, but would marry none of them. She was nearing thirty when, goaded by her mother's taunts about the cost of supporting her, she said she would marry the next man who offered, and did so. The bedding appalled her; she remained resentful and self-pitying. Probably both parties regretted the transaction; hut appearances had to be kept up. Eighteen months later 'this reasonably happy marriage' – as it was called in a subsequent lawsuit – produced a child.

The circumstances of a British Raj childhood are discouraging to parent-child intimacy. The climate is too hot, the servants too numerous. A ruling race has other things to attend to. A District Superintendent of Police is always on the move, and where Garrick White moved Constance White went with him, travelling in tongas or sweltering trains, assisting in the pursuit of criminals, observing the execution of justice (she came of a legal family, it may have been a hereditary penchant) and, from time to time, tiger-shooting. In her manuscript reminiscences, 'These Have Interested Me', she admits she was a bad shot and implies that she was dauntless – an uncomfortable companion. Beyond a few references to 'my infant' there are only three mentions of the child. One relates how she heard him bawling in the nursery and hurried in to reproach the ayah for not giving him what he wanted. The ayah explained this was really not possible; he was crying for the reflection of the moon in the river. Another tells how he paddled for the first time and announced that the sea tasted of salt, not pepper. The third mention might well have been the last. He became extremely ill with some stomach infection; the doctor said he must be removed to

England and that during the voyage he was to be fed on nothing but fluids, 'or he would die in screaming agony'. She obeyed the directions, the child wasted under her eyes and was near dead when a doctor travelling in the ship disregarded etiquette, stole the case, and revived the patient with biscuits. By the end of the voyage he was perfectly recovered, and had seen 'an Arab by the Suez Canal; sharks; later, a whale; my father giving whiskey to a monkey'.

This passage is from White's diary for 1941. He was in Ireland then, and being at a pause between one interest and another made notes for what may have been a projected autobiography.

'I spoke Hindustani before I spoke English,' he begins – a common enough claim among Anglo-Indian children; and his remembrances of early childhood –

> Standing with garlands round my neck, smelling beautiful, lizards whose tails came off and wriggled away by themselves, chargers thundering, tent-pegging, torch-light, bonfires to roast potatoes, dark faces, double-jointed fingers which clicked, velvet nights, brown feet, Chota Syce standing beside my cot with his foot in a basin of oil because he had been stung by a scorpion, grown-ups in evening dress by candlelight out of doors, a potter, fireworks, flowers, rains, heats, mangoes, parchedness, nights, flames in darkness

– are commonplaces of that vanished society. Not so this:

> My father made me a wooden castle big enough to get into, and he fixed real pistol barrels beneath its battlements to fire a salute on my birthday, but made me sit in front the first night – that deep Indian night – to receive the salute, and I, believing I was to be shot, cried.

By now the 'reasonably happy marriage' was showing its teeth. After the child's birth Constance White refused intercourse. 'The effect of this strong-willed, imaginative, selfish, beautiful, malingering wife upon my father was the usual one; he took to drink.' The wife took to pet dogs; when she flaunted their devotion to her, he shot them. As with his mother's dogs, so with his mother's child. In the circumstances, it wasn't an illogical assumption.

> There was a great deal of shooting in the air in those days. I am told that my father and mother were to be found wrestling with a pistol, one on either side of my cot, each claiming that he or she was going to shoot the other and himself or herself, but in any case beginning with me. If I woke up during these scenes, the censor of my mind has obliterated them as too terrible, but I believe they happened. It was not a safe kind of childhood.

White probably heard about the quarrels over his cot from his Aunt Ruth, Garrick White's sister-in-law. She recalls:

> My husband and I stayed with my brother-in-law and his wife in Karachi when Terence was about two years old. Even at that time things were not very happy in the marital line. My sister-in-law was of an extremely jealous nature and if the little boy showed affection for his father, climbing on his lap or asking if he could go out with him, she at once tried to provide some counter-attraction. She dismissed the ayah of whom he was extremely fond simply (she admitted this) because children 'must not prefer to go out with the ayah to staying with their parents'. The same insane jealousy prompted her to reprimand Terence when he wanted to play with Chota, a little native boy attendant, instead of listening to some music which she was playing.
>
> I don't want you to think that the fault was all with my sister-in-law. There were many things to put up with on either side.

Looking back, White bore his father no grudge and could find little mercy for his mother. He wrote in his diary after her death:

> She was clever and intelligent and wildly imaginative. You never knew who she was being – Joan of Arc on Monday, Cleopatra on Tuesday, Florence Nightingale on Wednesday. I adored her passionately until I was about eighteen, except

for the time when I forgot all about her because she was in India and I was with my grandparents. I didn't get much security out of her. Either there were the dreadful parental quarrels and spankings of me when I was tiny or there were excessive scenes of affection during which she wooed me to love her – not her to love me. It was my love that she extracted, not hers that she gave. I've always thought she was sexually frigid, which was maybe why she thrashed it out of me. Anyway, she managed to bitch up my loving women. She made me dote on her when I was at school.

She had a way of grinding her teeth.

His parents brought him to England late in 1911. The three stayed with Constance White's parents at St Leonards where Mr Aston had settled on his retirement. The quarrels got worse. Mrs Aston watered the decanters. After a year's leave Garrick White went back to India; eighteen months later, Constance followed him. The boy was left in the charge of his grandparents.

For six years I grew straight and rampaged and was protected.

I was brought up with three cousins, two girls and a boy, grandchildren also. Oh, the Christmas trees in the conservatory, and the antlers and weapons in the hall (each weapon had done a murder, or so I was given to understand, since the weapon of a murderer used to become the Judge's perquisite in India), and oh, the dining-room lift which we worked perpetually, and my own lovely playroom on the top floor (chock-full of soldiers, guns, forts, and zeppelins on strings) and my tortoise in the garden.

Sea air, roast mutton, the tidal surge of children rushing up one staircase and down the other ... It was so real to him as he sat writing in Ireland in the third year of another war that he reverted to the very phrases of those days, the chock-full playroom, the weapons that had done a murder. Yet even at his grandparents', where he was taken for granted as one of four grandchildren, where he could quarrel in his own defence instead of being quarrelled over, where there was nothing signal about him or debatable, nothing to be watched for, guarded against, repressed, even there a hand from India could stretch out and fasten on him.

> Contemporary photographs show a fat little boy in an Eton suit too tight for him, with rather thick lips. It was taken to send to my mother in India, and she wrote back that my lips were growing *sensual*. I was to hold them in, with my teeth if necessary. Since then I have been ashamed of my lips and now wear them concealed by moustache and beard.

In September 1920 he went to Cheltenham College.

This does not square with the statement in 'The Pleasures of Learning' that at fourteen or so his home and education collapsed about his ears. The Aston household, the only settled home he had known, stood firm; he was making the normal move from a preparatory to a public school. But late in 1915, after a culminating drunken assault by Garrick White, Constance White had come back to England. Though the boy remained with his grandparents, he must have overheard talk about money, and where it would come from if Garrick's drinking led to his dismissal. Nothing had collapsed, but cracks were running through the structure.

Cheltenham, the earliest of the Victorian public schools, with its traditional Anglo-Indian connection, was a natural White-Aston choice. It has a military side which trains prospective army entrants; White was placed in it. But the six years of growing straight and rampaging and being protected had not been enough to fit the boy for the school's thwack-about regime – a regime, when he knew it, based on the theory that education must be harassing and the harassing systematically applied.

> The housemaster put you on a thing called 'Satis'. This meant that you got a card which had to be signed by all your teachers each week. For three signatures of Non Satis you were caned – and even for one you wasted time in writing a large number of 'lines'. Once you were on Satis you had to do too much work, to save yourself, and this diminished

your infinitesimal freedom. Then the prefect would put you into the house platoon of the OTC. He would give you a punishment called Defaulters for each parade. This cut down the spare time to nothing. On top of these sorrows, there were a hundred pettiflogging exactions of time. A prefect would call out 'Orderly', and all we little creatures had to run to do whatever shopping, etc, he wanted. Then we had to clean our OTC equipment to Guards' standard. Between the upper and nether millstones they were able to crush us into crime.

My housemaster was a sadistic middle-aged bachelor with a gloomy suffused face. His prefects were lither and brighter copies of himself. He used to walk in front of one up the long corridor, trailing his cane behind him. The prefects used to beat us after evening prayers. I used to pray madly every night (or it seemed like every night): 'Please God, don't let me be beaten tonight.' I knew in a dumb way it was a sexual outrage, though I could not have phrased that charge. You had to go down a long passage to the gymnasium, where you took off your trousers and put on thin white rugger shorts. Then they came down, rattling their canes. All this was done with a kind of deaf-ear turned, a kind of surreptitiousness. It had the effect – unless something earlier had that effect – of turning myself into a flagellant.

By the time he was halfway through his school career, White was in the Sixth Form – hoisted by his wits above the worst persecutions and exactions, with a study to work in. Freed from the 'Satis' implication that work is something you do in order not to be penalized, he began to learn. He found a teacher. Forty years later, he wrote:

When I was a boy at what was then a rather cruel public school there was just one master who praised and encouraged me to be a writer. His name was C F Scott, and I shall be grateful to him till I die.

Among the juvenilia of this period – otherwise unremarkable – is an unfinished narrative poem called 'The Death of Oliver', The lines stagger under conventional-romantic trappings, but the narrative keeps going and the slaughter is done with brio.

> There, where King Marsil hewed among the press
> And all the Franks were mazed before his strength,
> Where Chernuble lay huddled motionless,
> And Turpin, whirling all his mace's length,
> Smote down two men at every clamorous blow …

If it was C F Scott who introduced the young White to *The Song of Roland*, Scott set him on the road to the *Morte d'Arthur*, and through the *Morte d'Arthur* to *The Once and Future King*.

In the summer of 1923, White passed School Certificate with credits in English, History, Geography, French, and Mathematics. By then he must have broken out from his original classification, for the actual certificate (he kept it) is endorsed: 'Mil and Eng Side'. By then he could justifiably forebode that his education might collapse about his ears. Six months earlier, Garrick White had petitioned for restitution of conjugal rights. Constance White countered by asking for a judicial separation, and got it.

Cases in which a husband sought restitution of conjugal rights were rarities, and this case, which extended over two days, was reported at considerable length.

January 25th, 1923, Evening Standard
Giving judgment, the Judge said he believed the wife even without corroboration. He accepted the story of the husband attempting to get into bed with a lighted lamp and of his making a public exhibition of himself at the dinner, as well as of the other episodes which the wife had described.

There was legal cruelty and also conduct on the part of the husband which prevented him taking proceedings against his wife for desertion because his conduct conduced to it.

He dismissed the husband's petition and granted the wife a judicial separation with costs.

Two months before the hearing, Garrick White had retired from the Indian Police – perhaps not unprompted; he had been reprimanded a little while before. Retirement pensions had not kept pace with the rise in the cost of living. England was full of the retired, the disbanded, the disabled, the ex-servicemen who had given up jobs to fight and found no jobs after the war had ended, and who were scraping up livelihoods as chicken-farmers, salesmen, secretaries to golf-clubs. Constance White presently joined fortunes with one of these – a cousin – investing with him in a small-holding where they struggled with pigs and poultry and bees and swindlers. It was this discouraging world that the boy had to face. Any thought of an Army career had been given up. Constance was looking forward to a time when there would be no more school fees to meet and when 'Dumpling' – she insisted on calling him 'Dumpling' – would be working, say, in a bank.

I shall never forget the day when I hadn't a penny left to pay for a stamp to put on a postcard which had to be sent urgently. The postman brought a letter from my son's headmaster saying By hook or by crook I must manage to send my boy to a University. He was so awfully clever it would be a sin not to give him a chance.

II Cambridge 1925–29

White left Cheltenham in July 1924, and for a year did private tutoring in order to earn his way to Cambridge. He entered Queens' College at the Michaelmas Term, 1925, to read for the English Tripos. He arrived poor, slightly older than his fellow-entrants and conscious of coming from a stuffy background. Cambridge was his first experience of a grown-up male society. R H B Snow, also a new arrival at Queens', recalls:

> I was attracted by this rather unusual character, maturer than most of us, and with a certain charm and wit. He got in the way of looking in for talks on poetry and at that time was keen on Sassoon and Masefield and often read to me from them. He was exceedingly hard up, and did Tutorials each vacation to help him pay for the coming term. Queens' (except perhaps for Potts) did not recognize his potential worth. He kept very much to himself but delighted to meet people.

In the course of meeting people, he won the acknowledgment of being given a new name. He became and remained Tim (via White and the chain-store firm of Timothy White, Chemists). The young man known as Tim was tall, with small hands and feet; he was a deft mover who did not drop things, stumble or collide. His eyes were vividly blue. Being projecting, they caught the light and were brilliant. Potts, while recognizing his potential worth, recognized something else: the turbaned portrait of Byron, by Phillips, he declared, was strikingly like White.

> My tutor was L J Potts, whom I disliked to the point of rage for about a year. It took all that time to discover that he was going to be the great literary influence in my life, as well as being the most noble gentleman I have ever met. He was ugly, with a ginger beard, and he was the only man who I have known to try to live up to his own rigid rules of decency and to behave himself. He also taught me to behave and

think. I believe he would have said that the decent person is he 'who sweareth unto his neighbour and disappointeth him not, though it were to his own hindrance'.

White wrote this in 1961, within a year after Potts's death. A pre-obituary statement that Potts was 'by education a moralist and by inclination speculative', and the fact that Potts, though much his senior by experience and digestion of experience, was only nine years older than he throws a more revealing light on the bond between tutor and pupil.

Another friendship with a young don developed when he began to attend 'Henn's Monday Evenings'. The young don was T R Henn, a Fellow of St Catharine's College.

I first met T H White in 1926. I had begun something that became known as 'Henn's Monday Evenings'. I merely told my lecture audience that I would be 'at home' on Mondays, 8.30 pm on, if they cared to come to my rooms in College. The gatherings usually broke up about midnight: numbers ranged from twelve to twenty-five or even more. Everything imaginable was discussed; my own part was to 'withdraw' and let the talk go where it would, though the nominal subject was the question raised in my own lectures.

They tended to bring along their friends. I think this was how T H White first appeared, since I was not actually teaching him. He very rapidly established himself as one of the leaders and 'characters' in the group: original and even violent in argument, delighting in various iconoclasms; full of recent reading (in particular Eliot). Great gaiety, a very strong personality; very truculent at times; talking vigorously and for effect; a strong desire to *épater la bourgeoisie*; apt to dramatize himself.

At the end of his first year, White was awarded a College Exhibition; in September he was recommended for financial assistance 'on the grounds of his ability, industry and economical habits'. Before then, the economical habits had taken him into the Arctic Circle. A particular friend of his was Ian Parsons, also a first-year man. During the General Strike in May, when the toiling bourgeoisie found itself being irresistibly succoured by hosts of hatless young men from the Universities prepared to drive anywhere and anything, they were active in London. Both of them now wanted to visit some unhaunted desert; neither of them could afford to spend a great deal of money getting to it. Studying maps of population densities, they decided on a walking tour in Lapland. They consulted a travel adviser and learned that in midsummer the snows are melted, the climate temperate, the rivers teeming with trout, the moors rich with game-birds feeding on cranberries. They could camp where they pleased and live off the country; some measure of protection against mosquitoes was advisable. It was the travellers' own good idea to add meat concentrates and some chocolate to their 80 lb weight of equipment. They set out – a handsome high-spirited pair, all laughter, enterprise and romantic friendship. But the climate of Lapland cannot be vouched for, and in 1926 the flush of summer was belated. The snow had not melted, or only melted into freezing slush. The trout were torpid in the icy streams. The game was scanty and evasive, the cranberries not ripe. Only the mosquitoes lived up to their report. Veiled and muffled, hungrier and hungrier, tormented by inflamed insect bites, their faces swollen as though with mumps, their tempers strained, the two young men wandered over the waste in search of food and fuel – for a camp fire was essential, both to keep off the mosquitoes and to save them from dying of cold. The rationed chocolate was almost exhausted and they were barely on speaking terms when White with a long shot brought down a merganser – a species of duck with rudimentary teeth. He threw it across a stream, and while he was searching for a place where he could ford the torrent pictured his companion devouring it raw.

At Abisko, on their return journey, each found a letter telling him he had got a first in the May examination.

In 1927 White put in for a Davison Travelling Scholarship. His application was backed by E M W Tillyard.

> Mr T H White of Queens' College tells me he is applying for a studentship to take him for a year to America and I should like to recommend him very strongly. I think he is admirably (and rather unusually) suited for an American scholarship – both for personal and academic reasons. He has wide interests and an unusually vigorous and inquiring mind.

Even if he had been chosen (he was not) he could not have taken up the scholarship. Shortly before his Tripos, Part 1, he went to a doctor about a pain in his chest; he had been fencing, and supposed he had strained a muscle; the doctor found he had pleurisy and diagnosed tuberculosis. 'I was told I had only six months to live.' It is unlikely that any doctor would have used these words to a young patient; they smack of Constance White, who would have been very likely to insert her own drama into the situation: 'The doctors told me you had only six months to live.' But a young man does not require a dramatizing mother to think himself under sentence of death and he would have been the readier to believe it (he was something of a dramatist himself) since the blow fell when he was doing so promisingly. R D G Laffan, his Director of Studies when he entered Queens' College, urged him to 'degrade' for a year; White insisted on taking his Tripos. He was in no state of mind to do well, and did not. Entrants for the English Tripos are allowed to submit an original contribution beforehand. White sent in an essay on Malory. Mr Henn, to whom he showed it, remembers it as 'wild, violent, very funny; clearly the germ of *The Sword in the Stone*'. White afterwards dismissed it with a 'naturally I did not read Malory while writing about him' and implied it was merely about sources. By then, he bore it a grudge. One of the Tripos examiners was a Malory expert, and – so the rumour went – had not been amused.

On June 21st, he was admitted to the Brompton Hospital and a week later sent to Frimley Sanatorium whence he was discharged on October 18th.

Mr Laffan, writing in 1965 to Potts's widow, continues the story:

I had approached some of my colleagues and asked them to subscribe for a fund to send Tim to the southern sun for a year. As far as I can remember, Munro and Sleeman and, I think, Arthur Cook, and I, all put up small sums. But James* came out with a whacking subscription of at least £100, perhaps £125. That settled the matter and I was able to tell Tim that there was £200 for him. As the pound went a long way in Italy at that time, his year there was assured; and off he went.

Among White's papers are five letters written from Italy to his mother. All are signed 'Dumpling'. They are affable, free, filially confident of her preparedness to do little jobs for him and quite without intimacy.

He arrived in Naples on November 6th and went on to the Hôtel Grotte Bleue, a small hotel on Capri. Determined to make Italy his schoolroom, he exchanged English for Italian lessons with the secretary, studied Italian grammar while lying down for the prescribed hour, wrote, and went every afternoon to have tea at Morgano's. This cautious regime was interrupted by a stomach-upset, which he attributed to Italian cooking and the high acetylene content of garlic-eaters' breath. 'The cook spent hours making the most filthy custards; everybody else came in as often as possible and said Speriamo.'

But by now he could converse in Italian ('the best thing for being sad is to learn something') and his insularity was melting among the linguists of the Grotte Bleue.

The secretary speaks four languages and is learning his fifth, one waiter (Giuseppe) speaks two and a half, the other (Costanzo, who took part in Mussolini's march on Rome) speaks two. The cook knows all the coarse words in every known language, and is training to sing in opera.

---

* L J Potts.

On Christmas Eve he was invited to dine with the staff. In honour of the occasion there was a bottle of Capri Spumante –

> a wine like cider with Lux in it. I compelled the entire company to drink your health. The cook sang a good deal of *Tosca* and 'Vous qui faites l'endormie' from *Faust*. Everybody became a little drunk. Costanzo unexpectedly let off the very detonating crackers which one buys in Capri for a festa.
>
> Then the business of the evening commenced. I had engaged with the two waiters to carouse on Anacapri, and we set out in the dark with the Capri crackers banging away endlessly in the distant piazza.

The carouse, with a very small Christmas tree and a very loud gramophone, was held in the parlour of an aged Hungarian, who brought out a liqueur 'brewed by herself out of 200 cabbage roses for two bottles'. The company was augmented by Costanzo's girl-friend and one of his brothers – 'a youth with a passion for standing on his head'. White produced a bottle of marsala. There was also (which added distinction) tea.

> At half past eleven the German waiter in spectacles asked me to play chess with him. At three o'clock I became conscious of the world again, having won both the two games. People were dancing or arguing or letting off crackers. Some had gone away to Mass, or had come back. Finally, we set off home. In front Giuseppe and Costanzo with one arm each of the commodious drab, three young heads together under one umbrella. Next Costanzo's brother singing dubious songs. Next myself and the chess-playing waiter, talking politely and gently – about the rain probably.

The two remaining letters were written from Amalfi. While there he visited Paestum, went for a day's walk with an Italian engineer over the mountains of the Sorrentine peninsula and won a prize in a competition got up by the hotel guests to raise money for the RSPCA. The prize was a pin-cushion. He also saw a mildish eruption of Vesuvius. Compared with the Grotte Bleue the Hotel Santa Caterina sounds tame; but it had its uses.

April 1st, 1928

My last week's amusements don't seem to have yielded anything worth writing about. I seem to have spent all day till three o'clock writing a new novel, which I suppose I shall give up when I'm halfway through.

It became *They Winter Abroad*. This letter concludes: 'Will Oolie be having puppies when I get back?'

There is nothing to show why he shortened his year in the southern sun. Perhaps he needed to earn his autumn fees by another tutorial. There was a further outlay to think of: Giuseppe had confided that he was unhappy and wanted to leave Capri, and White had offered to take him to England, paying his fare. 'If he mercifully decides not to come and I get my philanthropy cheap, I shall be able to do Rome, Florence and Venice after all.' In the event he was able to do Rome, where he saw Mussolini making a public appearance and – so he later intimated – was arrested as a suspicious character. In Naples he tested his command of Italian and of the Neapolitan dialect by passing himself off as a porter and guide to visitors.

In the same notebook as the draft of *They Winter Abroad* but written several months later is the first chapter of another novel, in which an expatriate Russian Jew called Spekter, living at Positano with a Clara and a Bella, is visited by an Englishman and an Italian boy. In a subsequent fragment, 'Tonino rolled out of bed at half past six awakening John.' It was to be a novel of homosexual love; a long, serious novel; a declaration.

In the autobiographical fragment, White said he left Cheltenham knowing nothing about homosexuality. Likely enough; it was wiser not to. At Cambridge it was ignominious not to know about it. Though he had a flirtation with a married woman older than himself and was spoken of among the Cambridge chaperones as a dangerously attractive young man (this reputation seems to have been gained on easy terms: one object of his attentions recalls, 'He spent the evening trying to prove that Queen Elizabeth was a man'), he fell in with the prevailing trend. In Italy, unsupported by English disapproval or approval, he had to decide for himself – or maybe have the question decided for him. Whichever way it happened, the experience was real enough to leave him temporarily disabled for treating it as fiction.

The draft of *They Winter Abroad* was written at Amalfi, hot and hot – written with a flowing pen and where cancelled, cancelled with a decisive one. The novel which he originally proposed to call *Of Whom the World** could not be so lightly undertaken. In August 1928, he began a new notebook which has survived from a parcel of his early papers (the vanished *Morte d'Arthur* thesis was probably among them) which lay for two years in an out-house. It has rotted with damp. Pages flake away as one turns them, part of the text is illegible. In this notebook, from August 16th to September 14th, in a series of long consecutive entries and writing with detached excitement, rather as though the subject had been set in an examination paper, he discussed the problem of how to live as a homosexual – partly as a preparation for the novel about John and Tonino, partly as a statement to himself. Is homosexuality inherent, assumed by election, imposed by circumstance? What are the advantages, disadvantages of a homosexual mating? Failing, after several badly damaged pages where a hypothetical baby is offered chewing-gum, to satisfy himself over the born or made question, he came to 'What makes the homosexual's life inevitably more tragic than the great percentage of quite normal people's,' and listed: loss of environment from choosing to fly in the face of the majority; social prejudice and a legal code compelling homosexuals either to go disguised into the world or to live as in a ghetto; the narrowed field of choice, rendered even narrower since 'not only must the paederast find a paederast but a paederast of an opposite specialization to his own. The incubus requires a succubus.' Another requirement is then foreseen; both

* 'Of whom the world was not worthy', Hebrews xi 38.

specializations are subdivided into destructive or constructive types: John, a destructive incubus, must find a constructive succubus.

> Intellectually, he should be made miserable – but physically and emotionally I can't help thinking that destruction may prove a very satisfactory passion.

After all this quadrilling, fulfilment may still be lacking.

> There must be something unsatisfactory about relationships between homos. This is deep and I can't quite get it. The actual sexual relationships must be equally satisfactory sexually in the case of both norms and abnorms; but sexual relations in themselves are not particularly satis[fying]. For love in its wider sense I postulate more than lust. A marriage between norms in which it was perfectly secure that interruption would always be used seems to correspond to the contract between paederasts. (This can never be altered.)

If the young man was sexually speculative, he was by inclination moral. He would scarcely have catalogued all the factors which make the homosexual's life inevitably more tragic if he had not felt drawn to homosexuality; but he wanted it on his own terms: monogamous, secure and exclusive.

But what he was steadily drawn to was authorship. The later entries in the notebook are increasingly concerned with the problem of how to write his novel.

> Novel-writing comes awkwardly to me – perhaps I am too young for the embracing views and interest in humanity which must go with it. For theory I am in my prime.

The problem of how to write was broken in on by the problem of whether to write at all.

> Miss Radclyffe Hall's novel about sexual perversion has been called a stream of garbage by the *Daily Express* and banned by the Home Secretary, a combination of which she should be proud.

After a reaction of 'What is the use of my continuing to write my book, which nothing will prevent me from doing', he considered 're-writing it without bedroom scenes or, if possible, but I feel this is impossible, purely allusively', or having it published in a translation abroad.

> Growsing is hopeless. I shall go on, collect my guts, face fifty thousand words of forced and accumulated time. One can't tell whether there won't be a tide to catch, some beautiful morning.

At Michaelmas he went back to Cambridge for his last year, a year out of step with his fellows. He must have felt outstandingly elderly. He may also have felt outstandingly mature, for he took back with him Chatto and Windus's agreement to publish a book of poems. The agreement had the usual royalty clause: 10 per cent on the first 1,500, 15 per cent thereafter. With a prudent if visionary eye on business he asked for 20 per cent on sales beyond 6,500. This was not quite so artless as it now seems. There was a market for poetry then and the Cambridge of I A Richards had a reputation for poets.

Mr Laffan in the letter to Potts's widow already quoted from summarized White's last year:

> He returned in great form, determined to have the examiner's blood in Part II; and sure enough in 1929 he took a tearing First Class with Distinction.

He also drew a little blood en route writing for the *Granta* and the *Cambridge Review*. The censorship was always good for a scratch. 'This limited and expensive edition will be beyond the reach of our little ones and the unemployed.' In his theatre criticisms for the *Cambridge Review* he was sufficiently engaged to object, at the risk of seeming old-fashioned, to a production of *As You Like It* which presented the exiled Duke eating what was not there and menaced by Orlando

> who comes in waving a sword he has not got. The arguments advanced are that small properties are not scenic. To stab a

man with a dagger may resolve itself into something quite abstract. When it does, there is every reason to do without the dagger. But such an action, in ninety-nine cases out of a hundred, is not abstract. On the contrary, the dagger for that moment becomes the one tangible and overwhelming fact: the stage, one vast and fascinated frame for it.

In a notice of Elmer Rice's *The Subway*, he carried engagement beyond the proscenium arch.

When, in the dreadful bedroom scene, the visionless voices announced to Sophie that she was going to have a baby and roared with hideous laughter, the audience simply rocked as well. That gave one something to think about on the way home.

As 'Our Cambridge Correspondent', White had several articles in the *Saturday Review*. In one of these – fired, I think, by a hearsay prejudice – he fell foul of the Fitzwilliam Extension as 'another example of the Menin Gate and British Empire architecture of the Wembley Exhibition'.

No part of this wing seems to be ornamented through an organic constructional growth, and no part is ornamented to accord with the main building in the mere pleasure of ornament. It stands with columns, which should have been fluted, merely weakened by a pointless parallelogram which might have been painted on a flat column in Pompeii, and with a massive cornice which is supported by no weight below.

He seems to have been reading Ruskin. He had also plucked – too hastily – some information from a *Guide to Cambridge*; but it was from his own bosom that he fetched the assumption that the protruding wing was to be complemented by another, which would hide a view of Peterhouse.

Next Saturday, he was answered by a Voice from within the portals:

Your Cambridge Correspondent is, of course, wholly entitled to his or her opinion on the subject. But, in imparting it to the world, why stray so far from the facts? He or she will be surprised to hear that not the interior but only the entrance hall was dealt with by the younger Barry, that no part of the building ever contained any cartoons by Rossetti, that the Marlay Extension was finished and opened in 1924, that there is nothing Doric about it, that the portion specially objected to was designed before Wembley or the Menin Gate, that this portion is the first side of an ultimate quadrangle, that it has no exterior columns, that there was never any idea of an E-shaped development, and that consequently the 'vista of Peterhouse which was one of the best in Cambridge' has not been disturbed or even so much as threatened.

Does it not seem deducible from so many slips in a short article that your Cambridge Correspondent is imperfectly informed as to what has taken place, is taking place, and is likely to take place in Cambridge. Of the knowledge of architecture displayed I say nothing.

I am, etc, Sydney C Cockerell
Fitzwilliam Museum

The Cambridge Correspondent replied – unconvincingly and rather pertly, but maintaining with a final blast of Ruskin that 'anybody who chooses to look closely at the Fitzwilliam Extension for, say, two hours' would agree with him. Mrs Malaprop considered that "Tis safest in matrimony to begin with a little aversion'. The friendship between White and Cockerell certainly began so.

Loved Helen and Other Poems – with a Latin dedication to Constance White – was published in March 1929, and chosen by the Book Society as its poetry recommendation for April. J C Squire, who saw the poems in proof, said of them to a friend, 'No one could read them without becoming interested in the author.' It is noteworthy that Squire, who had not met White, should have fastened on the person behind the book; Potts, who knew White very well, said of him that he was far more remarkable than anything he wrote.

To some extent, at any rate, White intended the reader to be interested in the author – as after reading on a succession of gates 'Beware of the Dog' one would begin to speculate what this redoubtable animal might be. With negligible exceptions, the poems are self-referring; many are self-pitying, others self-deriding; they carry an implication of someone sedately shameless, a passionate, melancholy, sardonic soliloquizer, indifferent to being overheard and suavely forbidding intimacy. They are plainly a young man's poems; but the young man seems unyouthful, much older than his pretence of being old. Recalling White at the time of the TB diagnosis, Mr Henn says, 'T H went all Byronic – "the young poet about to die"'. Byron, too, went all Byronic. A pose is a measure of self-protection. It is understandable that White, told he had tuberculosis (considerably more of a killer then than now), aware that he might die, realizing how intensely he didn't want to, should apply a pose of sophistication as a styptic to what was most sensible of his impending loss – his youthfulness. And as it is essentially grown-up to conceal one's feelings, these self-referring poems are self-revelatory not only where they are autobiographical – 'Pharaoh', 'To the City of Ka-Ka', 'Clouds are Beautiful', the movingly eloquent 'No Stone Unturned' – but in the author's determination to keep the reader in his place.* All this self-consciousness detracts from the effect of the poetry; but not from the effect of the book. Behind the student reading for the English Tripos who had marked and digested how Donne did it, and Patmore and Hopkins and Tom of Bedlam and

---

* 'The 'Helen' poems are not autobiographical. Replying in March 1929 to a *gentilissima signorina* in Positano who had given him Italian lessons he wrote: 'Lei ha dommondato chi e Helen. *No lo so!* La cerca in cielo e inare ogni giorno ma non posso trovarla.' ('You asked who Helen is. *I don't know!* I look high and low for her every day but can't find her.')

T S Eliot (even to supplying notes of reference, some of them so fatuous that it is hard not to believe he was pulling a sacred leg) and was discarding as fast as he might the influence of Brooke; behind the Harlequin who let off such disconcerting squibs; behind the sardonic young man who trailed so many long lines after him like mourning-cloaks, was a personality – mistrustful, vehement, curiously artless, far more remarkable than anything he had written.

And then it was all over – the dipping willows, the talk and stimulus, the old brick of Erasmus's tower and his portrait in Hall looking like Voltaire, the bicycles and the Mathematical Bridge: however often he saw them again, he would not take them for granted. He got his First Class with Distinction, and several impressive testimonials, and left Cambridge, where he had felt his powers, where he had been securely happy for perhaps the first time in his life, and where in Potts he had made a friend with whom he remained on terms of complete confidence.

III Prep School 1930–32

After leaving Cambridge White lost no time but immediately set about writing a book. The book was called *Three Lives* and he spent the autumn working on it in the Reading Room of the British Museum. The lives he chose were those of Joanna Southcott, Admiral Byng and Sir Jeffrey Hudson, Henrietta Maria's dwarf – disparate characters but alike in having made themselves famous and then being frustrated. The first two Lives are straight narrative, sturdily documented; in the third he tried a different approach, with Hudson, an old man in new times, recalling his haphazard career. The approach was ill chosen. He had not the technique to support it and this third Life seems sprawling and fictional. It is the first Life which foretells the writer; at a date when Joanna Southcott was a laughing-stock among the knowing, he had the maturity of mind to tell her story soberly and allow her her due: to be given credit for the sincerity of her delusion.

In 1930 he went as an assistant master to a preparatory school in the south of England. 'I feel that it's rather preposterous to teach Latin in a prep school after getting a First in English,' he later wrote to Potts. If the employment was preposterous, its perquisites were valuable: limited responsibility, regular holidays, time to call his own, freedom to pursue his private intentions. These were clear: as T H White, he would write a book on Gerard Manley Hopkins; as James Aston, he would write novels for profit. These symmetrical aims were complicated by a social ambition. Destined to be an army officer, he had chosen to become a scholar, and now found himself what he probably called 'an usher'. This needed to be redressed. He would become a Toff. He explained this to the not wholly sympathetic Potts.

February 2nd, 1931
I am sorry you can't be bothered with my convictions about gentility. It is an absorbing topic. As for snobbery, it is one of the best parlour games known to me – for persons not

among the gentry. The gentry don't need the game, for they have the genuine article. So when they want to play games they have to take to poetry and that sort of thing. Hence my desertion of poetry (my possession) for gentility (my sport).

March 24th, 1931
My blood-story was accepted by Messrs Cassells. I may be able to afford to be a quasi-gentleman after all. I am just going to start another one – the one I told you about, in which you are murdered by Laffan. Gerard Hopkins will take another year at least. My school holidays begin next Tuesday, and I'm going to Malvern to take a course in Advanced Equitation. This is all directed at gentility.

May 9th, 1931
My book on Hopkins came to a complete full-stop. I never got beyond the first joyous chapter of demolishing previous critics. I must be content to be a wash-out until I've made enough money to afford leisure. Then I shall write well, for I find I am naturally strenuous and should be driven into writing by having nothing else to do. This schoolmastering business is a bad idea really – however pleasant. So was your idea that I ought to be driven to write by writing for a living. The need of money has never driven me to anything but despair.

The need to write a book by T H White persisted. This emerges in a letter to Potts, undated, but written during his summer holidays.

My serious historical novel is giving much entertainment, though I have not yet written a word of it. I find that the two decades following 1840 marked the apogee of the second golden age in English civility.

White had a good, ranging nose for source-material; he was reading early *Punch*es. But with the end of the summer holidays the need to make enough money to afford leisure in which to write well drove him back on James Aston.

October 10th, 1931

I'm halfway into an attack of flu and struggling with one of my numerous unrequited love affairs. (I seem doomed to sterility, and can't help feeling it a waste. My body, poor creature, though as weak as a kitten at far too many points, is superficially well made, and seems so pathetically deserving that I feel a cad to baulk it all the time.) I am writing a book about a don called Mr Belfry, who goes to Italy a virgin, takes a mistress, falls passionately in love with her, is jilted because she falls in love with somebody else, and returns to Cambridge, taking up his duties where he left them off. I shall be pleased to have written this book, I suppose, though I hate writing it.

Next holidays I am going to hunt with a very unfashionable pack, on account of financial strain, but I hope to get my don's adventures finished then and have a little pocket money. Fame comes slowly, but I intend to have it sooner or later. For one thing my body (*q v supra*) can't have its sup until I can afford it. And all the time one's rosebuds are slipping away. Never mind, I insist on being a roué sooner or later, even if I have to wait till I dodder. I'm afraid I shall be a scandal as a poet laureate. I send you a poem, with my love.

TIMOTHY

Of the novels in this helter-skelter of composition, the blood-story, *Dead Mr Nixon*, was written in collaboration with R McNair Scott, a fellow master. White supplied the earlier chapters and the finale. His hand is obvious in the elegant casuistry of the principal criminals and in the last paragraph of the penultimate chapter.

He looked through the doorway with puzzled but contented eyes. He saw straight through Charles and the wall behind him. He left the house, passing the car, the road, the dishes and the landlady. He slipped at last through everything, leaving the body behind him to slip with gentle dignity to the ground.

The novel where Potts is murdered – an injurious picture of University life, in which both the victim and the College President are drug-takers – is *Darkness at Pemberley*. The murderer, named Mauleverer, escapes to Pemberley in Derbyshire, inhabited by descendants of Jane Austen's Elizabeth and Darcy, and lurks in its commodious chimneys. A scene where Mauleverer donnishly explains to a horrified hearer exactly how the murder was carried out and exactly why the law can't touch him is an early example of White's talent for irrefutability. The historical novel became *Farewell Victoria*. The book about the don in love is *First Lesson*. A youthful reader said of it that it was a good story, except for the heroine, who was more like a boy. She showed acumen. *First Lesson*, an Aston, was made over from that novel of homosexual love to which White had given so much thought and peripheral speculation in 1928. 'I shall be pleased to have written this book, I suppose, though I hate writing it.'

But the pursuit of gentility costs money, even if you hunt with an unfashionable pack, ride a hired horse, and wear boots without tops. Among White's many diaries is a solidly bound Hunting Journal, divided across the double page into ten columns: 'Date. Hounds. Meet. Distance to it. Horses. Wind and Weather. Scent. Coverts Drawn. Killed: to Ground. Remarks.' It cost seven and sixpence, in those days the price of a novel. The first entry is for September 10th, 1931. The hounds were the East Sussex, the weather was fine and cold with much dew; he went on foot, four miles to Crowhurst Park, and the day's score was one cub to ground and dug up.

> The digging up of the cub was an extraordinary and emotive spectacle. It was stopped up in a drain, and the latter was taken up by sections, slowly shortening the length in which it was free to move. When it had been located the chief digger tried to drag it out by the earthy scruff of its neck. But it was tightly wedged. After another effort at dislodging the cub, made complicated by an exceptionally keen hound who nuzzled to break in and scared the workmen, the pack

was cheered into the excavation, from which the muddy and somehow 'under-lived' pelt still protruded. They poured in with an exultant and deep cry, whilst the onlookers screeched them on. The pack engulfed and wrenched the creature out, pouring away from the hole in a circling whirlpool of silvery muscular bodies, deeply roaring. The savagery of the hounds was deep-rooted and terrible, but rang true, so that it was not horrible like that of the human. On the crest of the whirlpool was a dark tawny leg, cocked up. The worry lasted for half a minute, perhaps, before it disintegrated into separate hounds with separate parts of the body – a mask, a pad, a string of grimy guts. The only human who won my admiration was the huntsman; he stood apart, and with pink swelling cheeks decorously blew a formal note of parting.

Many people are shocked by the custom of 'blooding' young children. The blooding of a scholarly young quasi-gentleman might affront sensibilities too.

Two years later, White wrote in his Hunting Journal: 'Why hunt? A. (originally) desperation. B. (originally) snobbery. C. desire to excel in every possible direction. D. enjoyment.' 'This order is borne out by the dutiful tone of the Journal. He liked being on a horse, and jumping excited him; but his hunting lacked the savagery that could make it ring true. He felt no pack warmth, though the approval or disapproval of other riders affected him. He hopes he wasn't thrusting; he notices that the MFH looked angry. Twice he lost his temper with his mount because it refused a jump, and beat it atrociously – recording this with the same bleak objectivity as he did the breaking-up of the cub.

He used a different tone of voice about cubs of his own species, in the poem sent with love to Potts.

This pretty boy, mischievous, chaste, and stupid,
With bouncing bum and eyes of teasing fire,
This budding atom, happy heart, young Cupid,
Will grow to know desire.

Anxious Mamma, discern the signs of rapture,
Observe his sensuous wriggles in the bath.
His plump brown legs design their future capture,
Their virgin quelled, their tenderness and wrath.

Happy immoral imp, if this continues
He will, no doubt, grow up a shameless sensualist.
He won't despise his genitals and sinews,
Won't know that it is 'beastly' to be kissed.

Stuff him in Etons quick, and send him packing
To Dr Prisonface his breezy school.
That old rheumatic man with threats and whacking
Will justly bring this body to the rule.

Send your bright dreaming angel then to Dr Prisonface
So that he may be taught his 'beastly' loins to rule,
So that he may be learned what is and isn't cricket,
So that he may be a product of the good old school.

His legs are beautiful but he must hate them,
Starve them till sterile and when past their prime
He may be allowed to marry somebody exactly like him
And have a jolly good time.

Till then, for you can't quite kill his angel,
He'll fall at intervals and take a whore,
Shamefully take her in the night time and afterwards hate
himself
All the more, and do it the more.

He will convey the blight to his own marriage bed
Which will exactly resemble Dr Prisonface's:
Surreptitiously wrestling with his wife in the darkness,
Putting her with averted eyes through hasty shameful paces.

Dark and remorseful and dirty will be his copulation,
In Dr Prisonface's hell, among the wicked.
But never mind, he'll be a credit to the nation;
And we all hope, we all so hope, he will be good at cricket.

Prescribing (those whom White loved he prescribed for) books for Mary Potts to read after an operation, he recommended Masefield's *The Midnight Folk*. 'I read it all through to my form last term (illicitly).' The illicit reader was twenty-five – considerably nearer in age to his pupils than to their headmaster. Ten years earlier he was at Cheltenham College. He was back again in much the same atmosphere, though now on the other side of the fence. It was not a position to contain him. Combative and chivalrous, White was drawn to defenceless causes as others are drawn to lost ones. An incident had inflamed both his pity and his satire. Two little boys had been found in the same bed, and were expelled. White was charged to accompany them to London. During the journey, he asked what they had been doing. They admitted that they had been talking. Asked what they had been talking about, they replied, 'Buses and trains.'

On January 2nd, 1932, he wrote to Potts:

To all intents and purposes I have been fired from this school owing to my Socratic intransigence. There was nothing wrong, or anything of that sort, and Dr Prisonface had to invent a rambling, plaintive excuse about the lack of people to teach the boys cricket. Well, are you going to let poor Nelly starve?

Poor Nelly did not starve.

February 28th, 1932
I have succeeded by my own efforts, to a certain extent, and am to be the head of the English Department at Stowe from next September.

IV Stowe 1932–36

There is no record at Stowe how this appointment came about, nor who it was who supplemented White's own efforts. It may have been Tillyard. The appointment must have been a snap decision, for there was already a natural successor to the vacated post on the staff. But White's sudden appearance from nowhere in particular was not held against him. The supplantee says:

> I never questioned his qualifications to be English teacher, nor did anyone else think it odd. I do not think we knew, or if we did we did not care, that he had come on from a prep school; he had a First in English and obviously knew what he was talking about. He was different and exciting.

Different and exciting: that was what people were saying about Stowe and its remarkable headmaster, J F Roxburgh. It was different and exciting that a public school of less than ten years' standing was being spoken of as 'the new Eton'; that it occupied one of the great show houses of the Augustan Age, whose vast acreage of pleasure grounds, laid out in vistas, avenues and ornamental waters and admired by Horace Walpole, had stirred Sir Harbottle Grimston, another eighteenth-century visitor, to remark – rather breathless with admiration: 'The walk round is computed five miles, but the variety of pleasing objects, particularly of temples, obelisks, pavilions, etc, etc, take off the tedium so much that it appears to be less'; that a corresponding ambition to take off the tedium shaped the curriculum; that its headmaster was so free-minded that at a masters' meeting he put forward a proposal that bad reports should be edited by the boys they concerned.

Leaving the preparatory school at the end of the Lent term, White had five months to call his own before he went to Stowe. A project of 'a round of visits, and then to Paris to see a rich demising aunt, and thence to Warsaw, or any other convenient place for wildcats' boiled down into going to stay with his mother at Burwash in Sussex. From there, in May, he sent Potts a copy of a book, by a friend of mine, whom you may know. The only reason for the pseudonym is that he hopes to hold down a job in a public school, where parents are the oddest people and may find the book immoral. So the pseudonym leaves him and his headmaster (who knows) able to deny culpability if necessary.

They Winter Abroad by James Aston was published by Chatto and Windus. Their announcement stressed that Mr Aston's first novel had been written by an author of several other books, including a volume of poetry. David Garnett's review in the *New Statesman and Nation* made play with this.

A pseudonym has given Mr Aston a new freedom like a mask at a carnival: freedom to write as he speaks, to make any joke which comes into his head, to split an infinitive and to say anything he likes about anything. It is glorious. The novel is a description of a hotel for English people in Italy and the effect which the southern springtime has upon them, awakening desires which have been dormant during the winter.

Sex. Yes, indeed.

All nature stirs and quickens, the sun shines, the flowers shamelessly open their corollas promiscuously to every passing repulsive-looking insect, the birds sing and mate, lizards sun themselves and look about for other lizards – and the poor English, creaking like rusty stag-beetles, pour unfortunate confidences into each other's unwilling ears.

After regretting that Mr Aston had handled one of his characters too bookishly and another splenetically, the review ends:

But the wit, the brilliance, the jokes! Come, highbrows, come, gather and fall shamelessly upon the feast.

The feast had been prepared some four years earlier. James Aston's first novel was White's first novel too, and referred to by him in the notebook of 1928 as 'my Huxley novel'.

In August *Darkness at Pemberley* (by T H White) was published by Gollancz. Another novel by Aston was due for publication in the autumn. To give substance to Aston, press photographs of a bearded young man were got ready, White growing a beard for the purpose.

In the course of a letter to Potts (dated August 25th, 1932) he wrote:

> I must tell you that the Belfry book (which describes my experiences grafted on to your pre-marital nature, and which I hope you will recognize as complimentary – I have had to laugh gently at the hero now and then, to provoke sympathy for him and to save myself from being a prig, but the basic picture [of the man who recognizes responsibilities] is the greatest compliment I shall ever pay to anyone) will be out fairly soon in England.

That Potts's pupil should entangle himself in such a fluster of parentheses suggests embarrassment; but embarrassment from a sense of having made too free with Potts's pre-marital nature was not in keeping with White's character – or with Potts's either. Potts had a liberated mind, and was careless of social censure: finding that cabbages did better in his front garden than in his back garden, he grew cabbages in his front garden, flowers at the back. White, who rarely suspected himself of offending, certainly did not suppose that Potts would be offended. But he was afraid of being thought a prig. He had old-fashioned notions about goodness and honour, St Leonards and Cheltenham notions, which for his reputation's sake he was careful to hide. It was the disclosure of his old-fashioned esteem for Potts as a man with a sense of duty that embarrassed him.

The letter continues:

> Meanwhile (yesterday) I have finished my great full-length heroic picture of the XIXth century. I am not sure that it isn't as bad as everything else I have written, and if so, after the pirates (title, Rather Rum) I shall write no more.

'Rather Rum', which was never published, belongs to the same group as the two Astons. Like them, it has a holiday theme: in this case, a holiday cruise, promoted by a madman and passengered by type characters, is a cover for piracy. The characters are so typical that the residual effect suggests an amoral Bunyan. Potts thought well of it, and twice read it for revision. It was also read for revision by I A Richards.

In September White drove up the great avenue to Stowe in his black Bentley. At that time a Bentley was the right thing; his was old, it was probably bought second-hand; but it went very fast and was black. He was bringing a hunter too. Head of the English Department and hunting with the Grafton, he set out on a career of White-Centaur, half galloping animal, half teaching Chiron. The writer of his obituary in the *Stoic* (April 1964), recalling the impact of 'this daemonic and brilliant man', describes him 'coming out of school on a Saturday morning, pulling off his grey flannel trousers and revealed in breeches and hunting-tops before jumping into his Bentley to join the Grafton.'

Early in the new year the impact of the daemonic and brilliant head of the English Department was being felt beyond Stowe. On January 20th, he wrote to Potts:

> I am as usual in the devil of a mess. *First Lesson* was read by a parent of one of the boys here (the pseudonym having leaked out owing to the imbecility of Chattos, who keep on sending my correspondence to James Aston, Stowe, Bucks, with the result that, there being a boy here called James Ashton everything got wrongly delivered and the arrival finally of a photograph exploded the plot entirely). The boy came to me with the picture, asked if it was me, and turned over a considerable amount of correspondence which he had kept in a puzzled way.

The boy, now Colonel James Ashton, had a good eye for a likeness. 'The James Aston-THW identity was established when

I received a lot of portrait photographs. And although heavily bearded in the photographs I was able to recognize our new schoolmaster.'

To have written a novel under another name, to have carried a beard on the same chin, were not things to damage a new schoolmaster in the eyes of his pupils. But parents, as White remarked earlier, 'are the oddest people' – and one of the four wild horses (the others are the boys, the staff and the school governors) to whom headmasters are tied for their martyrdom. The Stowe files contain letters from several parents who, learning of the White-Aston identity, had read *First Lesson* and taken alarm. Mr Roxburgh now read *First Lesson* too, and was shocked by some passages in it. Standing by his young man, he maintained that the book was not representative of its author. Tillyard was invoked (which looks as if it were Tillyard who had supplemented White's own efforts), and replied that *First Lesson* was

> no more than the natural exuberance of youth calling attention to itself. As to White's personal character, it is quite unimpeachable, and any idea that the daringnesses of the book betoken a corresponding looseness of morals is grotesquely false.

White was asked to substantiate this.

> He wants me to write a letter of recantation, condemning *First Lesson* as 'an undergraduate scrape' and promising that James Aston will write no more such books.

The letter was written (it is so dignified and lofty that it almost gives the impression that White was exonerating his headmaster for having been involved in an unfortunate affair); and that was all – except that Mr Roxburgh also was asked to read 'Rather Rum'.

Many years later White looked back and did Roxburgh justice, saying in a letter to Sydney Cockerell:

> Roxburgh – whom I envied at that time and consequently

disliked but later, after leaving, made real friends with – was a genius. He allowed people enormous latitude to do what they enjoyed doing.

But the affair left him feeling resentful and (quite wrongly) imputing resentment to Mr Roxburgh by whom he pertinaciously expected to be sacked.

White at Stowe kept a Hunting Diary, a Fishing Diary, a Shooting Diary, a Flying Diary – but no Teaching Diary. In 1935 the English Department issued a pamphlet on grammar and composition for the guidance of boys doing the English syllabus. The section on composition was by White. It begins with a practical recommendation of 'good solid notebooks' and ends with the axiom: 'All rules exist to be broken for the sake of emphasis, but you cannot get your emphasis until you know the rules.' Among its 'Don'ts' is: 'Don't use "suddenly". Say the thing suddenly, shortly, instead', and: 'Don't start sentences with co-ordinating conjunctions. A full stop separates sentences, and it is illogical to follow it with a word that joins them.' The distinction between 'as' and 'like' is conveyed by: 'He looks like a fish but he behaves as a cow does' – a guide to insult which should fasten the distinction into any young mind.

Some questions jotted down in a notebook: 'Where at Stowe is there a bird's nest in a lion's mouth?' and 'What is George made of?' suggest the kind of General Knowledge he thought desirable (George is an equestrian statue of George II). '*La derniére poule est déja morte*', 'The Queen is finishing the King's stockings', 'Was your uncle's nose red?' presumably date from Dr Prisonface's time. They are demonstrably White's own work, for in a further sentence 'fromage' is spelled with two m's. The head of the English Department was an uncertain speller.

Here are some aspects of White as his pupils saw him:

Slim, wasp-waisted, with a red moustache and dark hair, he usually wore a polo-necked sweater, tweed coat and wide-cut grey flannel trousers, though he would sometimes put on a dark suit with a flaming tie and look demure. It was clear from the start that he regarded himself as a Sixth Form master, and it was believed that by the terms of his appointment he was exempt from having to supervise games or undertake the heartier chores that public-school masters were expected to shoulder, in order to enable him to write yet more scandalous novels. He introduced the new methods of literary criticism from Cambridge, and he brought an entirely new vision of life such as had never before been seen in the school. He set before us as an ideal *emotional* sincerity. This was an entirely new idea to the clever boys who were scoring off each other in the style of Aldous Huxley. He made one feel that truth might or might not exist. But what did matter was what you felt and whether your feelings were genuine, personal and sincere; and what was despicable was to serve up stock responses or clever aphorisms or second-hand opinions.

He was a very severe teacher. His irony was so withering. He knew who the clever boys were and he waited for them to expose their brash sophistication and their knowing allusions and then he would descend. He would languidly pour scorn on them and show them up and try to shame them into writing or saying what they felt. One of his tutees who experienced his teaching for two years said that after being taught by Tim one was impervious to rebuke or insult from other men.

Another:

Tim was then I suppose in his late twenties and a fairly Bohemian figure even by Stowe standards, which were not noticeably strict. He had an old open black Bentley and a red setter and among the boys enjoyed a reputation exciting, faintly discreditable and much envied on the strength of *Loved Helen* and *They Winter Abroad*, copies of which were eagerly sought after. In spite of this his teaching methods were strictly classical and any tendency to romanticism, or worse still sentimentality, was heavily censured. As a result he instilled a sound knowledge in me, his least promising pupil, of Aristotle's *Poetics*, Longinus and Quintilian, I A Richards's *Practical Criticism* and even *The Meaning of Meaning* and E M W Tillyard's *Poetry Direct and Oblique* which after all these years has never left me.

In addition to his tutorial with us he gave lessons to the school, large gatherings in the library which no one even thought of cutting. I remember him standing up, walking around, his gown flowing out (a very good-looking figure), talking fluently about I think Norman Douglas's *South Wind*, completely holding the attention of every boy there. At least in my time it was said that he had never given any punishment, lines and so on, to a boy, presumably because we were all much too interested to misbehave and he was never the type to invite ragging.

Looking back with adult hindsight, I suppose he was not happy at that time. I seem to remember remarks suggesting doubts about his talent and ability to write anything of merit. Lonely too perhaps.

Another:

'Write an essay on anything you like,' he would say to an audience of boys whose short lives had been spent in being told what to do. What he wanted was sincerity. 'What does it *mean*?' he would say. 'If you don't know what it *means*' – his speech was full of emphases – 'how can you claim the right to say whether you like it or not?' I can remember one painful afternoon when I had written a rather flatulent essay on John Donne saying how good he was and so forth. Tim then made me read out *A Nocturne upon St Lucie's Day* and construe it for him. I failed utterly. 'This proves you don't understand your own language,' he said. This savage kind of commentary was mixed with occasional interludes of modified encouragement.

In my last year I grew a little less afraid of him and a shade more sure of myself. But I was still dominated by him and accepted all his judgments. Some eighteen months earlier he had crushed my religious beliefs to powder by a passing remark about the immorality of postulation without evidence. Thereafter it never occurred to me to be anything other than an agnostic. When the countryside became a vocation for him I regretted that my family was based in London and that I had not been brought up as a countryman. When he sneered at A A Milne or Beverley Nichols and sliced to ribbons a book like *Down the Garden Path*, I sneered too – and naturally failed to take the point that his contempt was a covering for some uneasiness about a parallel that could have been pressed, however unjustifiably, between two latecomers to the non-urban scene. When he read out Hopkins's 'Pied Beauty' or 'Nothing is so beautiful as Spring' I got both poems by heart within the day and would recite them in exactly his manner. He had a particularly fine speaking voice and could modulate and vary his pitch and speed of voice with notable effect. When reading poetry, or the lesson in Chapel, he made great use of pauses.

Another:

He taught us about Wilfred Owen and Edward Thomas as part of the period of the First World War. I remember him reading Wilfred Owen's 'Parable of the Old Men and the Young' so effectively that there was dead silence. For Edward Thomas he did not restrict us to 'Adlestrop' but read us many and was particularly fond of 'A Private', which looking back I suppose represented the view of himself of which he was most proud. I know that he read and explained to me 'Fifty Faggots' so that many years later when a prisoner-of-war I could remember it without seeing it and got from it something I could not have got without it.

And another:

In his classes one always felt confronted by a person and not a performance. I think he put more feeling into his classes than most people (often using a rather Ophelia-like register of his voice) and probably came to find teaching a strain because of it. This was certainly so with his Present Day classes. These were supposed to be a commentary on current events or anything pertaining to them. The first one Tim gave was a sustained attack on capital punishment, on which he felt strongly. This was shortly followed by an attack on the goings-on of the armaments industry, then (1932) rather in the news. Another might have been called Trials of an Author, pointing out that at least one of us (there were probably about three dozen or more present) would be likely to take to writing books, and we might as well know the troubles in store.

He had a number of crazes – horses, aeroplanes, snakes, and so on. I remember the snake craze well, as we used to wander around the neighbouring countryside looking for them. I think this fitfulness of feeling gave an impression of reassuring amorality in him, and as he liked diffident and worried boys several of them (including me) went to him with their adolescent emotional troubles.

He was much attached to the ordinary conventional courtesies of civilized personal exchange. I remember once breaking a table lamp in his room (I had left, but came back for a meeting of the 12 Club, a cultural body). I wrote rather a perfunctory letter apologizing. He wrote back two letters timed to arrive by successive posts. The first said something like 'Thank you for your letter regretting having broken my lamp. In case you are thinking of buying me another one I may mention that it came from Heal's.' The second letter was long and avuncular, explaining that I ought in any case to have offered to buy another lamp, that in practice I might or might not have to, but honour would be satisfied, that only by observing these civilities could much emotional wastage over trivial things be avoided, that intellectuals and scientists (because they thought they were intelligent) tended to ignore the feelings of ordinary people, that they were a destructive force and the cause of all the trouble in the world, and so on, It was cantankerous, but extremely friendly.

Finally, two recollections of a non-scholastic White:

> When first he came to Stowe he had no gun. His shooting
> terminology gave him away as a novice. At fishing he was
> a relative beginner. I rarely saw him on a horse but was not
> impressed. Yet so wholehearted was his approach to these
> new pursuits that it was not only a pleasure to accompany
> him but very soon he became a most efficient performer.

> When Timothy White arrived at Stowe he fell in love with
> country things, horses and birds, etc, and I think it was
> probably due to the fact that having been brought up in the
> country and taught by my father to ride and about birds and
> wild life of all sorts that we found ourselves with common
> interests. I remember at the age of 16 driving his Bentley at 85
> miles an hour on the way to the airfield near Northampton
> where he was learning to fly. I was a very small 16 and I can
> remember that my feet would hardly reach the pedals and
> allow my eyes to see over the bonnet.

It was from this last boy that White learned to identify birds by
their song or way of flying. He was an ardent learner – though
what went into him as learning often reappeared with such
promptitude as teaching that people deeper into the subject
sometimes called him a smatterer. Potts's Cambridge comment
that he was more remarkable than anything he wrote was also
applicable at Stowe, where obviously he was more remarkable
for how than for what he taught. But smatterer or no, he held his
pupils' attention; their imagination, too, calling out an unusual
degree of solicitude – as though in the tall gowned figure these
adolescents recognized a hidden adolescent, someone unhappy,
fitful, self-dramatizing and not knowing much about finches.

In 1933, *Farewell Victoria* was published and 'Rather Rum'
reluctantly laid by. So much advice had been taken on 'Rather
Rum' that it became a sort of royal deathbed. The undertaking
that James Aston would write no more such books made it
difficult – since 'Rather Rum' was typically Astonian – to keep
the pseudonym. Yet the name of Aston had selling value, and

was not a thing to be thrown away. Potts with levity suggested Phoebe Aston.

White had consulted no one about *Farewell Victoria*. He may have felt shy about it, because it revealed his old-fashioned esteem for goodness and faithfulness. Its theme is The Good Man Suffering Adversity. The good man is Mundy, a stable groom at a large country house. His wife leaves him, taking their child with her; he 'lists for a soldier; when his army days are up it is chauffeurs not grooms who are in demand, but he finds employment as a coachman. His employer dies, he becomes a cabman, the only cabman on the taxi-rank, with a screw of a horse – but well tended. All his life he is patient, dutiful, unresentful and unfortunate.

In *Farewell Victoria* White allowed himself to write without sacrificing development to narrative. It goes slowly, because it has a great deal to think about: nature and human nature and the course of history and the changing English scene and the dogged English rustic – Piers, Hodge, the homeward ploughman, the Lincolnshire Poacher. Because of its theme, White put only his sadder self into it.

It is artless enough to contain a deliberate device: the theme in diminution. Mundy as a soldier takes part in the defeat of Isandula. The battle – described in rather Cheltenham terms – is over. Night falls. One tent only shows a light. In it sits the Commander-in-Chief, writing his dispatch about the calamity; he too is a good man suffering adversity.

A communication containing the lines

Refrain from sending of your beery letters
From hell holes Metropolitan to taunt your betters:
Idle apprentice, Prentice, and, O frockless Parson,
Where are you assin'?

is preserved in the Chatto and Windus files. But even when on these cheerful terms with parties who went so obligingly into Sapphics, White's fret about poverty obtruded. Also, he had resented some cuts imposed on *First Lesson*. Bent on getting them restored in an American edition, and influenced by a prospect of slightly more money, he disregarded his contract with Chatto and Windus and made a separate deal for himself while they were concluding a sale with a different American publishing house. There was an angry parting between him and Ian Parsons, who had first introduced him to the firm.

The wind was immorally tempered to the black sheep because F T Smith, the editorial director of Collins, liked *Farewell Victoria*, accepted it though he did not expect it to sell, and went on backing his fancy through two more unsuccessful books and several displays of creative captiousness.

Skilled killing was a part of White's compartmented character, and it may have been duck-flighting that took him to Norfolk in the summer holidays of 1933. At any rate, he was at Horsey, hearing the invisible sea grumbling behind the dunes, when he wrote to Potts:

August 5th, 1933
I am going to slowly divest myself of possessions and see what happens. My car has gone already (smashed) and I shan't buy another. After this season I shall sell my horse and stop hunting. Beer is my solution: probably a good one.

The only problem is how to support myself when they chuck me out of Stowe. The ideal job is farm labourer, but I am too stupid. I want to leave the upper classes.

Everybody at Stowe hates and fears me, or everybody that is bound for hell anyway. Unfortunately this includes the headmaster, so that I shan't have that job for long. If I can hang on till I'm 30 I'll try for the headmastership of a rural grammar school. I think I could bear that. But if only I could plough and sharpen a scythe and so forth. One feels so insecure without possessing any of the basic arts.

How Potts replied can be deduced from White's next letter.

September 16th, 1935

You are quite right in saying I shall never be a failure. Neither of us, now, will ever fail so far as to be successful. But the real success is to accomplish the first death effectively and early. I am getting on well with it. For me it will mean (1) no more writing (2) no more luxuries like cars and hunting and the upper classes. My motives for writing were never good and life has cured my snobbery. Well, it may not be an advance. One can't tell what it's like to be dead in this way anymore than in the other.

I am not coming to Cambridge just now. Why this is, I can't quite say. It is probably something to do with the fundamental lethargy which I share with Dr Johnson. When I make plans it costs me such an effort that I can't summon the energy to unmake them. Imagine the agony it must have given Johnson to go to the Hebrides. However, I suppose Boswell bought all the tickets. I wish I had a Boswell.

He didn't sell his horse, and his car was either mended or replaced. That winter he hunted as usual.

At a village in the Grafton country called Tingewick the Crown Inn was kept by Mr Jimmie Blaize and his wife, Flodie. Mrs Blaize had been the matron of a wartime hospital, and looked the part, for she was a big woman with a commanding presence. One of her earliest patients was a drummer boy. He fell in love with her, and wooed her so resolutely that after the war, and despite the disparity in age and weight, they married. They set up at the Crown Inn. They were childless, but there was plenty of young life about, for Jimmie Blaize bred red setters. White lodged at the Crown Inn during Christmas holidays, hunting and in between hunting, writing. In the evenings he would sometimes sit in the bar, sometimes in the kitchen. It was a small room where the red setters lay on chairs, on benches, on the lower shelves of the dresser, keeping out of Flodie's way. One evening, after he had gone up to his bedroom, he heard a light scratching at the door. When he opened it, a young bitch was on the threshold. She waited there, and looked at him.

Tired from hunting, rather drunk, flattered by the intensity of her gaze, he laughed and said, 'All right.' She came in, without demonstration, and slept all night on the foot of his bed.

From that night on, she considered herself his. With his head full of horses and hounds and shooting and the next book which would bring him a fortune and the salmon he would catch if he could get some salmon fishing, he did not realize this till Jimmie Blaize said, 'Well, she's evidently made up her mind. You'd better have her as a present.'

White wrote long after:

> I felt vain about this, and accepted the dog graciously. Yes, I can distinctly remember thinking of her as 'the dog', rather as one thinks of 'the chair' or 'the umbrella'. Setters are beautiful to look at. I had a beautiful motor car and sometimes I wore a beautiful top hat. I felt that 'the dog' would suit me nearly as nicely as the hat did. In this cheap, brutish and insensitive spirit, I embarked upon her great romance.

When he wrote those words he was reproaching himself; and probably he was kinder than he supposed. But he was not particularly attentive. He did not trouble to find a name for her, but called her Brownie, as the Blaizes did, shortening her kennel name of Brown Maid of Tingewick. And he could never remember for certain how old she was when she came to him. There are photographs of her in his Shooting Diary for 1934: – slender, leggy, newly full-grown, with the grieving Vandyke portrait expression of her kind.

By now White had finished the stately Hunting Journal and was using a series of small notebooks. One of these is lettered on its brown canvas cover FISH, and to show what manner of fish a photograph of a salmon is pasted on below. It was his first salmon, out of his first quick-running Highland river, his first experience of a wild free landscape. The river was the Beldorney Water of the Deveron, in Aberdeenshire. The month was April, with easterly blizzards and snow lying on the higher moors. It rained as implacably as the Ashtons – who had helped him to this fishing on a private water – had told him it would rain. For a fortnight he lived at the full stretch of his capacity for living, enthralled by the bareness and solitude and rigours of the scene, out all day, contented and predatory, with the noise of running water in his ears. For once, the happiness was more positive than the dream. He triumphed in the moment, and spent his last day – 'a happy day, for I forgot it was my last' – catching a few trout in order to be useful (the trout had a disease and the water bailiff wanted some for examination), scrambling about in the river or smoking on the bank with a mind detached enough to reflect on the crofter who ploughed with a horse and a cow. 'It is not a laughable spectacle really. There is something horrible about it. The horse is poor, but not a scarecrow. Somehow this makes it worse. And the man has a toiling face.'

Fishing is often called an art – which is another way of saying it is not notably dangerous to life or limb and that the fisherman who carries a flask thinks of keeping his circulation going, not his courage up. It may have been freedom from fear which accounted for White's great happiness on the Beldorney Water, and for the desistance of his usual clawing ambition – for ambition, too, is a whet to keep one's courage up. If so, he was to compensate; for the next thing he did was to learn to fly. The machines of that date were small and looked gimcrack. There was a prevalence of feats – rolls and loops and spins. The practitioners talked a baffling jargon with death grinning through the flippancies. You went faster than in any car, you rose more dangerously than over any fence, and the people who flew, who had machines of their own, who arrived for lunch removing furred helmets and unbuckling quantities of little straps, spoke of it with phlegm, as though it were nothing to them to have come down from heaven.

White bought his first flight in a travelling aerial circus near Buckingham. He had a recurrent nightmare of falling from a height, so here was a splendid new variety of insecurity to explore. It could be explored at little cost if you were lucky. The *Daily Express*'s scheme to encourage flying paid your training expenses if your instructor reported you as his best pupil. The scheme was in operation at the Northampton aerodrome, and White applied for instruction.

White's instructor was the veteran pilot Tommy Rose. This is what he remembers:

> Our little club had over sixty applications and I was busy from early morning to dusk giving trial lessons. They were of all sorts, male and female, and it was obvious the decision would be a difficult one. In the middle of this hectic period I heard a vintage roar and a young man arrived in an old Bentley and came into the office. His opening remark was 'I have come for a trial lesson for I have decided to learn to fly for nothing. I have to be back at the school by seven o'clock and my best time for the journey should be twenty minutes.' I pointed out that there were at least six people in front of him and that it was now four-thirty but he appeared not to hear. I tested three more and then young Mr White came up and said the others had 'volunteered' to let him do his test before them.
>
> Long before his half hour was up I realized that here was the winner. He had the hands of a horseman, his reactions were perfect and his intelligence outstanding. He was named as the victor and then the road between Stowe and Sywell was burned up by his Bentley every day.

In 1964 I met Tommy Rose, who had gone to live in Alderney, and asked him if White was a good flyer. 'No,' said the instructor, promptly and plainly, 'when he'd got what he wanted, he never went on with it.' White collected techniques – it was a part of his theory about the Renaissance or polytechnic man who could shoot and gut a hare in the morning, fell a tree in the afternoon and write a sonnet in the evening. If he saw an implement – plough or paintbrush – he wanted to use it; if he watched a skill, to practise it; and having got what he wanted, went on to something else. But when he took up flying he was after more than a technique. He wanted to learn a new variety of fear. He was drawn to fear, as people of a more straightforward courage are drawn to danger, and felt respect for it. Much later on, when he was discussing with a younger friend whether to take up gliding, 'he propounded to me his theory of deliberate fright. He reckoned that it was therapeutic to be fundamentally scared every few years to release adrenalin, re-awaken gratitude for life and generally shake oneself out of complacency.'

White was still learning to fly when Potts told him about a post at Uppsala.

I should love the job. They are sending me mad here. I was never born to mind my Ps and Qs. And I am beginning to find there is something horrible about boys in the mass: like haddocks. As for it only lasting 6 years, I don't mind that at all. There are only two worries. (1) Are there Nazis in Uppsala? (2) If I put in for it, do you really think I shall have annoyed my headmaster seriously, in the event of failing to get it?

White did not date this letter, but a promise that Potts should be rewarded by a Siamese kitten establishes that he wrote before June 18th, 1934, when Lady Chatterley, his Siamese, whose kittens he hoped to sell at a great profit, gave birth to an all-black litter.

Nothing came of the Uppsala project. Lady Chatterley was disposed of: she had been incompatible with his grass-snakes and White never liked her. A new project succeeded. The year before he had produced *Miracle at Verdun* as the school play. He had done it with enthusiasm, and successfully.

July 31st 1934. To L J Potts
I have suddenly found out that it is my mission in life to produce *Henry V* as communist propaganda, first at the Festival [Theatre] and afterwards in Moscow.

It's going to be like this:

Modern dress for real people like Pistol and Quickly.

Exaggerated or stylized modern dress for people with any reality at all: eg top hats, tummies and false noses for bishops, peers, etc. Some like Beaverbrook, some like Baldwin, some like the bishop in the Russian version of St Joan.

Full armour for Henry with Union Jack baldric and a Union Jack on a pin on his helmet – like a flag day only much bigger. He will carry a microphone throughout, and speak all his speeches at it. Anybody else who has a particularly bogus speech will be allowed to have the microphone pro tem, and indeed we will probably develop several sharp tussles for its possession. Crosses and Union Jacks suddenly looming out in glorious lights and stars upon the cyclorama. Poppies. Staff officers. Big gun battles. Prologues by newspaper magnates with heels on desks speaking into telephones for latest editions. Big business. Publicity. Empire. Reporters' interviews, flashlight photographs after Agincourt. No more paper. For Xt's sake help.

Stowe at that date was fashionably Red, and White had several pupils who professed and called themselves communists. Their opinions and actions – a petrol-soaked Union Jack was burned during an Empire Day celebration attended by a War Office bigwig – appealed to the frondeur streak in his character; he was excited and curious, and slightly dutiful. He probably felt that he ought to be a communist, as he felt that if there were Nazis at Uppsala he did not want to go there. Perhaps he even allowed himself the cloak-and-dagger thought that he would be endangered by going. George Rudé, a master at Stowe who was White's most intimate friend there, remembers an instance in point. Mr Roxburgh called a meeting at which he addressed his staff on the subject of Red Stowe: there even might be, he understood, communists among them – though he felt sure that any such were communists from the highest motives, good communists, etc. 'The moment the meeting was over, White rushed to see him, and began, 'I suppose you were talking about me.' Even from the highest motives, White could not have been a communist. His inclination was towards a William Morris kind of socialism, where ploughmen would not have toiling faces.

Professor Rudé told me:

He was a non-political animal, so he was always having theories. He believed in paternalistic Squires, he would have liked to be a paternalistic Squire himself; as he felt equally friendly towards farmers and farm-labourers he tended to bracket them together. He believed in using Christian names as a remedy against class, and felt that to be called Tim showed that he was accepted as an equal. There were two labourers he was particularly friendly with, Edwin and Arch. Edwin was bred in Wigan with an industrial background; 'Tim' came easily to him. Arch had been born near Stowe and had never lived anywhere else or been anything but a farm-worker. He'd try to say 'Tim', then he'd fall back into 'Mr White'. He was just as friendly – but Tim felt that something must have gone wrong – and blamed himself, of course.

At Stowe, there was no lack of people to hail him as Tim. He was a figure: a sort of robust Harlequin, plunging from one activity to another, self-confident, high-spirited and derisive. 'His height, his light sarcastic eye, gave him an air of magnificence which he was always ready to deflate by laughter', says the *Stoic* obituary. He was probably one of those people whom we consider amusing because they startle us. His sharp satirical wit and flights of extravagance were the more telling because of his quiet voice and active physique. 'A very sturdy, horsy, athletic sort of person' was the first impression of the pupil who went snake-hunting with him (the word athletic needs qualifying: White disliked organized games). The same pupil remembers

coming across him once in the lunch hour by the bathing pool, alone, lying on his face sunbathing, without clothes on. He said he often did this at that time because there was no one around to be shocked. He then said that there was no point in getting brown all over unless you had someone to go to bed with. He then said that people should go to bed together much more (and not just for sexual purposes), when they had nothing better to do, because it was natural and delightful to do so. Not only women, but men, boys, animals, even inanimate objects (he mentioned lamp-posts).

Perhaps the most significant thing about this incident is the situation: White was reposing – he may even, till the boy's shadow fell across him, have been at rest. He drove himself hard. Schoolmastering was a livelihood and subsidized the expensive hunting and shooting and fishing without which he could not have endured schoolmastering; but his mind was bent on the thought that he could write his way out – unless he could offend his way out by getting sacked – and so, either by making a great deal of money or by practising a compulsory poverty have time, at last, to write a whole-time book. After a day of teaching and violent relaxation and talk (he talked a great deal); after coming back from Edwin and Arch at the inn; after preparing work for the next day, and correcting essays and doing his duty by other intellects, he sat up writing the novel by which he would write his way out.

In *Earth Stopped*, the first of his Stowe novels, there is a character called Timothy. He is a novelist. He points out the manual labour involved.

> Write your own name a hundred times, and you will be bored; seven hundred times and you will be exasperated; seven thousand times, and your brains will be reeling in your head. Then realize that you have only written one tenth of a novel, and you will be lucky to escape the madhouse.
>
> And yet you haven't the full of it. Your own name can at least be written down mechanically. You need have no ideas. You can work like a sweated labourer doing piece-work in a factory. But the novelist has to write down different names: nouns, verbs, prepositions, adjectives, reeling across the page. They have to make sense. They have to produce ideas. All the ideas were produced long ago, by Adam, and yet he has to produce new ones.

In all probability this was remembered from the 'Trials of an Author' lecture. He had a wonderfully exact memory and economically made good use of it. It was a well-contrived economy to use his experience of hunting for a novel in the manner of Surtees, and to include a conjectural communist, and to sub-title it 'Mr Mark's Sporting Tour'. But it proved a mistake to invoke the shade of Surtees. *Earth Stopped* has none of Surtees's rotundity. It is haggard with intellect, and the reader is left feeling ungrateful for not being more amused when the author was being so brilliantly amusing.

Earth Stopped came out in the autumn of 1934. It ends with an unidentified hand dropping high-explosive bombs and chaos obliterating the Scamperdale country, thus preparing the way for its sequel. In *Gone to Ground*, which was published the following year, the chief characters of *Earth Stopped* have been drawn into an underground shelter where they find Mr Soapey Sponge and Mr Facey Romford, enjoying a hale old age of 112 with still quite a lot of bottles left. Like Boccaccio's plague party, they pass the time by telling stories. This Decameron device allowed White to include some short stories written earlier (it is always a satisfaction to find somewhere to deposit the poor things), to return to the Lappish landscape, to draw on his diaries, to embellish his experiences (in the fishing story he hooks a mermaid, not a salmon). The Countess of Scamperdale's story, 'The Spaniel Earl', is one of those written earlier. Its harsh, rather Swiftean fantasy develops a seriousness that accuses the rest of the book.

On March 1st, 1935, he dined with friends and stayed playing bridge till two in the morning, when they gave him a final glass of whisky. Roads were emptier then: driving down the steep hill from their house he saw that there was no traffic on the main road and quickened speed. He found he could not control the steering; he tried to brake, there was a noise of tearing metal, the car had stopped, his head had struck the windscreen, his nose and throat were filling with blood. The headlights were gone, but when he got out of the car he discovered by the tail light that he was blind in one eye. He walked back to the house he had left, and rang the bell. His friends were still up. Realizing that he was safe with them, he fainted.

He had crashed into a cottage at the side of the road, through a wall and into a room at the far end of which an old man was sleeping.

March 3rd, 1935
Several pleasant legends have begun to grow up about the accident. The first legend says that the Bentley had to be jacked up in order to extricate the old man's beard: the second that he slowly got up, put on his trousers, called his daughter and said, 'I think there is somebody trying to get in.'

These legends were reported to White as he lay in bed, able to use both eyes again, and go on with his diary. There is a Stowe legend also, recalled by the snake-hunter:

He was reported to have a lady whom he visited at night. Returning from one of these trysts he had an accident in his Bentley. The story was that driving back late at night, in what mood I do not know, he had driven straight through the wall of a cottage which collapsed around him. Bentleys being what they were the headlights remained undamaged. The two old people asleep in bed in the cottage, woken by the sudden collapse of the bedroom and finding two bright lights shining on them from a few feet away, supposed the Day of Judgment had arrived and Tim I suppose a rather bedraggled archangel.

Legend dies of asphyxiation when it gets among the educated classes. The version where the old man called to his daughter had the true note of folk story – the note that White listened to in village public houses, and put to good use in his later books.

The car accident was fortunately timed, for it supplied a full-close ending for the book White was now putting together from his various diaries – a book that gave him the minimum trouble since it was written already and only selection and tidying was needed. There is no record that he felt sanguine about it, though he called a committee of his friends to help him find it a good title. The title chosen was *England Have My Bones*.

Liking Stowe no better, still not sacked by Mr Roxburgh, still alive after the car crash, still failing to make money by his novels and now minus a friend, for George Rudé left Stowe at the end of the summer term, he decided to look for another post, and learned from the Appointments Board that there was a chance of a Professorship at Presidency College, Calcutta; and it shows how sad and sensible he had become that he made the first approaches himself.

October 1935. To L J Potts
The advantages are that it would rescue me from here, and give me a chance of seeing a bit of the world while I am still young.

The disadvantages are that I am not sure whether I want to see the world. I get on very well in England.

I am doing exactly three full-time jobs at the moment (a) being psycho-analysed (b) being an author (c) being a schoolmaster. As a relaxation I am learning to be a farmer.

No more was said of Calcutta, authorship or farming: (a) triumphed over everything else. Apparently his analyst had encouraged him to try a normal love affair. At any rate – for White was in the stage of blissful obedience – he cannot have forbidden it.

He reported to Potts:

It is most extraordinary. I am partially in love with a quite perfect barmaid, and spend six hours a day sitting in the pub, as temperately as is consistent with remaining in her good graces, staring at her. She doesn't feel anything in particular about me. I talk to her a lot. She has the mental age and morality of a rather nice Girl Guide. Dark hair, big dark eyes, boyish figure, protruding or rather *upstanding* bottom, giggles. I find that I make a *perfect* lover. I am so humble. When she is cross I just go on holding my peace for days, admitting her superiority and ordering drinks in a steady imploring voice. It will be irresistible in the long run, poor girl, and we shall be very happy. Anything but marriage is out of the question for her. We shall take a public house outside Cambridge, and you shall come to dinner every night, bringing masses of dons. NB You pay.

I am not really in love with her yet, or more emotionally than sexually, and I go on being psycho-analysed every day, dashing back to the pub the moment I have been done.

Is this very selfish? No, I really do like her in a queer little way.

Though he had qualms of conscience about this inclusion of the barmaid in *materia medica* he continued to follow the prescription. However, he wooed in vain. It was a setback, but he took it lightly. He had found faith, which was more to him than bringing it off with a barmaid.

In January 1936 he wrote to Potts:

— is the name. He is a very great man – must be, for cured cases such as mine are I believe most rare, if not unique. I am so happy that I hop about like a wagtail in the streets. Personally I think p a is the greatest thing in the world (how not, since it made me happy?) and if I had any guts I should write and publish my sexual autobiography, for the benefit of other poor devils. If only I had been the kind of person who went, ten years ago!*

My only outside evidence for —'s ability is that the man who gave me his address was a sadistic homosexual, and is now married and has a baby.

The coincidence of this encounter with a family man released from White's own quandary is not so very remarkable, perhaps:

---

* The sexual autobiography for the benefit of other poor devils was not written. But between 1957 and 1961 he kept an intimate record of his own poor devil state. He considered this the most important of his books ('It has cost more') and made a special bequest of it with the hope that its publication (at a date when it could no longer distress those it concerned) might contribute to a more enlightened and merciful outlook on sexual aberrants.

the quandary is not uncommon where the English public school system has prevailed. What is remarkable is that White appears to be hiding behind him.

He had not been frightened before. In previous letters he had been frank enough about his tendencies, in one, written soon after Potts's marriage, inquiring light-heartedly, 'How is Mary? Has she had any of those children yet – of which she promised me one for immoral purposes?' He had no reserves from Potts, and felt no compulsion to be on his good behaviour with him – if anything, the compulsion was to be on his bad behaviour, to resume the outrageousness of Potts's Byronic pupil. He boasted, lectured, complained, extorted, depended; he supervised his marriage – after protesting against it – gave advice on Mary's lying-in, trusted him entirely and relied on him exorbitantly.

In 1936 he found a new correspondent with whom he became a rather different White.

V Stowe Ridings 1936–38

During his first term at Stowe White wrote to David Garnett, inviting him to lecture to a group of senior pupils and offering him a day's hunting. Garnett replied that he had given up lecturing and did not hunt. On January 8th, 1936, White wrote again. His letter recalled *They Winter Abroad* and asked Garnett to 'glance at *England Have My Bones* by the same author'. Garnett replied:

January 10th, 1936

Dear White,

Thank you very much for your letter. A proof copy of your book has arrived. I have read most of it and I am enchanted with it. What a queer thing it is that we should like so many things – fishing is more to me than flying – snakes too I like.

I must say I cursed you horribly at the beginning. I can only just endure reading about people who actually catch fish. I have never tried for salmon alas. If I could catch a salmon I should die happy.

The letter – a very cordial one – included an invitation to come to Garnett's home, Hilton Hall, and have a flight in his Klemm plane.

White replied:

January 15th, 1936

Your letter was better than a salmon. I didn't know whether I ought to have written to you. I don't know yet whether I ought to be writing this, because after all one's affairs are rarely of interest to other people. But the length of your letter makes me bold.

I don't think I can get over to hazard myself in your Klemm, or not for some weeks because I have sold my car. I am selling everything and giving up everything except fishing, so as to be able to write as I think. Among the many things that I am afraid of was public opinion, and so I tried to write to please it. *England Have My Bones* is the same thing really: a facet only of all the things I should like to say.

Now I have grown up a bit and think (at 30) it is time to face the issue. I hope to get out of Stowe by the end of this summer term, and live in Scotland on £200 a year – which I think I can earn by writing. I want to get married too, and escape from all this piddling homosexuality and fear and unreality. That is why I wrote soliciting your good graces. Actually I would rather have no money at all than be a schoolmaster, but it would be nice to have a little cash in hand. So I wanted EHMB to have a chance.

It was the beginning of a friendship that lasted till White's death – a friendship which, reversing the usual order, ripened into acquaintance; for they met seldom, and never for long at a time. In fact, they were better apart. When they met, they got on each other's nerves. White's veneration made him emulatory; he wanted to impress, and showed off. This offended Garnett's fastidiousness and rather baffled his good will. But the veneration and the good will remained.

'Edward, who nursed almost every writer of outstanding talent for fifty years ...' Garnett's words about his father are applicable to himself; he has inherited Edward Garnett's eye for promise and concern that it should be rightly developed. One of the functions of a nurse is to keep children out of harm's way. The review of *They Winter Abroad* was calculated to present James Aston as an answer to the intellectual's prayer for intellectual light entertainment. The full-page review of *England Have my Bones* in the *New Statesman* for March 7th, with its genuinely felt praise and blame ('He has real power – and is often tiresome'), hauled T H White out of the ranks of entertaining writers, gave him a shake and told him he could do better.

In a letter to Potts White remarked: 'My style previous to EHMB was constipated.' At first sight, the explanation seems obvious: in *England Have My Bones* he was assembling from his Hunting, Fishing, Shooting, Flying and Miscellany Diaries pages about activities which he enjoyed: his style was easy because he was considering no one's pleasure but his own. But where in *England Have My Bones* the entry for May 17th ends: 'This journal is about fear,' the corresponding entry in the Flying Diary runs: 'This book is about fear.' He had a book in mind. As White could scarcely take pen in hand without thinking of a book, it is not perhaps of much importance whether he was writing a diary to turn into a book or writing a book that would read like a diary. Whichever way up it came, the variants between the constituting diaries and the book are slight: an adjective taken away, a slang idiom adjusted, a politer word substituted; and here and there an interpolation, usually to be regretted, of earlier fine writing. The book's sustaining merit – it has some queer lapses – is its persuasive love for outdoor pursuits, which fetched a signal compliment from James Agate, reviewing it: 'It is about subjects in which am not even faintly interested. It is entrancing.'

The book did very well; strangers wrote to him to say how much they enjoyed it. One of these was John Moore, also a writer and a fisherman, and a committed airman. White liked him so much that having behaved ill-manneredly at their first meeting he wrote to apologize.

– all that Café Royal stuff and the champagne. I'm sorry about it, but what else did X Y expect? I brought him because I knew neither of you, and if you had both turned out to be cads, I should have been able to set you at each other and remain unscathed myself. It was a defensive measure. I wanted to be talking to you, much less brilliantly and more slowly, but by the time I got the opportunity it was too late and I was too tipsy.

This was written from Dalmally in Argyllshire, where he had gone in the Easter holidays to fish for salmon in the Orchy. The letter ended, 'Wish me a good fish. They do run up to 40 lb – or might.'

On April 29th he caught a thirty-pound fish, and sent it to the Garnetts. By now he could picture the receivers and the threshold it would be lugged across. He had lunched at Hilton Hall at the end of January, when his host's first impression was of someone strikingly tall with 'brilliant blue, rather blood-shot, unhappy eyes'. There must have been talk about animals; in his *billet de digestion* White undertook to bring a fox-cub for his hostess when he came again, and a grass-snake. 'Do you by any chance care for hedgehogs?'

From Dalmally he wrote to Mr Roxburgh, resigning his post. He told Potts:

> It needed courage because my analyst has only got me about one quarter of the way. *England Have My Bones* has made a profit of about £500. I don't know what my future is going to be, if I have a future. The barmaid is a complete write-off.
>
> I caught a 30 lb salmon in Scotland (which is a big one) and sent it to David Garnett. I wonder how he contrives to be happy?

'I doubt if there is anybody living who likes being alive as much as I do' – so he had written to John Moore after a day when he had climbed to the watershed between Glen Orchy and Glen Strae. Being happy was a different matter. Fishing was a way to it – he had been happy at Beldorney. Fishing, writing, a cottage somewhere; John Moore was invoked:

> Do you know of a cottage (one room) within reach of your Wye salmon with a free trout stream handy and nice neighbours who will invite me to shoot half a dozen times a year?

The conjectural cottage became more substantial when it suddenly seemed he might not get there. His mother's cousin cut loose from their joint small-holding; she rose to the crisis and telegraphed intentions of suicide. Having dissuaded her, White learned that her last quarter's alimony had not been paid. For a dreadful fortnight he faced the thought that just when he had renounced a salary he would have to keep her and, having made himself homeless, might have to live with her. It was a false alarm: the belated alimony was paid, Mrs White was reconciled to existence and proposed to visit him in his cottage later in the year. John Moore, to whom White recounted these anxieties, was struck by his 'cool, steady, uncompromising dislike, lacking in compassion'. Lack of compassion did not wipe out the sense of filial duty. White never broke with his mother, wrote to her, helped her with money, would at the pinch have tried to live with her; but her woes wrung a dry heart.

A new proposal superseded fishing.

I had two books on the training of the falconidae in one of which was a sentence which suddenly struck fire from my mind. The sentence was: 'She reverted to a feral state.' A longing came to my mind that I should be able to do this myself. The word 'feral' has a kind of magical potency which allied itself to two other words, 'ferocious' and 'free'. To revert to a feral state! I took a farm-labourer's cottage and wrote to Germany for a goshawk.

It was a cottage on the Stowe estate, built for a gamekeeper. It stood in woodlands, half a mile from the road. Notes of Victorian pheasants reared and killed were still legible on the door of its barn; there was a badger's sett nearby and a fish-pond with carp in it. Water had to be raised from a well, sanitation was an earth-closet, but it had the practical advantages of being in a known neighbourhood, with a rent, barn included, of five shillings a week. Here, for the first time in his life, he would have a home of his own. He spent a hundred pounds on carpets and curtains, bought mirrors and a highly ornate second-hand bed and laid in a stock of tinned foods and madeira (Scythrop Glowrie drank madeira in his tower, and White was an admirer of Peacock). On July 29th he left Stowe. Two evenings later he fetched the goshawk from Buckingham railway station, a light weight, bumping and screaming in a canvas-covered basket. Taken from its nest in Germany it had travelled to England by air, then on by rail to Scotland; thence, swopped for a female, to the falconer in Shropshire from whom White bought it.

I picked up the clothes basket in a gingerly way and carried it into the barn. I had only just escaped from humanity, and the poor gos had only just been caught by it.

The bird's jesses had been knotted into the basket. He untied them, and left it alone to recover. After an interval he put on his falconer's glove, went back to the barn, took the bird on his wrist and momentarily looked at it by the light of the hanging oil lamp. Then, correctly, he looked away: hawks must not be eyed. It gave a leap of rebellion, fell off his wrist and hung upside down on its jesses, flailing its wings. He was prepared for this too. It is called bating and would happen a thousand times.

He was impatient to begin – too impatient to consult the Shropshire falconer or to find out if there were any contemporary manuals on falconry. Unwittingly, he achieved the distinction of being perhaps the only twentieth-century falconer to man a bird by methods Shakespeare would have accepted as traditional. Nowadays a hawk is acclimatized to man by a process analogous to running-in a car. It is moved, little by little, from entire seclusion to a background of daily life. It associates its keeper with the food he leaves with it, it comes to think of him as an appurtenance and finally consents to be handled by him. It is then manned and ready for training.

The old method of 'watching' the bird is based on the fact that birds, like men, sleep by night. White, standing in the barn with Gos on his fist, patiently replacing him when he bated, whistling to him or repeating poems or stroking his talons with a feather or offering a bit of fresh-killed rabbit, always attentive to him yet always scrupulously aloof, patiently and unyieldingly and sleeplessly keeping him awake for three nights running until the wild bird abdicated from its feral state and fell asleep on the gloved hand, was as much a figure out of the past as the ghost of a ballad falconer would have been. 'It is strangely like some of the eighteenth-century stories of seduction,' David Garnett said of the resulting book. But seduction is only half the story. Eighteenth-century seducers knew their business: in the story of White and Gos, two virginities met together.

For six weeks White kept a day-book, entering, sometimes barely able to keep his eyes open, the uncertain progress of Gos's training. Sandwiched among these are his own domestic works: cleaning grates, scrubbing floors, shooting rabbits and pigeons for Gos's victuals, making bookshelves and a kitchen table, house-painting. He was putting a coat of blue paint on the front door when Gos escaped. With the kindest motives he had lengthened the bird's tether by six yards of tarred twine, a twine which he knew to be defective, since it had broken before.

I saw the end of the twine lying loose, with no leash tied to it. It had snapped quite clean. Gos was gone.

It meant that I could not publish what I had written about him, of course. Failure. My living depended on writing about him, as the fascination of owning him had depended on it: but not now.

His retainer of £200 from Collins was on the understanding that he would offer them a book yearly. (This is the £200 he referred to in the January letter to Garnett.) He had a book, but did not offer it. 'I have just finished an absolutely bloody novel about schoolmasters – a mean-spirited and sour book,' he wrote to John Moore at the end of October. The novel is called *You Can't Keep a Good Man Down*. Its theme is that if you have been a successful schoolmaster you forfeit all hope of succeeding in anything else. White wrote it during his last year at Stowe, and under the name of Dr Prisonface made himself a warning to himself. As a flogging headmaster, as a tutor to little boys, as the seducer of a barmaid, as the twitching prey of the barmaid's mother, as a hanger-on, as a farm-labourer, as a beggar, he tumbles from failure to failure. At the end, shuffling hungry and penniless along a country lane, he meets a stranger who is White redeemed from school-mastering – a free spirit who trains labradors and is happily married to a good cook. The book had been shown to Potts, who pronounced against it: it would have done White's reputation no good to recall James Aston. But White traduced it when he said it was sour and mean-spirited: it is funny, heartless and humane.

In November he wrote to John Moore from the Buckingham Cottage Hospital where he was waiting to have his appendix out.

I write this in considerable distress, since, although suffering no pain and never having suffered it, I have just had to make the decision in cold blood for myself. I have always been terrified of the knife.

It has made me feel cleaner in some obscure way. I think I am brave and master of my soul after all. And it was necessary that I should unthrone the self-centred tangle which my life has become, by adventuring the life. (They say it is only five thousand to one.) So many people have been to see me and sent me things, people for whom I would never have stirred such fingers myself. It has been a happy humiliation.

White's letters to his friends show him being a slightly different White for each one of them. It wasn't something put on, it was more in the nature of an adjustment. With John Moore the adjustment took the form of a slackening of tension. John Moore's outlook on him suggests why.

He was beautifully unprincipled in some ways, indeed quite amoral, but with the marvellous saving grace of complete loyalty to his friends. At least I always felt I could trust Tim – making allowances for the wild winds that moved his spirit – but even if I had felt I couldn't, wouldn't have minded very much because I was fond of him in an easy way which didn't demand that he should never let one down or fail one.

I think he was 75 per cent of his time unhappy and often very unhappy; probably about nothing in particular. Terror and awe mysteriously affected him. He couldn't bear to think about death; he was quickly cast down or lifted up according to how his writing had gone. He was a dead serious writer. This I imagine was what mattered to him most.

He was a self-tormented person and I imagine he saw himself very much as Lancelot in *The Ill-Made Knight*. He was very subject to fear in little things – absolutely terrified of aeroplanes though he forced himself to learn to fly. He both liked and hated to scare himself by driving very fast along narrow country lanes at night – he had an old Bentley, I think. At the end of such a drive even if he was a bit tight you could see how frightened he had made himself. It was a deliberate thing. Do you remember Edith Sitwell's account of John Mytton in *The English Eccentrics*? She sees him as driven along at a great pace 'racing, driving, jumping, hunting, chased always by a high mad black wind'. That is very much how I see Tim in those days – chased by a mad black wind. Not always distraught, of course, sometimes gay, often wildly enthusiastic, tremendously moved, especially by natural beauty, then often quickly lapsing into melancholy because that beauty was so transient.

In February Garnett was offered a fishing on the Wye and invited White to join him. While they were breakfasting their first morning a carrion crow settled in the garden and cawed persistently. White remarked: 'There will be a death in one of our families today.' An hour later Garnett got a telegram telling him of his father's sudden death. Writing to Garnett, White commented:

> I do not think the corbie was entirely a coincidence. The presence of the crow was a coincidence, but not that we talked so long about it. You said at some length exactly what your father would have said. I cannot explain this properly and do not quite mean what the words would seem to mean, but I think that fathers do actually persist in their children. There was a link at that moment, like the link which brings carrier pigeons home or works the wireless. Your father came to you then and took refuge, got inside.

He was back at Stowe Ridings by the beginning of April, having done 'the first third of a book which I hope to call Burke's Steerage'.

Burke's Steerage, or The Amateur Gentleman's Introduction to Noble Sports and Pastimes, is White's *Te Deum* at having come out on the further side of trying to be a Toff. It is comprehensive – 'In shooting foxes the Amateur Gentleman will make sure that he is alone or absolutely sure of his company'; succinct – 'When these creatures [salmon parr] have lived the correct time in the river, as laid down for them in the Lonsdale Library, they go out to sea and eat cod'; exhaustive – 'Hunting, being carried on in the winter months, is almost the only gentlemanly occupation (tobogganing can scarcely be called so) which does not expose its devotee to the danger of being struck by lightning'; helpful – 'The hunting hat is specially strengthened and has a little leather bag to fall into, so it is no good wearing the one you bought for funerals.'

White had fallen out of conceit with *England Have My Bones*, saying of it that it had a beautiful thought on every page. (Possibly it stung his pride that the book he had taken no trouble about was praised when the others weren't.) *Burke's Steerage* was calculated to alienate his *England Have My Bones* public, and duly did so; when it came out in 1938 it did not go beyond its first impression. English sportsmen quite like being laughed at: *Burke's Steerage*, serenely sardonic, laughed at their sports.

Though in the mortification of losing Gos, and losing him so discreditably (for if the bird had been properly manned he should have come back to the distracted trainer who was walking from one dripping tree to another, whistling 'The lord is my Shepherd' in the teeth of a gale and holding out a rabbit leg), White felt that book and livelihood were gone too, he got over it and ordered another goshawk. She arrived in mid-April. He called her Cully. The falconry book would be written after all – in a more experienced manner. He inquired about getting a pair of merlins, applied for membership of the British Falconers' Club, and began to correspond with its secretary, J G Mavrogordato. On May 8th he accepted an invitation from Garnett. 'I can release my two badgers, but shall have to bring Brownie [his setter bitch] and the goshawk.' A week later he wrote to say that he could not come. Brownie had pleurisy.

He knew that Brownie was jealous of the hawks and felt her nose put out of joint. He had tended her when she got a thorn in her foot, and after that she made several attempts to regain his attention by limping and holding up a sound paw. When she went off her food he commented, 'Brownie is on hunger strike as a protest against the hawk.' In fact, she was developing distemper, which is usually a mortal affair with a grown dog. Six years later, in the 'Biography of Brownie' written for his godson, William Potts, he wrote:

She had decided to die.

She had had it for a day before I noticed, but when I did notice, the miracle happened all at once in my heart. Something in her dying look at last penetrated my thick skull. I wrapped her up in the best eiderdown; I bought bottles of brandy and port and stuff to make junket. I had a veterinary surgeon every day and even a human doctor twice, and I sat up beside her, day and night, with hot water bottles, for a week. She got rennet every two hours with a teaspoon of brandy, and I told her over and over again that if she would not die I would not keep hawks any more, or go to cinemas or to dances or to any place where she could not go as well.

But I couldn't stop her. She got weaker and weaker, and it was awful to hear her breathe, and the doctor and the vet were useless, and you could hardly feel her heart. At last came a minute when I said:

'In a quarter of an hour she will be dead.'

Then I said: 'Well, there is nobody left in it but me and Death! We will fight it out. I can't possibly make her any worse, so I will at least do something to see if I can make her better.'

He looked up Distemper in the *Encyclopaedia Britannica*, and found a rather half-hearted recommendation of quinine.

I gave her half a human dose, which burned her weak throat but she was too feeble to cough it up. When the quarter of an hour was up, she stood up on her shaky legs and was sick. The next time the whey came round she actually drank it, instead of having to have it poured down her throat.

That night she suddenly ran out into the darkness, or rather tottered out, and vanished. It was pitch dark. I stayed for hours calling her and walking about the wood with candles, but I could not find her and she did not come back. At last I knew she had died in a ditch, so I went back to the house and cried myself to sleep, but I got up again at dawn, and went to look for her body. I was calling and looking when she staggered out of the wood, not quite sure who she was or who I was, and I carried her home in floods of tears, but they were quite needless. She was cured.

They were both cured. The trick of withholding his heart, which shows so odiously in the courtship of the barmaid, was gone, abolished by the shock of finding himself essential to a living creature. 'I have always wanted to be somebody's best friend, but never succeeded' – so he once wrote to Potts. 'I have no friends, only acquaintances. You have no idea how curious it is to live one's whole life like a cat.' He remained unsecured, sharp-clawed and suspicious: these were in his lot, like the caution which his lot enforced on him. 'His own amorous feelings were, I think, all for boys, and he was very very very careful about them' (Hugh Heckstall Smith, in a letter to the author). But his loving feelings were less strictly guarded, and at the realization that he might lose Brownie's love before he had allowed himself to love her 'the miracle happened all at once'. He dared to risk his heart on something that might be dead in another twenty-four hours. Whether or not this made much difference in his cat's life, it made a great difference to his next book.

Brownie was so sure of their new relationship that he was not even held to his promise. He went on keeping Cully and two sparrowhawks and presently added an owl, whom he called Archimedes:

the poor starved tawny, taken and kept for two months by a small boy who did not understand an owl's stomach, and subsequently murdered by a local family of tawnys. I was sleeping out at the time, and he had come back to me with one eye blinded, and I had done my best for him. For the two days which his vitality left him, he would not leave me by an inch, and at night he slept on my head, while Brownie slept on my feet: three beasts on one camp- bed out of doors.

Readers of *The Sword in the Stone* will know that Archimedes did not wholly die. On October 5th White wrote to J G Mavrogordato:

I have to come up to Wen some time in the near future to hand over a manuscript to my publisher.

This was the manuscript of *The Sword in the Stone*.

January 14th, 1938. To L J Potts
I have £41 in the bank. No book has been published since the last you heard of – *England HMB* – but there is one in the press. I think it is one of my better books, so probably nobody else will. It is a preface to Malory. Do you remember I once wrote a thesis on the *Morte d'Arthur*? Naturally I did not read Malory when writing the thesis on him, but one night last autumn I got desperate among my books and picked him up in lack of anything else. Then I was thrilled and astonished to find (a) that the thing was a perfect tragedy, with a beginning, a middle and an end implicit in the beginning, and (b) that the characters were real people with recognizable reactions which could be forecast. Anyway, I somehow started writing a book. It is not a satire. Indeed, I am afraid it is rather warm-hearted – mainly about birds and beasts. It seems impossible to determine whether it is for grown-ups or children. It is more or less a kind of wish-fulfilment of the things I should like to have happened to me when I was a boy.

I have also written a book called *Burke's Steerage or the Amateur Gentleman's Introduction to Noble Sports and Pastimes*. It is a short, cheap thing, doing for sport what Cornford's *Microcosmographia Academica* did for your damned university. But it is not good.

Writing books is a heartbreaking job. When I write a good one it is too good for the public and I starve, when a bad one you and Mary are rude about it. This *Sword in the Stone* (forgive my reverting to it – I have nobody to tell things to) may fail financially through being too good for the swine. It has (I fear) its swinish Milne-ish parts (but, my God, I'd gladly be a Milne for the Milne money) but it is packed with accurate historical knowledge and good allusive criticism of chivalry (I made the fox-hunting comparison with some glee) which nobody but you will notice.

In fact, *The Sword in the Stone* had allowed him two wish-fulfilments. He gave himself a dauntless, motherless boyhood; he also gave himself an ideal old age, free from care and the contradiction of circumstances, practising an enlightened system of education on a chosen pupil, embellished with an enchanter's hat, omniscient, unconstrainable and with a sink where the crockery washed itself up. As Merlyn, White had the time of his life: the brief dazzle of being head of the English Department at Stowe was a farthing candle to it. There was also the pleasure of discovering a Kingdom of Grammarie where there was room and redress for anything he liked to put into it: for the poor starved tawny who there feasted on dead mice cupboarded in his master's cap, for the crockery in the Stowe Ridings sink, for the friend's spaniel who had impeded their walks by winding her lead round their legs and became King Pellinore's brachet, for the excessive earnestness and lacking final Gs of Advanced Equitation, for his own remarkable memory which enabled Merlyn to remember all the things that hadn't yet happened. With this went the satisfaction of serving under Malory – a Master whose service imposed freedom. Except in the *Midnight Folk* pastiche of Madam Mim – later cut out – White showed his veneration for Malory by writing like himself.

The letter to Potts was written from Wells next the Sea, in Norfolk, where he had gone for goose-shooting. Two months before, writing to Garnett about possible journalistic work, he had said: 'What I want to do is to shoot a goose!' There is nothing to show what gave him that ambition; but it must have been strengthened by Malory's Merlyn, who came disguised: 'all befurred in black sheepskins, and a great pair of boots, and a bow and arrows, in a russet gown, and brought wild geese in his hand'.

From Norfolk he went back to Stowe Ridings.

White's earlier diaries had been about his activities. In 1938 he began to keep a diary about himself. It begins:

> This day, Wednesday the 25th of March, 1938, I began to construct the first air-raid shelter I ever made, at the beginning with sorrow and perturbation of spirit, but afterwards with honest interest in making the thing secure.
>
> But the human brain can be unmade so quickly, and it takes so long to make a book out of the brain, that I must at the same time begin to write in order that when the whiff of murder comes stealing something may be left behind.

At that date, poison-gas was the foremost dread. It was the wrong guess; but the assumption that a further war would involve civilians was correct. The book White had in mind was intended for survivors of those civilians who by their sheepishness, mental laziness, and good feeling had allowed themselves to be bossed into war by their governments. Such survivors must learn to think for themselves, and form some sort of International Front against warmakers.

> Bianchi! Veit! Strange Russian into whose language I cannot even translate our own name [he could not translate it into German either]. You love your countries as I love my dear one, and it is for that reason that I refuse to shoot at you. I hope to run away, as I beg you to run away, refusing to identify *England* or *Russia* with Chamberlain's policy or Stalin's.

At that date it was uncertain whom we should be told to fight.

The thoughts he wrote down (they are really more in the nature of expostulations) stem from the same wishful socialism as his public-house visiting at Stowe. The common polyglot man, he believed, was a man of goodwill, the same goodwill which rendered him the inattentive implement of war-makers. This belief was dashed by a conversation with a local farmer, who had done him many kindnesses and for whom he felt great affection. 'He was England for me; was Britannia with her honest trident on the penny.' This man had been a prisoner in Germany in the 1914–18 war, had worked as a labourer, had seen hunger hardening into famine. The English escort who came to entrain returning prisoners brought white bread. White's friend ate till he could eat no more, then threw the rest of the bread away. The German civilians watching, hurried to pick it up. He put his heel on the bread and trampled it. 'They are damned by their extraordinary minds, they are sainted by their extraordinary hearts', was the best White could make of it.

He spent Easter with his mother. She was always unlucky to him. When he got back he found that Cully, the goshawk, was dead. She had been left in the barn, with a boy coming to feed her. The windows of the barn were blinded with strawberry netting. She had entangled her foot in the netting and so hanged herself.

Both goshawks were lost to White through economy. Gos had been tethered to the bow-perch with defective twine. The barn windows should have been secured with a much stouter netting. It needs moral stamina to buy the better article, and White had not much experience of spending money prudently instead of thriftily. By now he had very little money to spend. Goose-shooting is expensive; an ordinary gun will not carry far or thwackingly enough, and for winter dawns on mud-banks you need Merlyn's wrappings. White had spent on his expedition to Norfolk because he hoped to recoup by *The Sword in the Stone*. 'This book will make all our fortunes,' he said to Mr Smith of Collins. When this seemed likely to come true, the English publication was put off from February to July, to give time for it to be considered by the American Book of the Month Club. The forty-one pounds in the bank dwindled to nothing, swelled to an overdraft.

June 13th, 1938

CREDIT

I have a cottage at 5/- a week, and it is a very beautiful one, but I don't own it and can't lease it.

I have credit until July 1st at the White Horse in Silverstone, at the Tingewick Co-Operative Society, at Harrison's Stores Buckingham, at Markhams (ironmongers), Busby (Market gardener), Smith's (Bookseller), Boots (Chemists), and I could probably get credit at some more.

I have had enough to eat.

I have a mother living, but apparently imbecile through what seems to be paranoia, a father, judicially separated from that mother, whom I have not seen for 16 years, a red setter bitch that I love more than anything, a little owl (*athene noctua*) whose life I have saved if she lives, a tawny owl (*strix aluco*) about six weeks old called Silvia Daisy Pouncer, and a dozen set traps to feed them with.

My cottage is furnished with several thousand books. I know one great man, David Garnett.

In the garden I have a dozen delphiniums, two dozen hollyhocks, some dahlias, golden rod, Michaelmas daisies, chrysanthemums, nasturtiums, eight guineas worth of flowering shrubs, two peach trees, two fig trees, six sumacs, four cherries, two apples, two plums, some red-hot pokers, lilies, spring bulbs, irises and geraniums and salvia, two rockeries in good trim and twenty pole of lawn mainly just sown and doing well. There is also a dovecot without any doves in it.

I have my faculties.

DEBIT

I can see, feel, smell, touch and hear: but there is no wife or child to see, etc.

I owe the bank £67, and they will not let me owe them more. There is no capital at all.

I have consumption, or was once locked in a consumptive home for six months, and I drink much too much.

Nevertheless I look healthy enough to be conscripted or shamed into volunteering for the next massacre of innocents,

My gum boots make my feet sweat.

Though he was living on credit, and the shadow of war neared or veered, and his mother paid him a return visit, his diary shows him enjoying a happy summer domesticity. 'A young strix can live well on four mice a day, and the athene only needs two. Both can, after a bit, take beefsteak if it is cut up small.' (The supply of mice was kept up by Stowe boys who trapped for him.) For himself, 'A cabbage makes a very good dinner,' he noted, and elsewhere records, 'My dinner of shredded wheat with cream and golden syrup.' 'My Lilford owl gave in today. I put an old coat on, and she sat on my shoulder for two hours, under the apple tree, sometimes nibbling my hair and sometimes speaking with little squeals, as of a small expiring concertina.' The owls (both were too young to fend for themselves) answered his need to have something depending on him but he had no sentimentality about them.

One of the boys who brought Eldrich (the athene) thinks he wants to keep him as a pet. But I hope to make it clear that he can never win the tolerance of this owl now. It is only by performing all the duties of a foster-mother that one can achieve a sort of desperate tolerance from these creatures.

On the way home from Silverstone I drove with my arm round Brownie, calling her: red setter, sorrel, Indian red, royal sovereign, red-hot poker, sanguine, nut-brown maid, goldfish, marmalade, conker, vixen, crust of bread, 18 carat, carrots, mahogany, chrysanthemum, bloom of rust and blue of shade. In fact, she is my Pocahontas, my nonpareil.

On July 2nd his two merlins arrived: 'Such meek and noble beauties.' 'Each merlin weighed exactly five ounces.'

July 6th, 1938
Two things happened today which have never happened to me before. I got a cable of more than a hundred and fifty words from America, and, in the evening, I was rung up from that continent at the rate of about five dollars a minute. This strange conversation, backed by the sea-like roaring of many thousand miles, was occasioned by the even stranger possibility of wealth and fame. Today I am faced with two paths, in the one of which I may remain a sort of philosopher without money, in the other of which I may lose philosophy and all occasion for it. It seems that the American Book Club may be prepared to choose *The Sword in the Stone*, if I will alter three chapters. It may mean selling 150,000 copies.

The owls come in shy secrecy every day to the food which I leave out for them, and Balin and Balan are growing down their feathers with a healthy firmness. Today Balin settled on the hack-board while I was cutting up meat on it, and even accepted a fragment from my lingers, with a dainty snatch.

The merlins were named out of the *Morte d' Arthur*, but for ordinary purposes were called Red and Black, after the colour of their hoods. They were amenable to training, they came to his whistle, they enjoyed motoring, they flew to the hand (he had to train himself to carry two birds on his wrist). His only difficulties were remembering their sex ('I must get into the habit of thinking of them as masculine: the trouble is that they are so sweet') and overcoming his scruples about procuring small birds for the initial kill.

July 31st, 1938

Last night I knew that the time had come for the illegal flight at a bagman.* But I was at my wits' end to get 2 live bagmen, till Graham** thought of the martins in their nests. We took two, and I put them in a covered cage in the coal cellar, where the darkness would keep them quiet. First thing in the morning I went out determinedly and let them loose.

August 5th, 1938

I spent the day rushing about like a madman. First of all the old 1927 Austin finally broke down halfway to Buckingham. It boiled over, all the wheels fell off, the hood fell in, and I left it in the middle of the road. I walked to the New Inn Farm and rang up London to hear that the American Book Club had chosen *The Sword in the Stone* after all. It had seemed too good to happen to me, so we had not counted on it. But now the Austin having faithfully expired at just the right moment, and how it held on for so long I don't know, I bought a Jaguar on the spot, had it in my possession by the evening, and will be off to Wales tomorrow.

He took Graham Wheeler with him. Angus Bellairs and two local naturalists went too.

In Radnorshire Balin flew so brilliantly and with such fire that White gave up all attempts to remember his sex. (He was thinking in terms of falcons – the female falcon is the grander bird.)

I flew Red at a ringing lark, who took her up almost out of sight, and half a mile away. Red stuck to her like a bull-dog, and, in their manoeuvres for height, sometimes the lark seemed to be chasing the hawk, as each took advantage of different currents of air. But suddenly, there were two merlins. A wild merlin had joined in! Now was the height of glory, as

* Live bird, tethered, used to provoke man-reared hawks to their first kill.

** Graham Wheeler, a local boy who helped with the merlins.

wild hawk and trained one took company together, and flew the lark down to earth like two roadmen hammering on a crowbar in turn. It ended in one perilous vertical stoop of perhaps 500 feet, like Satan's fall from heaven. In a moment all were gone like meteors into the trees round the farmhouse on Rydithon side, and it was over.

He drove on to Wiltshire. There were larks over Yarnbury Camp, singing above the noise of the army's gunnery practice. The nearest hotel was at Heytesbury.

At the Angel, the hawks provoked less than the usual amount of comment and the landlord said, 'Of course you know Major Allen?"
'Well,' said I, 'I know of a Major Allen by repute.'
'He lives next door.'

Before the day was out, White had paid his respects to Major Allen and gone out with him. The merlins killed three larks – 'but they were all easy birds'. In the presence of this great falconer White was modest, even about Red. For three days, he was a pupil in heaven. On the third day there was more to thrill him. Siegfried Sassoon, living at Heytesbury House, invited him to lunch, where other guests were Ralph Hodgson and Sir Sydney Cockerell. 'I find it is very nice to meet humane people,' he wrote to Garnett. But on August 22nd he wrote in his diary:

I have either been cutting the hawks too sharply, or else weathering in today's hideous downpour upset them. Black made two good efforts, but Red suddenly collapsed and lay almost dead on the hand. Major Allen, who was there, felt her breast and pronounced it fat. He was puzzled.

The next day Red, who seemed to have recovered, was flown and killed a lark. White thought one flight and a little playing with the lure would be enough. Red stooped to the lure, but half-heartedly, and then perched on a molehill. White knelt down, offering the lark.

She swayed and sank down quietly on her right side, laid her sweet little head across the lure, since it was too heavy to hold up any more, and she was dead.

White waited for Major Allen's verdict: Red, in perfect condition, had died of heart failure. He left Heytesbury next day, and a week later, having made sure that Balan was able to provide for himself, let him go.

Sir Sydney Cockerell had retired from being Curator of the Fitzwilliam Museum at Cambridge, but not from connoisseurship. Meeting White at Heytesbury he discerned a character he would like to add to his collection of acquaintances, and invited him for a visit to Kew. (In all probability, he knew the identity of his Cambridge Correspondent, but he did not say so.) In the course of the visit, White was asked to wash his hands; when he had done so he was allowed to examine his host's treasured manuscripts and early books. Cockerell also showed him the Roxburgh Society's facsimile of a twelfth-century bestiary, and undertook to get him a copy. The visit included the first of many small bestowings – photographs, postcards, cuttings from catalogues – which Cockerell was to give him. It is an unexpected Exhibit A. White stuck it in his diary, with the note: 'This immodest picture was given to me by Sir Sydney Cockerell, to whom it had been given by the gentleman, who appeared to be proud of it.' In the immodest picture it is Miss Shirley Temple, dimpled and glossy, whom the gentleman, his white handlebar moustache brushing her ringlets, appears to be proud of.

The English edition of *The Sword in the Stone* came out in August. It had great praise from reviewers who liked it (it was that kind of book) and by September White noted that he had nearly £500 in the bank. Circumstances devalued this. It was the month of the Munich Crisis. Hitler was about to invade Czechoslovakia, whose integrity England and France were pledged to preserve.

September 12th, 1938

Six months ago I said I would run away from war, if I could accumulate enough money to flee the country. Well, I have accumulated it, but the strange thing is that I cannot flee.

Whether I have yielded a citadel in this decision, or captured one, I have not lived centuries enough to tell.

September 21st, 1938

Tommy Osborne came to me, with Mrs Osborne, in order to fit me with a gas mask. It was a foul thing in which it was almost impossible to breathe, and when I blew out breath its rubber made a noise like a fart. But Tom is one of my dearest friends, a farmer of genius and energy who has farmed with love for forty years: but Mrs Osborne is the finest cook in England, whose chickens are the only true chickens I have eaten since I was a child – and the obscene thing they brought with their true love was a token of slaughter, was a thing they ought not to have been allowed to touch with a pair of tongs.

They came lovingly, and helped me with fumbling, farming fingers, to fit the badge of human degradation over my shrinking face. They talked about my garden, shy at the rape at which they were assisting (but what else could they do?) and all left the scene of beastliness degraded … But Mrs Osborne had tried to help by wearing her best hat.

White grew up into a period of war memorials and declarations against war. The post-combatant generation felt little compassion (their age-group was too near that of the lost generation), but a massive intellectual repudiation. War was a brutal bungle. They at any rate were not going to be taken in by it. White with his OTC certificate was not going to be taken in, though the romantic hero-worshipping side of his character laid him open to an incompatible admiration for warriors – especially if unfortunate. 'Lord Chelmsford stood at last in the tradition of commanders. He was now among the immortal generals of defeat.' White wrote this passage in *Farewell Victoria* with sincerity. With equal sincerity, he would have stood no nonsense about the immortal generals of Passchendaele and the Somme. Now he was trying to make up a divided mind. His physical reaction was as pure as an animal's. He must have trembled like an animal when the gas mask was fitted over his face, and would have torn it off and rushed into the woods if he could have escaped into spontaneity. But the Osbornes were kind, and sorrowfully doing their duty, and Mrs Osborne had put on her best hat. Was he to fail people like these, and the England they stood for?

But then, was he to be false to his convictions and to poets who also stood for England – to be a post-consenter to the deaths of Wilfred Owen and Edward Thomas?

September 23rd, 1938
We heard on the wireless that Chamberlain had failed to see Hitler all day and the negotiations had presumably broken down. I wrote to Siegfried Sassoon, David Garnett, J F Roxburgh and Sir Sydney Cockerell, asking them if they could find me an *efficient* job, if war broke out.

If he could not be usefully made use of, he said, he would enlist as a private soldier one month after hostilities began. The four answers concurred in telling him to wait for something where his qualifications would be of service.

Long entries in the diary show his suspended mind as he watched the reactions of people in public houses, who listened to the broadcast of Hitler's Sports Palace speech and to news bulletins; and heard a woman crying because Chamberlain was working so hard and getting no sleep. He seems like a man in the lightning-slashed darkness of a midnight storm, attentively studying what lay within the beam of a small electric torch. If he read newspapers, there is no sign of it. Once the circle of his torchlight is crossed by a flight of Jews from London, buying local cottages – and resented. Unable to settle to anything and uneasy in his solitude, he moved to the hotel at Wheatley.

All night I could not sleep because of the difference between Stowe Ridings and the main Oxford–London road. All night the lorries went by at regular intervals, carrying aerial torpedoes, they said.

He drank, he listened, he looked on. He was no nearer knowing his own mind when Chamberlain came back with his tidings of peace and safety and capitulation:

> the tired voice of the old gentleman of seventy, who had been flying to and fro across Europe with his umbrella and his baggy overcoat on the wrong buttons, talking to us without theatricals: with a voice of love and culture and decency which did not threaten.

Possibly his hero-worship fastened the more feelingly on a Chamberlain to whom the umbrella and the baggy overcoat added an ornament like defeat.

He stayed on at the Wheatley Bridge Hotel, where in November David and Ray Garnett visited him and the conversation about writers and war took place. By living in a hotel he was relieved of housekeeping and could give his time to writing. He was again working on the *Morte d'Arthur*.

November 4th, 1938

Dear Sir Sydney,

Can you tell me what is the proper sign for an illegitimate union in a family tree? I have written a play about King Arthur and I want to print a family tree at the beginning.

It is a very good play.

When Hayley finds out what you cannot do
That is the very thing he'll set you to.

We all have our inner Hayleys, urging us to the thing we cannot do. White could not 'pitch' his dialogue to a tension to carry development of action. His Hayley seized on this and made him write, or begin, several totally undramatic dramas. Two years before he had written to Garnett, 'I want to make a play out of Sir Walter Raleigh. Can you tell me what *one* book I am to read as far as the history is concerned? The fellow's character I understand already: it is my own.'

On November 26th he fetched Cockerell from Kew and drove him to the Wheatley Bridge Hotel to spend the week-end. This was the week-end when Cockerell recalled eminent funerals and everyone was so animated and participating, and at the end of which their host wrote the sad impromptu summary of his early training in insecurity.

The next week-end was spent at Hilton Hall, where David Garnett showed him the special edition of *Seven Pillars*, and his copy of *The Mint*. He comments on the latter:

> He seems to get his swearing just wrong. There is a sort of rhythm about obscene language. T E Lawrence misses it. He hates it, listens to it like Swift (sporting in the filth he loathes, in order to punish himself), gets its perspective wrong, and faintly misreports it.
>
> We had a lovely week-end, very bracing to have to talk truthfully.

Some of the truth must have been home-truth. In a subsequent letter to Ray Garnett, White said, 'Thanks to David's care over the week-end, I only drank 2 pints of beer yesterday.' The letter ends, 'Thank you for being kind to me.'

This was written from Wells next the Sea, where he had stayed the previous winter for his goose-shooting. It pleased him to be hearing Norfolk speech again: 'But although I can get the vowels, I cannot get the cadence, which makes the whole thing.' But he wanted more geese and perhaps less company, so a week later he moved to the New Inn, Holbeach St Mark's, on the Lincolnshire side of the Wash. Holbeach St Mark's is a hamlet in the parish of Holbeach – which consists of 71,000 acres of land and 11,000 acres of water.

He wrote in his diary:

December 18th, 1938
The winter has come at last, with half an inch of ice in the pails. Unfortunately I got up too late and so I was not more than half a mile out from the bank when the first party of

geese arrived. They saw me, still walking out, before I heard them (it was very dark) and made a detour to the N so then I slumped down in a small drain which could not hide me, and watched several skeins going to right and left, low enough, but out of range. In a lull I got back to the big creek and later had a V come directly over, just shootable if you chose to be inhumane. I did so choose (it was my first chance) and heard the shot go swash among them, but they were too high. Afterwards I must have seen four thousand. They kept coming for nearly ¾ of an hour. But too high. Brownie behaved well, sitting nicely on a goose bag on the frozen mud ledge of the creek. I knelt on it, and was blue-cold, in spite of waistcoat, jersey, tweeds, muffler and overcoat and mittens. It was a lovely morning.

It was his state of mind that made it lovely – as he walked out beyond the frontier of the sea-bank, so outstandingly a moving shape on the expanse of the marsh that the geese in the dark sky saw him before his pricked ears heard them; as he knelt, an early morning worshipper, on the frozen saline mud; as he kept in mind the controlling sea and how when you saw the tidal water turn in the creeks you could still take your time, unless a high tide flooded over the marsh, when you must hurry before it.

It was a hard winter. There were six inches of snow when the postman brought his copy of the Roxburgh bestiary, on the shortest day of the year. He wrote (it was 'Dear Sydney' now):

The bestiary arrived this morning. I can't tell you how happy I am with it. By pure, unforeseen good fortune it has come slap at the right moment, just when it was the very thing. I get up at 5.45 in the snowy morning and am on the salt marsh till half past eight or so, when I come back to a ravenous breakfast in this tiny beer house. In the earth-closet an Arctic subterraneous blast desiccates the fundament. Then, all the morning, I am free to sit before a blazing fire in the parlour. Fortunately I always refused to learn Latin at school, and I find great difficulty with the abbreviations, so the Beasts will last me for months, at a page a day. I am so physically healthy (there is the evening flight as well, at about 3.30 in the afternoon, so that I am simply distended with sea-air and icebergs and dawn and dark and sunset), so hungry and sober and wealthy and wise, that my mind has gone quite to sleep (a healthy sleep) and exactly relishes to saunter at a page pace. Generally I read at a gallop, but with this it is to be first a paragraph and then a snooze. All that miserable drunken autumn is over for me, and I feel fit to fricasse (can't spell it) an Ypopotamus ... I am living *sobrius et castus et spiritualitus*, and the author is quite right in saying that *Tunc congaudunt mihi angeli et omnes virtutes celorum*. The latter are in this case Pink-footed Geese.

It became steadily colder: so cold that Brownie, for all she wore a little flannel coat, had to sit with her hind-quarters in the goose bag and his woollen mittens on her front paws; so cold that the Baltic was frozen over. Drifted snow lay five foot deep; with the snow-covered ground reflecting the moonlight the geese disregarded time-keeping and made their flights as the fancy took them. Many of them were flying inland for better feeding-grounds and flew so high there was no getting a shot at them. White continued to go out before dawn and before dusk. He ate in the kitchen with the family and slept in a feather bed. But he had lied to Cockerell. His mind had not quite gone to sleep.

The story he had begun to write was called 'Grief for the Grey Geese'.

Its theme is the contest between the geese and the goose-shooters: the shooters equipped with guns and abetted by the experience of local men who serve them as guides; the geese equipped with wings, long sight, a power to communicate among themselves, and their immemorial habit of society. In the ranks of the goose-shooters there is a renegade. He was a General Christie and had lately been getting queer.

His queerness was this: he said you ought not to shoot geese.

It does not much matter why General Christie went mad. The poignancy of General Christie's situation was, not that his wits were unsettled, but that he had come to

Staithebeach-next-Sea three years before his affliction happened, in order to be a goose-shooter. The general had been a quick learner and, in the years that he had been studying to slay the geese at Staithebeach, what with his naturally receptive brain, his knowledge of birds and his previous experience of shikari, he had managed to pick up as good a working knowledge of the best places to wait for geese as any professional guide. He knew where the geese would come in, as well as that could be known, and he knew for certain where the guides would wait for them.

This was what made the situation curious. Tom Nesbitt would not have cared how mad the general was, if the general had not known where Tom Nesbitt would be waiting. For, if the general chose to station himself a hundred yards in front of Tom Nesbitt's ambuscade, and to wave his arms, the geese which were on the point of falling into the ambuscade would swerve away. There was no law to prevent the general doing this, and he was a brave man whom it was impossible to intimidate. If he did it, he could save the geese which he had begun to love. He had done it, moreover, twice.

It is a pity White did not go on with this book. Judging by the fullness of the layout and the slightly lumbering gait of the narrative, he knew he was breaking new ground and was taking it seriously. There is evidence that he had been thinking about it for some time. On September 9th he wrote in his diary: 'I shall make off for the east coast in a week or two, with three novels in preparation,' and on his second day at Holbeach St Mark's he consoled himself for an unfavourable wind with: 'I am here, really, only to observe.'

He observed very closely, and set it down very plainly. The shooters, the guides, are planted in a definitely East Anglian landscape. Since he had less than two months more to spend in East Anglia, it may be that the book died when he took it away from its native air. The geese have a landscape of their own, and they and it survived.

It was four o'clock in the morning and it was January. The place which they were in was apparently boundless. It was a kind of no-man's-land, but so severe and without comparison that it was no-thing's-land also. It was not England. England has fruitful fields, warm windows, human beings – who often love one another – and church steeples or houses which stick up. Neither was it the sea, whose waves go up and down. The sea is full of character and mood and feature.

The place was quite featureless. Nothing stuck up on it. It did not move. It had no warmth or light or any particular colour. It did not give one the impression one was living at any particular time. One could not say: This place seems to have stepped straight out of the Jurassic period, or the Pliocene, or anything like that. For there was no time here at all: it was always one time, always had been, and always would be, whether it was day or night.

Timeless, featureless, horizontal, not England, not sea – it was an hiatus in the world, which had been given up to wind and sound and temperature.

It was hellishly cold in this desolation. The straight line of the sea roared to the north-west – it was low tide – in accents so remorseless, so vast, so terribly powerful and perpetual, that one dared not listen for long. Two miles away to the south-east, there were three lights. They were in England. Between the lights and the sea, down this unutterably lonely and awful corridor of sound and wind, the east wind howled. Even during the daytime the sky would be the same colour as the mud, so that to lie on those miles of sand and mud waiting for the widgeon would be like lying in the wind itself. You would not be in England, nor in the sea, but, more peculiar than this, you would not be on the earth either, nor in the sky. You would be lying horizontally in the east wind, which would blow horizontally also – a stratum horizontally howling and being. The wind in this place had no human characteristics: it did not punish or lament or exult or despair. It was mindless, in a country without mind.

VI Doolistown 1939

At the turn of the year Garnett visited White at Holbeach – a visit that had long consequences. Learning that his friend was going to Ireland in February to fish for salmon on the River Dee, White was fired to go too. Garnett ascertained that the only formality Brownie would have to comply with was to be issued with a sailing-permit by a customs officer; White bought new waders. (Gone were the days of his admission before their earlier fishing holiday: 'Personally, I have no waders. I take off my trousers.') On February 22nd he arrived in Ireland, having travelled in the bowels of the ship because Brownie was not rated as cabin-folk. The fishing on the Dee was poached, so the party decided to try a day on the Boyne. Within quarter of an hour Garnett had a salmon. White failed to get a fish. Mettled by this, he decided to stay on till he had caught a great many fish – the Boyne must be full of them, since it had yielded one in a first quarter of an hour; and in the intervals of fishing he would finish *The Witch in the Wood*. He supposed it would be a matter of a fortnight or so. Ray Garnett walked across a couple of fields to a farmhouse. It was called Doolistown, the owners were called McDonagh, they would be pleased to take a lodger. White moved to Doolistown next day. It was to be his home for the next six years.

He was by nature a settler. The nomad is rooted in his nomadic life: settlers, rooted in themselves, adhere. Their home is where they are. White's Irish diaries are streaked with execrations and bewailings: there is no one to talk to; there is no sense in Ireland; there are no fish in the Boyne; there are no books in the telephone booths. The elegant imperturbable handwriting fills page after page, with only one mention of the Stowe Ridings cottage where he had lived 'snug as a badger' – and that as evidence of his Irish heredity.

> We spend endless pains in painting our houses and ironwork
> with gay colours – no houses are so clean and often painted

as the Irish, and in no country are the iron railings so often and so defiantly coated with the wildest shades – but they all fall down quite soon. My own love of vermilions and frightful clashes is evidently inherited from my father's side. It is from him that I got the fierce enthusiasm for painting all the woodwork in my cottage an unsuitable shade of blue. Then I abandon the cottage to mildew and corruption, and all the blue peels off, and no doubt the whole thing will burn to the ground.

The Journal that broke off on December 30th begins again:

March 3rd, 1939. Ireland
Meath and Louth are what you might get if you brought Norfolk to the boil – only all the fields are much smaller. A country of bubbles: you can see sixteen small hills wherever you stand. Mrs McDonagh says that fairies are so high, holding her hand two or three feet from the ground. Quite possibly, for the country is on that scale also. Mrs McDonagh has twice heard the banshee. Mrs McDonagh's house: a beautiful 18th-century structure now painted pink, standing in 70 acres of land. The mattress is of straw; outside sanitation; oil lamps; hundreds of cheap religious pictures. Yet the chairs and sideboard are Chippendale, the spoons solid silver, early Victorian; I drink from Bristol glass. Mrs McDonagh says every day: 'You will get a fish today, *please* God.' This is a prayer, passionately genuine and spoken with intensity.

Some Irish flavours: An old donkey in a field. His hoofs have been neglected, and have grown round in a circle, like the shoes worn under Richard of Bordeaux. Field gates off the roads are built (the uprights) of stone, as solidly as park gates in England. Nobody gets up early. Living religious belief. It has had the effect of making me say my prayers and stop swearing when my casting line gets into a tangle. Also I have given up spirits for Lent. Beggars do not cringe or bless the English. They ask the money as a right.

Later he noted a further Irish flavour. 'Calves aged as much as eighteen months are dishorned with a saw: they stand in the field, bloody and bedimmed.' White had a sadist's acute intelligence for pain (when he hooked a salmon he was so conscious in himself of the steel lodged in the living flesh that he could not 'play' it till it was safely exhausted but dragged it in to the bank). He saw the calves with a stern acceptance; he felt with them, not for them. They were part of the country where he was in the process of becoming an inhabitant. If he had stayed on in north Norfolk, in 'the spare, dear, flat, rich winter country, and the ugly four-square squatting homestead', he would by now have been frequenting the prevalent chapel and listing among East Anglian flavours the stoning to death of stranded seals. In County Meath he was going to Mass and acclimatizing himself into Roman Catholicism. It was the easier because he had been happy in Italy, where the staff of the hotel had been so friendly and accepting, where arms had gone so naturally round waists. Irish manners are not so free, and Irish Catholicism is severer. I doubt if White ever had his arm round Lena McDonagh's narrow waist (she was a thin woman, with a kind anxious face); but Brownie took to her, she could cook turnips like butter, she gave him a rosary, a gospel done up in a cover like a pork pie, a medal of the Little Flower for Brownie's collar (when Brownie lost it, it was replaced with a medal of Saint Bernard). White gave Mrs McDonagh an Infant of Prague. He could not have done better, for the Infant of Prague must always come as a gift, not be bought outright. White says nothing of this, he may have done the right thing in ignorance; in any case, it was the right thing. She was a very kind woman, and he felt great affection for her. In the end, quite without intention, he wounded her to the heart.

White lent himself to being received, as long as there was no patronage in it. Received as a hopeful Catholic, he began to think about it.

April 2nd, 1939
Nowadays I have to say a rosary with the family, every night before we go to bed. Mrs McDonagh bought me a

beautiful one as a present. Luckily I know how to say it; but only in Latin, and am received as a hopeful Catholic. The extraordinary bray with which Mrs M gives it out. We reverently follow, and accomplish the whole in about seven minutes. I have strange feelings about this. They are of love for the people but lack of communion with the thing: like somebody trying to be sick, when he has been sick. I hope it is right to do this.

April 4th, 1939
In Ireland the Catholic Church is still alive, still the young bride of Christ. Like all newly-married couples, the spoons and furniture and wedding presents which they have are new. No old churches greet me, only chapels absolutely up to date – new glass, new stone, new whitewash. It is the difference between the living and the dead, and, as in so many cases, the living are less beautiful.

He had got so far by the end of Lent; but not further.

Good Friday. A magpie flies like a frying-pan.

April 26th, 1939
Conscription is now seriously spoken of in England, and everybody lives from one speech of Hitler's to the next. I read back in this book at the various tawdry little decisions which I have tried to make under the pressure of the Beast: to be a conscientious objector, and then to fight, and then to seek some constructive wartime employment which might combine creative work with service to my country. All these sad and terrified dashes from one hunted corner to the next.

Father Dempsey made clear to me the Church's attitude. To the Church, man is a beast, dangerously withheld. No Pope can intervene too much, any more than one can curb an African python. A touch here and there can be administered, in the hope of staving off the worst catastrophes, but the worst catastrophe of all would be to be enfolded in the python. The Church must keep clear and try gently. The layman is a ravening beast, governed by worldly ambition.

I could fight in defence of the freedom of this man, and win a gaudy grave like Rupert Brooke's, or I could die for him and be forgotten, like Edward Thomas or Wilfred Owen. On the other hand, I could abandon worldly life, like the Church. I could renounce ambition and life among men by going into a monastery or into the ministry. In this case they would leave me alone.

But my nature is not monastic; it may be non-cooperative, but it is free. It is a raptorial nature. Hawks neither band themselves together in war, nor yet retire from the world of air.

This last sentence holds the germ of an idea which later on was to become a preoccupation.

May 5th, 1939. To Sydney Cockerell
I have very little news. I have finished the second volume of my Arthur series. It is called *The Witch in the Wood*, and I am bringing it over to England next week. I shall only spend a couple of days there, invest a little money, get rid of the book, and fetch my car. Then it will be back to Erin. My father was a Gael.

I have made up my mind about this war at last. I am not going to fight in it. You Anglo-Normans can do as you please, but I am a Bard, and, according to the convention of Druim Ceat (AD 590) my person is inviolable. (Also I ought to be immune from taxes, but the Inland Revenue have overlooked this.)

Seriously, I shall refuse to fight or run. My most important business is to finish my version of Malory, and so I shall tell any tribunal which sits on me. I cannot finish it if dead; I am the only person who can finish it. I have been at it unconsciously ever since I was at Cambridge, when I wrote a thesis on Malory; anybody can throw bombs.

The convention of Druim Ceat would have appealed the more to him since he now had money enough for Income Tax to be alarming. In the past he had been one of those small-selling writers who could say, with Dryden's Blest Shepherds: 'Over our lowly Sheds all the storm passes.' But *The Sword in the Stone* had changed that. In the fiscal year 1938–9 he had made £1,885 2s. 10d. ('It all seems to have gone somewhere.') A large cheque had come from the USA in May. Willy-nilly and unconsulted, White was due to be serviceable to his country.

He decided to leave Brownie behind during his trip to England.

> I think it may be good for her to be gently introduced to abandonment in case European war or some other act of God may make such an abandonment necessary and final in the future.

This forced him to an admission which he cannot have liked making.

> My mother was (is) a woman for whom all love had to be dependent. She chased away from her her husband, her lover and her only son. All these fled from her possessive selfishness, and she was left to extract her meed of affection from more slavish minds. She became a lover of dogs. This meant that the dogs had to love her. I have inherited this vice.

May 25th, 1939
Crossed on a Wednesday morning, and was horribly sick. The Captain called it choppy. Fixed plays with BBC.*

Tried to settle Disney contract.** Phoned Mavro about peregrine and merlin. Delivered *The Witch in the Wood* to Collins. Joined the AA and arranged photographs and triptyques for hours. Dined and went on to Humbert's, with P Frankau, Compton Mackenzie and the Foreign News Editor of the *News Chronicle*. Sat up until 5 am. Fetched car from Stowe. Arranged with bank about investing £1000.

---

* This was a six-instalment arrangement of *The Sword in the Stone* which the BBC ran as a Sunday afternoon serial.

** The Disney organization had asked for the screen rights of *The Sword in the Stone* for purposes of a cartoon version.

> Stopped night at Feathers, Ludlow. Called on Stevens at Walcot Hall – a sort of paradise – and inspected the gerfalcon which I have bought from him. All this time living on practically nothing except champagne and glucose tablets (result of crossing). Caught Holyhead boat, with car, on Sunday night. So much for a dreadful interlude.

So much for the England of his bones. The day after his return he took Mrs McDonagh for a drive to Tara.

> Approaching it from the south, one could see nothing: it seemed to be going to be a frost. Stopping at a likely place, next a dingy Protestant chapel, we walked into a field full of sheep. Suddenly it was obvious that we were on the hill. It might have grown below us, a magic mountain. It felt as if we could see all over Ireland. There were no picture-postcard booths, barbed wires or adjacent military camps. Only this superb empty down-swell, hanging over Erin, its close-nibbled good sheep-turf with so much blood of hostages and high Kings, the mounds of the raths and a statue of St Patrick. The great banquet hall seemed to be called in Irish 'The Not-One-Person-Room'. This struck me as a fine descriptive word, and I was proud of being able to find it out for myself. I should add that the 'Not-One-Person-Room' is possibly a figment of my own brain. Looking at an article by L S Gogan on getting back this evening, I find he derives it from 'House of the Central Visitation'. It doesn't seem to matter how you derive these things, for O'Murchair blithely asserts it as 'House-of-Mead-Circling'.

> *May 30th, 1939*
> Yesterday was my birthday. I felt vaguely that this ought to have some significance for somebody, but it hadn't – not even for me. 'Mind you,' said Gorman's brother who works in a bakery, 'fishing is a great pass-time.' I thought how my whole life was a pass-time, I am passing it as best I can until I am dead.

He was studying Erse; he was reading Irish history; he was thinking about becoming a Catholic, and conversing with Father Dempsey; he still had hopes of getting a salmon out of the Boyne; he was keeping a brimming diary, full of conclusions about Irish farming, Irish character, Anglo-Irish relations, which he might make into a book; if he had been committed to Wandsworth Jail, by the end of three months he would have been writing a history of Wandsworth, with sections on its geology, botany, bird-life, etc, together with a dictionary of prisoners' slang and an analysis of what was wrong with the penal system and suggestions how to improve it. Wherever chance had directed him, his active, loquacious mind would have borne him company – very much as Brownie did, since he hadn't got complete control of either. But at times one has the impression of this faithful mind looking up at the man and saying, 'Master, why are you so sad, all of a sudden?'

At the beginning of June he drove westward into Co Mayo, where he looked at various shooting and fishing lodges he might rent, tried to get a young peregrine and inquired about possibilities of winter goose-shooting. The lodge he fell in love with was not available but he found another, called Sheskin, which would do. Erris, the desolate region of bog and mountain between Ballina and the sea, was a new Irish flavour – a heather ale. 'Suddenly getting out of the car I rushed across a moor and, stripping myself naked, plunged into a small loch as warm as toast, to the surprise and embarrassment of F B [his travelling companion].'

June 10th, 1939. To Sydney Cockerell
My next and third volume in my Arthurian cycle will have to be about Sir Lancelot. Lancelot was the Bradman of the day, and I think it is only decent that I should have a smattering of his tools. At present it is as if I were writing a history of Bradman, without knowing the shape of a cricket bat or a set of stumps. All I want to know is how to put armour on, how it articulated, what were its special problems, etc. I want to know how the stuff works. Perhaps I ought to add that I

am following Malory in assuming that King Arthur lived at the same time as himself. He thought of the Round Table as a contemporary – just as Shakespeare dressed Caesar or Macbeth in armour – and so I am assuming the Arthur dates to be *second half of 15th century*. Why hasn't somebody written a book which will tell me how such a knight put his stuff on, fought in it, etc, and what effect it had on his movements? Where did he get his blisters? What was his field of vision? What movement was the most difficult to make? What were his vulnerable points? You will see what my troubles are. If only there were some collection of armour in Dublin I would go there and ask to be dressed. Unfortunately I am over six foot. And anyway who would expect to find anything in Dublin? The whole of this country is kept together with bits of string.

Sydney Cockerell replied that White could not know anything about armour without seeing and handling it; and added: 'I cannot fit Lancelot into the decadent 15th century.'

On June 25th White drew up one of his balance sheets:

CREDIT

1. I have written offering £45 a month for Sheskin Lodge, Co Mayo, in September. This has two or three miles of the Owenmore and 10,000 bad acres of grouse, one living-room, 3 double bedrooms, 2 single bedrooms, bathroom, lavatory and kitchens, etc. We might get between 6 and 60 salmon, and between 20 and 50 brace of grouse, ccording to the weather and season.

2. I have written offering £4 for a pair of eyas peregrines, a falcon and a tiercel, and arranging for them to be sent by air to Baldonnel Airport.

3. I have been offered the mastership of the Kill Harriers and accepted them provisionally.

4. I go to the Trim schoolmaster every week for an evening, and do an hour's prep every morning, at my Irish.
5. I have not drunk anything for a week, and hope to stay teetotal for three months, by which time I may have learned to drink in moderation.

Added in pencil, 'NOTE: I did not.'

DEBIT

The quenchless fear of war, which would smash all these innocent eccentricities and which also robs profits in the bookselling world even when it hasn't broken out.

June 30th, 1939

The two peregrines arrived last night, feather perfect, no down and already flying. A jolly day preparing for them, knocking up a hack house and stringing barbed wire round it to keep off the cows: then fetched them from Baldonnel (the thrill of seeing the aeroplane land – a resurrection of old excitements): then looking the lovely birds over and taking them out to the hack house (so much arrangement and deftness and pre-consideration – falconry is like treason, it is all plotting) and sat up till 2 am sewing lures. I have made a charming hood for the falcon.

White's plan ('out of experience, not out of a book') had been to keep the birds shut up for three or four days.

By giving the last feed late, I hope to help the dangerous moment when I leave the hack house open for the first time. I suppose it will be dangerous, owing to the hawks being already flying. But they should be lazy after their food and *there will only be an hour or two of daylight left*. So I hope they will stay on the roof overnight, a good step towards accepting the house as home.

A letter from J G Mavrogordato discouraged this plan. It came too late.

July 3rd, 1939

This day I loosed the two hawks, having given them a cut feed in the morning. The falcon dashed out immediately, bumped on the barbed wire, hoisted herself over the hedge and disappeared. Watchers from the farm say that she rose again some hundred yards further on, and took a wide circle round the Lawn,* vanishing from their view behind the farm. I came away at once, and, about ten minutes later, saw through the glasses that the tiercel was on the ground outside the hack house, flapping his wings like a small prep-school boy doing Sandow exercises. The cows, which were complicating matters, gathered round him in oafish curiosity. He attacked two and chased them away. Then he also took to the wing. We stood at the upstairs window till dusk, but never saw the falcon again. The tiercel took three flights in all, finally ending up in the high poplar just above the hack house as darkness fell. This is where I wanted him.

July 4th, 1939

At 6 this morning I went out to feed, and there was the tiercel, still in the poplar. Foolishly I let him meet my eye, and he dropped out of it on the further side. Even yet it might have been well, only this bloody wind. Every time he took to the air, the air must have conveyed him towards Connemara. It still blows, and no doubt they are ten or twenty miles away.

'Falconry is like treason – it is all plotting.'

Much the same can be said about authorship. In both, the plotting must include plotting against oneself. The birds were lost because White did not plot against his besetting hurry. They were, however, totally lost; nothing more need be done about them. By a similar failure to plot against himself he had let his mother get into *The Witch in the Wood*; and this resulted in a letter from his publishers to say that the book would not do; would he please reconsider it. On June 28th he wrote to tell Potts:

* A meadow by the house.

The Witch in the Wood is Book II of a projected 4 books about the doom of Arthur. Book III will give the Lancelot-Guenever tangle and book IV will bring the three tragic themes together for the final clash. The three tragic themes are the Cornwall feud, existing ever since Arthur's father killed Gawaine's grandfather; the Nemesis of Incest, which I have found frightfully difficult to introduce without gloom or nastiness; and the Guenever-Lancelot romance. You know, the real reason why Arthur came to a bad end was because he had slept with his sister. It is a perfectly Aristotelian tragedy and it was the offspring of this union who finally killed him. Morgause (the sister) is really more important in the doom than Guenever is, both through being associated with the Cornwall feud and through the incest theme (for her son Mordred finally brings the doom). I had to show her as a bad mother and the kind of person who would bear more of the incest onus than my hero. Error or Frailty.*

Potts was sent the typescript and asked to decide. He demolished White's special pleading by advising him to get Lady Madge out of his system. It is easier to deride than denounce a person you are afraid of; and White's expedient with his mother had been to hark back to Lady Madge Calcutta, the rowdy Cleopatra of 'Rather Rum'. His next expedient was to play her down into unimportance. In the end, he made 'a dark Celtic witch' of her. But whether Morgause is a farcical strumpet or a dark Celtic witch, Constance White inhabits her and invalidates the book by being hated as an actual person. The real incest theme of the story is the maternal rape on the child; it was this that cast White back into the nursery language of 'nasty'. He was so incapable of facing it that the Malorean knot of doom is never tied: Arthur and Morgause glide past each other in a granny.

On July 18th he noted another Irish flavour in his diary:

There was in Trim about forty years ago a beautiful girl with auburn hair, but she lost her wits. She went mad in the

---

* The Aristotelian stipulation for Tragedy.

Catholic church. She walked to the pulpit, looked up at the priest (who was preaching) with her head on one side, and said something about a man who lives in the Navan road. She was caught hold of, and taken out. She had a brother and a sister. Thirty years later the sister died, a poor worn-out thing, broken with milking and feeding the brother for whom she kept house. When she was safely buried, it turned out that she had done other feeding too. Dr O'Reilly said to Dr Brady: 'You had better go down and see what you can find out.' Dr Brady did not like going, but he went. He said to the brother, in the front room: 'I hear you have another poor invalid within?' The brother said it might be so. 'I have not seen her for thirty years,' he said, 'but it might be so.' Dr Brady asked if he could see the invalid. The brother considered no reason against it. But he would not go himself, as she was terrible wicked at times. He gave the key to Dr Brady, who opened the room door. The room was quite dark and Dr Brady could only see a great shape standing in it. He shut the door quick and locked it, as he was afraid.

Eventually they got her away in an ambulance from the back door, and she is living in the asylum now. For thirty years she had lived in the locked room in the dark, without seeing a human soul. They just opened the door and pushed the food in at the crack. Sometimes she would get up and dress, but more often she only lay with her devils. When they got her out she weighed more than twenty stone.

White had devils to lie with too. At the end of a letter congratulating Cockerell on his seventy-second birthday he wrote: 'I have not drunk *any* liquor for a month.'

Sydney Cockerell's dry loving-kindness to the younger man did not stop at sending him pictures and catalogues, supplying him with books, answering questions about armour, heraldry, pedigrees, scribal contractions of Latin, and putting up with a good deal of contradiction and polemic. He loved him seriously enough to be seriously concerned about his drinking – and once, at any rate, to admonish him. White pasted the admonition into his diary.

On the flyleaf of a 13th-century Bible once in my possession is this 14th-century observation:

	Primo letens et gaudens
	Secundo sanctus et sapiens
Proprietates	Tercio tristis et amens
ebrii	Quarto debilis. Fine stultus
	et moriens, et omni sensu et
	omni bono carens.

No admonition, however delicately conveyed, and no concern, however affectionate, could have done more than stave off the next relapse; but Cockerell's scrupulous detachment made it possible for White to respond without feeling obliged to employ the *letens et gaudens* convention that drinkers drink for the fun of it.

July 22nd, 1939. To Sydney Cockerell
This drink business. Like most humourous writers (I suppose I am a humorous writer, even if I can't spell it) my life is in fact a melancholy one. I suppose nearly everybody thinks their lives are especially unhappy, so I am no exception to the rule. I used to drink because of my troubles, until the drink became an added trouble. Then I thought I had quite enough without it, so I stopped. After the first month I tried one Sunday to see if I could drink in moderation like any normal person, but I found, I couldn't, so I had to stop altogether. If I ever find that I can take a normal sup I shall go back to it out of politeness to other people, but it seems an illogical thing to me to take intoxicants unless you want to be intoxicated. There has been a good deal of drink going on in my family for some generations. Well, there it is, anyway. The one bright spot in the whole melancholy business is that I can honestly say I don't feel any better for giving it up, and now I never go to sleep before 4 am.

What a comfort to think that Tolstoy wrote *War and Peace* seven times. I bet he rewrote the last chapters most of all, and that is why they are quite unreadable. *The Witch in the Wood* is nearly sending me mad.

Cockerell, having insinuated that drinking was a mistake, now reverted to his wish for an earlier Lancelot.

You will think that I can never hold my tongue but last night there arrived from the Pierpoint Morgan library a publication out of which I have clipped the accompanying illustrations. They are from the MS of Camelot which I described in 23 careful pages (mostly very small type) in 1913. They will show you the sort of Lancelot that I think of, not the 15th-century fellow.

White stuck this letter into his diary, together with the reproductions from Morgan MS 705–806, with 'c 1290–1310' in Cockerell's minutest script.

July 28th, 1939. To Sydney Cockerell
Nothing that you could have said would have persuaded me, but the picture did the trick. I am half sorry that I decided on the 15th century, but it is too late to change, and anyway I am only half sorry. The consolation is that it is an imaginary 15th century. I am putting myself as far as possible in Malory's mind (which was a dreamer's) and bundling everything together in the way I think he bundled it. The subject is too long to explain except by word of mouth, but I am trying to write of an imaginary world which was imagined in the 15th century. Malory did not imagine the armour of your century (he imagined that of his own, and I will stick to him through thick and thin) but he did imagine dragons, saints, hermits, etc. I state quite explicitly that we all know that Arthur, and not Edward, was on the throne in the latter half of the 15th century, at the beginning of my second vol, and that we also know that the land of Lothian was then largely populated by saints who lived in bee-hives. By this deliberate statement of an untruth, I try to make it clear to any scholar who may read

the book that I am writing, as I said before, of an imaginary world imagined in the 15th cent. That is the best way I can explain it shortly and it may reconcile you to my date. You see, half of what Malory imagined in his 15th cent was the stuff of your cent but the other half wasn't. So I am taking 15th cent as a provisional forward limit (except where magic or serious humour is concerned – for instance, it is a serious comment on chivalry to make knights-errant drop their 'g's like huntin' men) and often darting back to the positively Gaelic past (the kind of date you think of) when I feel that Malory did the same. Will it satisfy you, then, when I tell you that both Malory and myself were charmed by the picture you sent (Malory has just told me that I am welcome to speak for him) and that we often think of Lancelot just like that, only we prefer to dress him in our own contemporary armour, just as Shakespeare dressed Macbeth or Caesar. Malory and I are both dreaming. We care very little for exact dates, and he says I am to tell you I am after the spirit of the *Morte d'Arthur* (just as he was after the spirit of those sources he collated) seen through the eyes of 1939. He looked through 1489 (was it? – can't trouble to verify) and got a lot of 1489 muddled up with the sources. I am looking through 1939 at 1489 itself looking backwards.

Here there is a drawing of White with a telescope looking along a dotted line of sight at Malory with a telescope who looks along the line of sight at an armed figure in a posture of defence, labelled 'Sources', who is looking in the same direction as do White and Malory.

Swept on by the pleasure of a little Art, White takes a fresh page, writes, 'Perhaps one could draw a diagram like this'; and draws a much improved White, dressed for shooting, at the top left-hand corner of a triangle, looking down through his telescope at a much more expressive Malory in a gown, at the base of the triangle. Malory is looking up to the word Sources at the triangle's top right-hand corner. White looks both downwards at Malory and along the top of the triangle towards Sources. Two lines of sight are projected from Malory's telescope: one, his Malorian view of Sources, the other, White's view of Sources via Malory. Thus White has direct view of Sources, a direct view of Malory, and a further view of Sources as seen by Malory.

> You see, Malory sees the sources through the eyes of the 15th cent and that is all he sees. I see Malory + sources. That is why I had to take 15th cent as terminal forward limit, but I assure you we are both immersed in a much earlier dream world. You could say that I allow anachronisms up to 15th cent, unless I want to introduce them on purpose. I will explain this properly when I see you.

The words 'I will explain this properly when I see you', refer to White's hope that Cockerell would visit him. He had a vision of all his friends coming to Sheskin Lodge in Co Mayo, all to be gloriously entertained, all to be delighted.

To the socially ambitious young man who took a course in Advanced Equitation, it was so grand to be able to rent a lodge in a wilderness and there spend the autumn shooting and fishing that even to be a guest at such a place was beyond hoping for. Now he could do better. Thanks to *The Sword in the Stone*, he would be host. On July 14th he had written to Cockerell:

> I have taken a shooting and fishing lodge for the month of September. From the 1st till the 11th of that month I have staying with me David Garnett and his wife (a splendid woman) and two sons, also J G Mavrogordato, the secretary of the British Falconers' Club. We shall have about half a dozen falcons with us, and will be out all day either fishing or shooting or hawking. The place is absolutely desolate, nothing but a flat bog ten miles square surrounded by high mountains (the Childe-Roland-to-the-Dark-Tower-Came kind) and the nearest neighbour is about eight miles away.

But we could fit you in if you cared to come. You know how uncomfortable everything in Ireland is, but the place has a water-closet and a sort of bath actuated by Calor gas. I suppose there will be nothing to eat except grouse and salmon. Or, if you would like to come during the second half of the month, I would try to get congenial company.

Grouse-shooting begins on August 12th. His first intention had been to rent Sheskin Lodge for the opening of the season. Its owners, however, wished to be there themselves during August. 'My husband says the grouse are never wild,' the lessor's wife had written. 'We did very well with them last year in September. In every way we consider Sept a better month for both fishing and shooting – than August.' It was settled that he should begin his tenancy on August 31st. The postponement was vexatious, but did not much signify: Hitler had been bought off with Czechoslovakia, everyone had again settled down to living on the slopes of a volcano. After the loss of the two hawks, the postponement may even have seemed providential, for if the replacing pair were to be flown with credit at Sheskin the month of August would not be too long for training the tiercel and accustoming the elder bird.

They were to arrive on August 2nd. He bought a majestic new diary to match their advent. It measures 16 inches by 10 by 2, weighs 8½ pounds and is bound in solid, parchment-covered boards with a spine and corner pieces of unbleached linen. He gave it a frontispiece. The British Museum's coloured postcard of *Chand Bibi Hawking* (a present from Cockerell) is stuck in the centre of the page, and framed in arabesques drawn freehand in red, green and violet inks. The design is Alhambra-Gothic, but Ireland is acknowledged by minute green shamrocks dotting a trellised ground. The first page is also decorated in freehand. A dragonish hawk, mantling her wings and emitting a long, writhing vermiculation, forms the capital and displays, if the vermiculation is studied attentively enough, the date: 2.vili. xxxix. Descending from the hawk are two intertwined serpents, opposed. The jaws of the upward serpent menace the hawk's talons; from the jaws of the downward serpent dangles a sort of tassel on a cord which at the foot of the page enlarges to frame a cross draped in a priest's stole. White, who was proposing to become a Roman Catholic, had considered the priesthood as an alternative to becoming a combatant, though only to reject the idea. But if this illumination was a personal statement he was still keeping the possibility in mind.

The entry on this splendidly prepared page records the events of August 2nd – but was written three days after.

> The inter-mewed falcon 'Cressida', who killed 44 grouse last season, was due to arrive in Dublin this morning. Just as I got into the car to fetch her, a telegram arrived saying she was not coming. In the evening my *ollaim** arrived, suggesting we should go into Dublin to see a play at the Abbey Theatre. His brother-in-law was a friend of the author's, and we could pass an evening with him. I was so tired, through never going to sleep before 6 am during the last month and then having got up early to fetch the falcon, and then the fury of knowing she was not coming after all, that I took two small glasses of whiskey to bear me up during the coming evening.

The theatre had only two seats left, so White, the *ollaim*, the brother-in-law and his wife made a night of it, drinking and talking till six the next morning.

> I was dragged out of my bed at the Wicklow Hotel at about 10 o'clock by an enraged *garda*, because I had apparently parked the car in the exact centre of Dublin. I was still tipsy when he got me up, the first time I ever recollect getting out of bed drunk. One is teetotal for six weeks, thus getting insomnia; when the insomnia has brought one to the lowest ebb, the thing corrects itself automatically. Back to the water-waggon.

Still tipsy, the party drove to Dun Laoghaire to collect the tiercel, which had travelled from Shropshire overnight. Tipsily inseparable, they drove back to Trim.

* His Irish teacher.

I recited the whole of Don Juan's long speech in Flecker, and all of us sang all the way.

Well, anyway, we got the poor tiercel home, and I resigned myself to the inevitable aftermath. That evening I simply threw down his food for him at the block, and left him alone. Next night I remembered to tie it to the lure, but left him alone to feed on it. Today, his second day in Ireland, I sat with him rather longer, and he took a very good bath.

August 6th, 1939

I took him for a walk on the fist, unhooded, round the field they call the Lawn, for twenty minutes or so. It was interesting to watch (or sense, for I still seldom look at him) while he watched me carrying him across the Lawn. It was my means of locomotion that interested him, and he could not keep his eyes off my legs. I suppose a biped mammal is rather peculiar.

When White filled up his form for *Who's Who*, he wrote under the heading RECREATION: 'Animals'. Recreation is an impoverished word: it must re-acquire its original meaning if White's answer is to be properly understood. He did not treat animals as pets, or as a pastime or a hobby. He turned to them for a renewal and enlargement of his being. Even with Brownie, who refused with the whole unscrupulous force of a strong and supple character to be non-possessed, and whose death in a few years' time was to maim his heart, he never stooped to being a Lord of Creation. His observations, such as the one on the tiercel's interest in his legs, may startle us into feeling entertained; but they are serious; they spring from a participating recognition of the creature's authenticity. And if he disliked an animal, it was on a basis of equality. He did not have to despise them, or hold them to blame.

August 10th, 1939

Yesterday, after a day of practically neat hell, I contrived to get the famous Cressida home to Doolistown at half seven this evening. She had been put on the wrong trains, etc, the Horse Show was on, also a race meeting, and it rained incessantly. There were no books in the telephone booths. However, by luck and bulldog tenacity I discovered the wretched bird halfway between Dundalk and Dublin, and eventually got her home. Fed her by simply throwing down beef beside her block and left her to recuperate from the far worse hell she had been in herself.

It was a bad beginning. Honesty compelled him to admit that Cressida had been the greater sufferer, but he had suffered too. The two exiles took against each other from the start, their excitable English natures chafing against the fatalism of the Irish rainfall and the Irish character.

I came in at 6.30 to my own tea, and read the newspapers till 8. Then I went out to take Brownie for another walk, and strolled past the blocks, just to have a look. Tiercel looked fine. Cressida was not visible. Not visible? Behind the block? In the long grass? Surely this was impossible. Even when I saw the end of her leash, lying on the grass, it seemed to take a long time to realize.

It was a strong plaited leash, which I had plaited myself out of nine bootlaces. They were plaited three strong. How she had contrived to unravel the knot at the swivel end, I don't know. But she had contrived it,

She had flown into a tall beech tree.

I stood respectfully some way from the tree and waved the lure every now and then. Cressida made it perfectly clear that (a) we had never been properly introduced, (b) she was fond of fine evenings in beech trees, (c) she would not be hungry for several days and (d) that lures were things she had long grown out of.

All the next day he watched her flying round about the farm. That evening he baited a draw-string trap, took a chair into the garden, and sat down to wait with the trap cord in his hand, motionlessly enduring midges. Cressida flew round, balancing appetite and caution. At last she was within the circle of the cord, and feeding. He began to pull his end of the cord.

I saw that one leg was in an ungainly position, which she kept pulling against like a woman patting her hair while thinking of something else. I knew the trap had worked.

With his unwieldy human pounce he caught her by her jesses just as she realized she was held by the leg. 'Mrs McDonagh, coming out then, exclaimed "What luck!" The unkindest cut of all.'

By the next morning, Cressida had almost unpicked her second leash.

Cressida was White's first experience of a mature, practised hawk. He could teach her nothing. She taught him a great deal. She unpecked his knots. She discarded her hood. She stabbed him in the wrist and drew blood from his chin. She distracted his attention from the tiercel, whose education he should have been completing. One night she compelled him to climb a high beech tree, searching for her among the foliage with a weak electric torch – and all to no purpose except that he was reminded how Sir Lancelot had also climbed a tree after a falcon. She was arrogant, crafty, beautiful and highly accomplished; she had worms, was too fat, was a screamer. It was as though he had married a full-grown wife. 'Hawks are extremely angry creatures,' he noted, 'and anybody who associates with them becomes atrabilious himself.' Except for one calm day when he lunched with Lord Dunsany at Dunsany Castle, and thought him 'a decent, amusing, interested, selfish, vain, enlightened fellow', the diary shows on what even terms a man and a hawk can contend. Of the two, he was the disadvantaged one; he admired her beauty and her accomplishments. She flouted his accomplishments and made plain her dislike for his person. 'I must be patient,' he wrote. 'I am annoying Cressida. She is much too fat.'

For August 24th he drew another freehand illumination. It follows the layout of the earlier one; but the dragonish hawk is replaced by a laidly worm whose head is a skull, and a second skull dangles at the end of the cord instead of the cross and stole. 'War seems almost certain now.' The laconic entry is isolated in the middle of the page, beneath a note on Tolstoy's view of Napoleon and above a record that when he hissed like a snake at Cressida to see if it would stop her screaming, she flew straight at his face. Only at the last was there a relenting.

August 26th, 1939
Flew both hawks loose on Balivor. Tiercel behaved perfectly, so did Cressida. Sitting beside Cressida in the sunlight, on that beautiful bog, admiring the blue-powdered feathers of her back as she plucked the fluffy fur off a light-coloured rabbit, I nearly rose above the desolation of these days.

Opposite this entry is a sprig of heather neatly glazed under a Cellophane panel. He had a childish piety for keepsakes. In the diary of 1938 a tiny claw is similarly glazed, with the inscription: 'Red's first lark'.

August 29th, 1939
Today my telegrams from faltering war-guests are beginning to arrive.

But the guests he had most at heart did not falter. Garnett, who a few days earlier had been asked if he would work in the Air Ministry's Department of Intelligence if war broke out, and had agreed to, was crossing to Dublin on the night of August 30th. His wife and two sons, holidaying in Co Kerry, would be driving to Sheskin on September 1st.

In *The Familiar Faces*, the third volume of his autobiography, Garnett describes his arrival in Dublin:

Tim White was waiting for me at Westland Row. Ireland suited him, and he seemed even larger, his beard bristling in all directions, his gestures huge. He had been shopping in Dublin – buying tea, coffee, Gentleman's Relish, Bath Olivers, cartridges, flies for sea-trout, dog biscuits, raw beef, claret and sherry. He welcomed me with open arms, told me about his shopping list, and led me to the long Jaguar SS.

He had fixed a wooden bar across the rear seat, and perched upon it were the two peregrine falcons, hooded, I think, and with their jesses fastened to the perch. Their beaks and talons were curved like scimitars and razor sharp. I looked at them nervously before getting into the front seat and Tim said: 'Brownie will have to sit in your lap. They can't reach you unless you lean back with your head resting on the rim of the seat.'

Brownie and I remained huddled and leaning forward all the way to Mayo. After Crossmolina, we drove along a narrow straight road across bog and moor, and then turned off at right-angles down a metalled track for Sheskin Lodge. The country was moorland, heather and bog like Yorkshire or Durham, but flatter and duller. At last we reached an acre or two of rhododendrons, in the middle of which stood a Victorian house of slate and stucco with a small lawn in front and stables behind.

They fed the hawks, and drove off to dine at a hotel in Crossmolina. There they heard on the wireless that the international situation had worsened.

September 1st, 1939
In Ballina, at the Imperial Hotel, we heard at 10.30 this morning that war had broken out between Germany and Poland. We got a wireless, which doesn't work much, and came out to Sheskin, where I spent one of the most miserable days of my life.

Ray Garnett reached Sheskin that evening: till then, the two men kept up a waiting-room téte-a-téte. They were friends, but their friendship was largely a presupposing friendship, founded on the letters they had exchanged with so much cordiality. Each had his picture of the other. Both pictures were slightly out of focus, for both men had disproportionately stressed the love of outdoor pursuits which first drew them together. From this grouse and salmon footing the impact of war tossed them into the realities of friendship, its clash of interests and temperaments.

White turned in on himself. 'I only wanted to keep quiet and be alone and behave as if I were already dead.' Garnett was strained outward. He did not know when a telegram might not come, summoning him back to England. He did not know what news a telegram from his wife might not bring – only that it was a long journey from Dingle and that a mortal disease was lodged in her. Leaning out of their separate miseries and incomprehensions, they tried to be kind to each other.

> Ray did not turn up till after nine o'clock at night, so I had Bunny on my hands all the time. His attitude was that he must do things, or else go mad, so I took him for two or three hours on the moor, and read to him, and made him talk about things. The thing which worked out best was when I asked him to come and cheer me up instead of making me cheer him up (implied, not said), which resulted in him doing this most sweetly.
>
> In Poland living souls are being blown to atoms. The English wireless has fled from London to Scotland: it talks and talks about regulations for calling people up and hiding lights and buying food. On it Chamberlain talks of war. Meanwhile we, in our outpost of the spirit with nothing but heather to see, have no longer the heart to fly the hawks at all. They get fed listlessly at the block once more, and the wireless finally packs up. Why mention the hawks, or ourselves, or anything, or trouble to make these marks with ink?

He made a few marks with ink on September 3rd and September 15th, when he wrote to Cockerell about finding 'something truly sensible to do'. But the diary remains a blank.

In *The Familiar Faces*, Garnett recounts a day's hawking when only one covey of grouse went up and Cressida flew in the wrong direction; a day's fishing when the midges drove them from the river-bank; and a last day.

> The strain of being without war news proved too great and Ray and I drove into Crossmolina. When we got there we heard that England and Germany were at war; there were

a few men shouting in the street. When we got back to Sheskin I found a telegram from the Air Ministry asking me to report as soon as possible. We decided that I should return to England next morning but that Ray and the boys should stay on at Sheskin Lodge until we knew better what the war would be like.

VII Belmullet 1939–40

Among White's MSS is a fragment which begins:

> Another lodge which I held in Mayo was called Sheskin – and there the most learned man I know came with his family to stay, in August. He was a burly white-haired genius. His eyes were asymmetrical owing to some accident in childhood. The slight independence of the eyes – not a squint – gave him a wild and terrible expression sometimes, which was backed by the frightening weight of his erudition but which had nothing to do with his immense, active, purposive benevolence. He was an agnostic whose conscious creed was having a heart. He came of a literary dynasty which had been among the philanthropic despots of literature for nearly a century. He was the kind of person who, not rich himself, would send a hundred pounds to a struggling author if he believed in him; who could be thrown into a passion by insincerity or meanness; whose goodness was an intentional effort, like running a race. For more than twenty years this genius had been the censor of my mind.

Out of this beginning – but some time later and coloured by a different mood – came 'Losing a Falcon' in *The Godstone and the Blackymor*. By then, White had skinned over his disappointment. In September 1939 it was fresh and raw. Behind his flourish of lodges in Mayo the truth stands out in the two words, 'in August'. If he had been able to rent Sheskin in August, the hawks would have been flown, the salmon grassed, the friendship explored and secured; what came after would only have made those days more glowingly memorable, like the ball on the eve of Waterloo. But when he took up his diary again his hopes had gone for nothing, and he was recovering from influenza and in a frenzy of mortification.

September 21st, 1939
I suspect that this war may be the end of such civilization as I am accustomed to. I don't mind much.

I asked myself before I got the flu: if I fought in the war, what would I be fighting for? Civilization. Not England, qua geographical boundaries; not freedom, that is always in the mind; not anything except what I call civilization. But I can do much better than fight for civilization: I can make it. So, until Arthur is safely through the press, I have ceased to bother about the war. I have vaguely volunteered for the Ministry of Information, with the mental reservation that I won't do anything till Arthur is over.

Ray and the boys left this morning. I get on better with Bunny than with them. I really like Ray very much, but more in small doses. It is like living with Mrs Be-Done-By-As-You-Did. A week ago she suddenly had convulsions after dinner and I had to drive for the doctor.

The doctor told White it was an attack of hysteria. White in his petulance half-believed it – though he also knew better.

This is an absolutely untrue picture of her, for it leaves out the essential thing, which is that she is dying of cancer. Take this in, and she is the greatest hero I have ever met.

White was ambitious and emulatory. Scholarship, flying, ploughing, milking – what he saw others doing he had to do too. When he began to write, ambition and emulation spurred him through his earlier books and carried him on into a serious engagement with literature. At that point, their usefulness was over; but one cannot dismiss elements in one's character as though they were grooms and housemaids, or have them mercifully put to sleep like animals. War, however censoriously accepted, is a challenge to display one's abilities. And David Garnett, whom White admired above all his other friends, had gone back to an England at war, already equipped with a job, while White remained with the women and children.

He finished the Sheskin tenancy alone, in the rainy autumn equinox. Insecure characters suffer a great deal from mortification but little and briefly from remorse. His dream of gloriously entertaining delighted guests had come to nothing and he had been a grudging host. But Sheskin remained.

> I was alone for dinner, with one candle,
> Reading a book propped against it about the stars.
> There was a grouse and wine and outside the French window
> Nephin waited for Mars.

Nephin, sounding so much like a person in Blake's mythology, is a mountain. It pleased him to have mountains in sight, after the unadventurous landscape round Doolistown. During the rest of his stay at Sheskin he was happy. He was alone, and undistracted; he was writing poems; Brownie kept him company (she must often have heard him muttering lines into shape in the house's silence); if he wanted conversation, there was Joyce, the keeper, whom he liked. Besides, Sheskin had the charm of being an island – an island in time; he did not have to debate with himself if he would stay, how long he would stay. His tenancy would run out, and he would go. Some time or other, he would come back.

> Sheskin, the music of your name and your waters
> That night when there was an inch and a half in the
>   rain-gauge
> And all round the lodge and from the spouts of the veranda
> You chuckled: we were waiting for a flood.
> Sheskin, your lovely lonely tunnels of rhododendrons,
> The absurd monkey puzzlers and riot of vegetable vigour,
> And the dragon blood of the fuchsias in forests, and
>   primroses
> And peas in September: all this in twenty miles of bog.
> Sheskin, your grouse whose crops startled me spilling sweet
>   heather
> Under the falcon's foot and blood-spotted train, and sea-trout
> With tiger fins, and red salmon who would not take,
> Even with all our prayers, leaping, leaping out of the
>   Owenmore.
> Sheskin, oh Sheskin, all the things that are Sheskin,
> As beautiful as infinity: please let me come back to you
>   in peace.

Please be there, and let me be there to come back,
Back to our secret stream which harps into the deep basin
Under the old kiln where they used to dry malt for potcheen,
That ice-clear summer stream of music fizzing with bubbles,
Sliding over the flat slabs to the little waterfall,
Is you, Sheskin; is me, Sheskin; oh Nephin, and Slieve Car,
    be true.

He freed the hawks and drove back to Doolistown. There he began to consider his third Arthur volume, *The Ill-Made Knight*.

October 4th, 1939
What kind of person was Lancelot? I know about half the kind of person he was, because Malory contented himself with stating the obvious half.

Malory's Lancelot is:

1. Intensely sensitive to moral issues
2. Ambitious of true – not current – distinction.
3. Probably sadistic or he would not have taken such frightful care to be gentle.
4. Superstitious or totemistic or whatever the word is. He connects his martial luck with virginity, like the schoolboy who thinks he will only bowl well in the match tomorrow if he does not abuse himself today.
5. Fastidious, monogamous, serious.
6. Ferociously punitive to his own body. He denies it and slave-drives it.
7. Devoted to 'honour', which he regards as keeping promises and 'having a word'. He tries to be consistent.
8. Curiously tolerant of other people who do not follow his own standards. He was not shocked by the lady who was naked as a needle.
9. Not without a sense of humour. It was a good joke dressing up as Kay. And he often says amusing things.
10. Fond of being alone.
11. Humble about his athleticism: not false modesty.
12. Self-critical. Aware of some big lack in himself.
    What was it?

13. Subject to pity, cf no 3.

14. Emotional. He is the only person Malory mentions as crying from relief.

15. Highly strung: subject to nervous breakdowns.

16. Yet practical. He ends by dealing with the Guenever situation pretty well. He is a good man to have with you in a tight corner.

17. Homosexual? Can a person be ambi-sexual – bisexual or whatever? His treatment of young boys like Gareth and Cote Male Tale is very tender and his feeling for Arthur profound. Yet I do so want not to have to write a 'modern' novel about him. I could only bring myself to mention this trait, if it is a trait, in the most oblique way.

18. Human. He firmly believes that for him it is a choice between God and Guenever, and he takes Guenever. He says: This is wrong and against my will, but I can't help it.

As with Raleigh, so with Lancelot. 'The fellow's character I understand already: it is my own.' But this didn't go for a heroine.

October 10th, 1939

Much more important question than what sort of person was Lancelot is what sort of person was Guenever?

She must have been a nice person, or Lancelot and Arthur (both nice people) would not have loved her. Or does this not follow? Do nice people love nasty ones? Arthur was not a judge of nice people or he would not have had a child by Morgause. And Guenever hardly seems to have been a favourite of Malory's, whatever Tennyson may have thought about her.

She was insanely jealous of Lancelot: she drove him mad: she was suspected of being a poisoner: she made no bones about being unfaithful to Arthur: she had an ungovernable temper: she did not mind telling lies: she was hysterical, according to Sir Bors: she was beastly to Elaine: she was intensely selfish.

Yet I have already had one unattractive woman in the epic – Morgause – and it goes against the grain to have two, especially if Lancelot is to love her.

Nice people do love nasty ones. But it seems to lower them somehow.

What is to be done?

Guenever had some good characteristics. She chose the best lover she could have done, and she was brave enough to let him be her lover: she always stuck to Arthur, though unfaithful to him, possibly because she really liked him: when finally caught, she faced the music: she had a clear judgment of moral issues, even when defying them, a sort of common sense which finally took her into a convent when she could quite well have stayed with Lancelot now that her husband was dead.

Was this a piece of clearsightedness or was it cowardice? One way to put it would be to say that she grasped the best of two men while she profited by it, but afterwards betrayed them both. When there was no more to be got out of the Arthur-Lancelot situation she preferred the convent. The other way to put it would be to say that she finally recognized her ill influence and thought it best to shut herself up.

She was brave, beautiful, married young by treaty. She had very little control over her feelings, which were often generous: cf her tears, weeping as though she would die over Lancelot's recovery.

Guenever was like most women, Elaine like most girls. Elaine never developed the adult feelings of the average woman: jealousy, possessiveness, self-reference. She remained a poor little thing at the mercy of her fate, like a child sent to bed by the governess when it was bedtime and taken out of bed by the governess when it was time to get up. She could make little effort to control Lancelot's fate. She managed to get a child by him, but never offered to direct or force him afterwards. She just offered him her love. She did not – was not in a position to – demand anything in return.

A girl and a beggar. A pathetic figure. She had nothing to offer him except love. He must have found her boring as a companion, but felt the flattered protective affection which men have for shooting dogs.

Guenever was not a girl, but a grown woman. She exercised control, demanded return, felt jealousy. She must have been a passionate lover.

Could she be a sort of tigress, with all the healthy charms and horrors of the carnivore? Is she to eat Lancelot as Morgause ate Arthur? It seems to make him so much less the man. Yet both he and Arthur were hero-worshippers. Do people hero-worship tigresses? Arthur looked up to Merlyn and Lancelot looked up to Arthur. Were they both lookers-up, who needed a tigress to look up to?

Like a man on boggy ground, who leaps from tussock to sinking tussock, he zigzagged from conjecture to conjecture. The nice person gives way; he lands on someone insanely jealous, maddening, suspected of poisoning, faithless, hot-tempered, a liar, beastly to Elaine, intensely selfish. It seemed a foothold; but the creator's plain common sense that another Morgause wouldn't do tumbled him off it. She is a nasty person with some good characteristics. This tussock gave way when he began to examine her reasons for entering the convent; the first is base, the second posits an entirely different Guenever. At last he landed on the tigress 'with all the healthy charms and horrors of the carnivore'. He could have looked up to a tigress himself. Exhausted, he sank down on the tigress – though in the event, he revised her.

Earlier in the diary he noted: 'I dislike the shape of women very much and can scarcely bring myself to draw it.' This follows a hesitant and chocolate-box drawing of a sphinx. Guenever is his only full-grown woman drawn without dislike of her shape. He drew the breastless girl in Maria, otherwise he was only at his ease with women when they had grown shapeless: Mother Morlan, the Queen of Flanders's daughter whose nickname in the family was Piggy, the cook in *Mistress Masham's Repose*, Mrs

O'Callaghan. The woman of his dreams, if a woman figured there at all, was a Nannie – the ghost of the ayah he had loved and whom his mother had sent away.

Guenever was not all. There was also the Holy Grail. He had seen it coming for some time but had dodged it. Now it was unavoidable.

October 16th, 1939. To Sydney Cockerell
I was reading through the literary controversy about the Holy Grail between your two pals Dr Evans and George Wardle this evening and now I am going to sail into the mêlée myself. I am not an authority on sources – which I don't care a fig for anyway except that I am grateful to them for having presented themselves to Malory – but I do think I am an authority on Malory. I also consider he was the greatest English writer next to Shakespeare.

Now this is the one fact I want to obtrude into the Wardle-Evans fracas – MALORY DID NOT WRITE THE GRAIL BOOKS IN HIS OWN MORTE D'ARTHUR.

Having given you a line-space to digest this bombshell, I shall retract it. I thought it was worth exaggerating, in order to give you a shock and make you attend to business. As a matter of fact I have no reason to suppose, and do not really suppose, that Books 13–17 were really written by another hand. But I am perfectly certain that there is something very queer going on in these books. Ascham said that Malory was all 'open manslaughter and bold bawdry' – a just and flattering criticism. But from 13 to 17 there is an absolute change of attitude, how absolute you will realize when I tell you it is from 'open manslaughter etc' to EXACT CATHOLIC DOGMA. Another peculiar, though more literary, feature, is that the format of the epic alters in these books. They suddenly assume the form of *Gesta Romanorum* – ie narrative succeeded by moral. At the end of each chapter you find a bit which says 'By the white hart was signified the spotless body of our Lord', etc, etc.

What I mean by the sudden obsession with priestly dogma, is that in these books suddenly everybody is faced with questions such as: SHOULD YOU COMMIT MORTAL SIN, IF BY DOING SO YOU COULD SAVE THIRTEEN LIVES? The whole of the Grail books in Malory are devoted to these dogmatic dilemmas – AND NONE OF THE OTHER BOOKS.

Now one last, and comparatively piffling, comment on the Wardle theory that the Holy Grail was some life-giving bucket carried about by Celtic fairies:

Why should not the Holy Grail (Malory's Holy Grail) have been neither more nor less than the Holy Grail? I don't know what it was before, because before Malory I consider that the whole story was childish, but at any rate by Malory's time it was perfectly sensible to write about a genuine search for a physical object. I want to say that the search for the Grail was as reasonable in the time which Malory thought he was writing about as the search for your own umbrella at the lost property office.

Though it was the *Gesta Romanorum* aspect he stressed to Cockerell, White might equally as well have pointed out that Books 13–17 contain a considerable element of life-giving buckets. For almost a year he had been busy making himself over as a Gael; one might have expected him to welcome so many hermits and enchanters, the speaking forest in the adventure of Sir Melias, Sir Percivale's fiend-horse. Instead, whatever he might have felt as a story-teller, he halted on the threshold of Book 13 for a scholar's reason: he was pledged to Malory's story, not his own.

Cockerell replied that wherever the text of Books 13–17 came from, Malory had accepted it. White, though still of his first opinion, had meanwhile found his way round the problem. The search for the Grail is carried out by persons convinced they are acting reasonably; but the wonders and miracles are narrated by those who sought. This expedient also enabled him to express his personal opinion of Galahad ('the little beast was brought up in a nunnery and was "seemly and demure as a dove"') through the mouth of Sir Gawaine 'in a black temper, with his head bandaged'.

At Sheskin he had noted in his diary:

> I have had once or twice for a minute or two, but through shame hesitated to record, a sensation of pleasure in this present war – as seen from the safety of Sheskin. It gives brio to life: so long as you are not in it.

At Doolistown, he had to listen to reports of a war he had repudiated among listeners to whom that war was a source of news they felt no personal concern with – like a flood in India or a famine in China. And the war was the Phoney War.

> *October 20th, 1939*
> There don't seem to be many people being killed yet – no hideous slaughters of gas and bacteria.
> But the truth is going.
> We are suffocating in propaganda instead of gas, slowly feeling our minds go dead.
> And on the wireless – it seems as if it must be hundreds of millions of times a day – the foulest and cheapest and vulgarest and most debasing. They sing or play nothing but 'We'll hang out the washing on the Siegfried line' or 'Run, Adolf, run, Adolf, run, run, run.'

> *October 23rd, 1939*
> Siegfried Sassoon sent me a present of *Rhymed Ruminations* today, one copy of the 75 he has printed of it. It was a blessing which I can't write of, because for several hours I have feared I was going mad.
> The war as one hears of it over the wireless is more terrible than anything I can imagine of mere death. It seems to me that death must be a noble and terrible mystery, whatever one's creed or one's circumstances of dying. It is a natural

thing, anyway. But what is happening over the wireless is not natural. The timbre of the voices which sing about Hitler and death is a sneering, nasal mock-timbre. Devils in hell must sing like this. And they must iterate their wickedness in the same way.

I found myself grinning at some joke on the wireless today (every syllable on it makes one jump nowadays, like a rifle shot – not for fear that the news will be bad or that I shall be shot, but from fear that it will be another murder of human integrity: I really do physically jump at every syllable, and have had to turn the wireless low), found myself grinning at the jokes about Hitler, and then found that I was not amused by them, but that it was a nervous grin. And it sank on my face, like an unattached garment, from grin to glare, from glare to grimace of agony. I could feel the muscles falling from one tension to another as if my trousers were coming down. 'Berlin or Bust' sings the wireless, and suddenly I find I am a madman. I am grinning like a comedian, then a wolf, then a lunatic, then a devil in hell.

The arrival of Siegfried Sassoon's poems allayed his sense of isolation. He pulled himself together, blued some petrol, and drove into Dublin, where he spent £10 on books, bought a grand pipe and some bottles of champagne. The books were 'mainly meaty Russians like Tolstoy and Turgenev'. Ray Garnett had told him he should read the Russian novelists. 'Then I came home, put myself on a diet of biscuits, toast, fresh fruit, two raw eggs a day. Today I am practically safe, and with no convulsions.'

October 30th, 1939
Autumn was on the night and the place Erin
Where I had paused in my pace to the grave faring.
Wheesht blew the winds as I walked the stairing,
Creaking the treads old and the candle casting
Melancholy movements of me on the mouldy ceiling.

The above was to be the beginning of a long didactic poem about Ireland, but Henry Hall's band was turned on, and I had to stop. It is not that I am feeling insane any longer, but that you cannot very well write poetry to Henry Hall. This evening a poem of mine (the one about Sheskin) won a competition on the Irish wireless! I feel great pleasure about it.

Among the bits and pieces written at Sheskin is a sonnet. It was White's fatality to find nothing difficult; but he worked at the sonnet and in its first line: 'Minds of less madness in more rural days', 'more rural' was arrived at after half-a-dozen alternatives. During October and November he was writing poetry, mainly using lolloping uncorseted lines held together by alliteration, of the same breed as the poem interrupted by Henry Hall but richer in language, as though he were moving towards some kind of bardic Parnassian. Then, as if the closing couplet of the sonnet had chimed on in his mind, he made a sudden turn:

This sooty grouse, yet tawny and touched with red
Weighs handsome on my hand, although he's dead.
One wing reflects the sky. A steely light
Gleams from the primaries he oiled last night,
The twelve steel swords on which he wove his flight.
His crop of heather which my falcon split
In footing him, spills on my hand. Each bit
Is cleaner than cook's salad, fresh and green
With lilac buds surprising to be seen.

All this without an erasure, only a marginal note against the 'twelve steel swords': 'or is it ten?"

It is the characteristic glory of Dryden that his heroic couplet is authentically pedestrian – that it goes on its way through narrative and argument and parenthesis and polemic with its feet on the ground, whether with the gait of a deity or of a rational man. White had never achieved a walking prose – a reason why Siegfried Sassoon wished for a book by White which could be read slowly; he never even achieves pedestrian prose in the pejorative sense; when he writes badly, he writes like a lecturer. But in the last two months of 1939, like a man bewitched, he wrote five poems in heroic couplets as though to the manner born, so sure of his medium that he could trust it to browbeat any rebellion in the reader.

– Two hours later the mainland
Received a man, a saucepan in his hand.

'You have the opportunity to write a masterpiece'– so David Garnett wrote to him after reading the first draft of *Mistress Masham's Repose* – and went on to reproach him because he was not taking the opportunity seriously enough. It is tantalizing to think how near White was to another masterpiece; how the vein of heroic couplet and the wish to write 'a long didactic poem about Ireland' and the stretch of time to call his own were all trembling to come together, like drops of quicksilver; for everything was there: the theme was full of variety and opportunities for contention and satire and elegy and the odd and melodious nomenclature of Ireland; he was in the ascendant of his powers, engaged with Ireland but not subjugated by it, and handling the verse form which is above all others the most apt for being judicious in, and the least apt for his besetting faults of hurry and triviality.

But the last of the five poems in couplets was written on the island of Inniskea, and Inniskea was the starting point for a wild-goose chase that took him a long way from the heroic couplet.

It was for real geese that he went back to Co Mayo in November. With no particular idea how long he would stay, he went to Belmullet, a remote little town on the coast.

November 26th, 1939
Healion's Hotel, Belmullet. Shot 2 young white fronts this evening on L Carrowmore. Heavy birds. It is difficult to work out the habits of these creatures in country with such a large selection of loch and sea – but I outwitted them this time. Looking upon the noble corpses in the hard hail and scudding moonlight of the bog, I determined on a saga.

That same night he wrote a poem, analysing the conflict between his venerating delight in the prowess of *Anser albifrons*:

– Wind, moon, tide, show our tactics, we prevail
By skill in elements

and the vehement delight of opposing his prowess to theirs:

– Drown me the tide may, or my lead down you
In the heart-tumbling dive and thump I joy to view.

He had trouble with this poem. There are several drafts and discards, only the first three lines:

– You two, lying there, you two at my feet
Dark, done-for dummies on the darker peat
I did you in, I made you into meat

are constant, and the last:

– It was because I loved you that you had to die.

In the upshot, he resolved the conflict by shooting no more wild geese. Eventually he gave up shooting, though before then he was once, deliberately, to aim at a man.

Westward of Lough Carrowmore a narrow isthmus between the tidal waters of Broad Haven and Blacksod Bay carries the road from the bog of Erris to Belmullet and hence to the near-island beyond – called the Mullet because its contours resemble those of the fish. A track twists across it, dodging the wind as much as may be, and brings one out in face of the Atlantic and the range of outpost islands: Innisglora, the two Inniskeas, and Duvillaun.

December 14th, 1939
Last night the whole hotel was kept awake by a priest, who came in very drunk about one o'clock in the morning. He spent most of the night falling out of bed and howling: strange moans of torture and the crash of furniture in the room above mine. I know this priest and had cracked a bottle of whiskey with him two nights before. This man had it in his power to ruin lives which had slipped, to interfere with commercial enterprises. All simple men, and all women,

treated him with placating diffidence. He knew all this, and, with coarse gaitered legs crossed before the fire, accepted the propitiation, the superstition, the whiskey and our awe. Yet I am only amused if a Protestant clergyman gets drunk. Yet in a few months I may be a Catholic myself.

And if a Catholic, then on to the priesthood? The process of mind is clear. White's drinking bouts need not stand in the way of him being well-thought-of by a parish, any more than Mat Talbot's alcoholism prevented Dublin esteeming him a saint.

As White never became a Catholic the drunken priest would have had no importance in his story if the diary did not go on:

> One of the things he told me was the kind of supreme poetry which you only get in the land of the Gael. In the great disaster of Inniskea (1927), when 10 men drowned in an enormous, meaningless squall which only lasted about half an hour, two men were swept ashore alive on an upturned currach. One of these men, sitting safe in a public house, continued automatically to make the motions of baling with a saucepan which he held, clutched immovably in one hand, for two hours after he was on shore.

The Inniskea of the disaster was the south island (the north island had long been uninhabited). White was drawn to it by a variety of motives. He would be sure of getting wild geese there, so his Belmullet friend assured him – too friendly to mention that the Inniskeas were a preserve. He would be challenging a danger, since a winter storm might maroon him there for a matter of weeks. He would be a Crusoe, and on a deserted island – for after the disaster of 1927 the remaining population had been evacuated to the mainland; he would be a ghost-ridden Crusoe, trespassing among ruins so recent yet so absolute. It would be an extreme experience.

In the third week of December, a few days before the shortest day, he was put ashore, with his dog, his gun and a hamper of food. The men in the currach felt uneasy as they rowed away. They had done their best for him, showing him the hut where fishermen kept their crayfish and lobster pots, the store of driftwood for firing, the well. But it was a bad time of year for such an adventure, you could not be certain of the sea; for that matter, you could not be certain of the man; he might break his leg; he might go mad. And at the same time they were wild with curiosity to know how he would get on, and sat up for hours that night talking about him.

He lit a fire; he ate; he looked at the objects about him and listened to the noises outside; he comforted Brownie, who gave him courage by being more afraid than he. He wrote his poem about the disaster of Inniskea and the island God, clung to by the island's inhabitants because it was native and always at hand when rough seas cut them off from the priest and the Mass. At dawn he went out and shot six barnacle geese, a brace of them with a left and right. On the afternoon of the third day the motor-boat on its way back from the Black Rock lighthouse took him on board, and that evening he was in Belmullet, and writing in his diary:

I felt lonely standing on the white sand in the twilight.

The 'Letter from a Goose Shooter' in *The Godstone and the Blackymor* begins with the same words and follows the diary almost word for word except for this private lament:

When I was in this place my mind was filled with lucid prose, simple and worth writing. I treasured it up, already arranged and ready for paper: but now I cannot put it down. There, belief in God was natural and observation of the world absorbing. All has gone, in a few hours, coming back to Bedlam.

If I had written on Inniskea, I could not have written mannered prose, or written anything for effect. It is miserable to sit with the wreckage of that world about me, trying to salve a few pieces of it.

'What he wanted was sincerity.' It was the demand he made of his pupils at Stowe, the touchstone by which he judged their writing. This entry – it is almost the only instance in those voluminous diaries where he expressed an artistic, as apart from a censorious, conscience – shows him making the same demand of himself, and grieving because he could not comply. Perhaps he was more aware of what was lacking in his prose because his recent poems had come so much nearer to having it.

February 1st, 1940
To Inis Cé again, in a 3-man currach. We got out and in nicely between the weathers, but had no geese. An old heron wove her way to the island as we left.

At this point, he set out on a wild-goose chase. It was all as Irish as could be, so Inniskea was given its correct spelling, and the ambiguities of the Irish language – even more pliable than the House of Mead-Circling, etc, which he met at Tara – closed round him.

The Godstone's name was the naomhóg, so far as I can catch it by ear. But naomhóg means a canoe – or cot. Naomh = saint or holy (adj) and oge = youth. Og (adj) = young. Taking naomh as a noun (saint or holy one) and óg as a dim suffix (young, little) you could call him The Holy Little One. On the other hand there is something interesting about the canoe or cot. Cot? Crib?

Then there is neamh = heaven (the Little Heaven) and néam = brightness (the Little Brightness). Again, neamh (neg prefix) gives a *contrary* sense so that neamh-óg might mean the Not Young. Finally neamh-ad = ill-luck.

The west of Ireland is traditionally hospitable; even if your motives are mistrusted (White's soon were) your wants are succoured. White wanted information; information was given. Translation was supplied too, for Sean Glynn, an Irish-speaking Land Commissioner whom he had made friends with at the hotel, came with him on journeys of inquiry. The statement that this Young, Old, Bright, Heavenly, Unlucky, Canoe or Cot-shaped Object (never set eyes on, broken by (a) pirates, (b) a priest, and given a yearly new garment of (a) blue serge, (b) red flannel) had been stolen from North to South Inniskea because its presence improved the potato yield encouraged White in the idea that he had come on the remains of a fertility cult. The object was also alleged to calm or enrage seas; and for a brief time the name in the ordnance map of a headland on the South Island, Carrickgubneptune, suggested a wider hypothesis.

> Could the Little Holy Man have been a Greek statue – got here heaven knows how? Note: Neptune, connection with the sea (he could calm it), necessity to dress him, fertility (a naked statue would suggest this), size (he was small enough to be (a) broken by a priest, (b) taken out and sunk from a currach, (c) described as óg). Perhaps it is a wild conjecture.

He gave up Neptune, noting in the margin, 'Obviously a shipwreck', and fastened on Father O'Reilly who cast the Godstone into the sea and was dead within the year.

> If this insistently repeated story is true, it should be possible, by finding out when Fr O'Reilly died, to fix the date of the Godstone's committal.

This hope wavered when Father O'Reilly turned into two Father O'Reillys.

There was perhaps a clue in the story as first told to White and which he used in the poem written on Inniskea. In this version the Godstone was taken ('in chains' according to one informant) to a museum in Dublin. The clue led nowhere; Dublin museums disclaimed all knowledge of the Godstone.

It was not the Godstone itself but a rumour of it which had been carried to Dublin

> by some Protestants, who were very kind to the islanders and gave them food, etc, and the result was that the trustful islanders told them all about their naomhóg, and the Protestants went away, promising to come back in six months with plenty more food. No sooner had they arrived in Dublin, however, than they wrote to the *Irish Times*, saying that on the island of Inniskea there were people who called themselves Catholics who worshipped a pagan idol.

And it was to combat these slanders that Father O'Reilly 1 broke the Godstone, Father O'Reilly 2 cast it into the sea.

White had been careful not to offend sensibilities by obtruding his theory of a fertility cult. He now began to suspect that some of his informants were being careful not to say too much in case he wrote to the *Irish Times*. When he met a schoolmistress of the vicinity, who distinguished the O'Reillys and gave a coherent account of the story, his suspicions were deepened. 'A woman of strong character and even stronger Catholic prejudices', she would help him to know as much as was good for him, but not more. Yet she had a turn for antiquarianism, and was sufficiently in sympathy with his researches to fall in with his project of a discreetly worded questionnaire to be filled out by her schoolchildren after interrogating their elderly relations.

At the end of February, he broke off for four days fishing. Throughout all these inquiries, conjectures, and intentions (a list of 'immediate things to do' included 'to try the newspapers of 1876, to find out dates of the Fenian cycle, to pursue the history of the races on the island, to save up 2 old remaining old women until I have definite questions to ask them, to get my copy of *The Golden Bough* over from England as soon as I can'), writing letters, visiting museums and gravesides, listening to everybody and trying to maintain his reason (the questionnaire would be a credit to any researcher, and only one of its twenty-four questions turned out to be totally beside the point) White held to his opinion that the Godstone was evidence of a fertility cult. On March 5th he had himself rowed to the North Island. There, among graves and thorrows and vestigial rubbish heaps, bones of men and animals, shells and carved stones, he began to change his mind. The bareness and antiquity of these remnants, the touching dimensions of the ruined chapel – 'no larger than a very small room' – the short-legged crucified Christ incised on a gravestone and the piety which had left the skull at its foot lying undisturbed, touched his heart. And his heart was more accessible than his head. He re-routed his thoughts, and accepted the consensus of the answers to his questionnaire and the statement of old Mrs Padden:

There was a stone in Inniskea shaped like a pillow, and the natives treasured it as the relic of a saint who lived at one time on the island, they said it was the saint's pillow worn in the middle like the shape or mark of a head.

On Easter Monday he drove to Doolistown, intending to be baptized by the priest at Trim. He bought some books in Dublin but the baptism did not take place. When he got back to Belmullet he found a letter from David Garnett, telling him of Ray's death, and enclosing a letter from her, one of the two letters she wrote on her deathbed. 'I would have liked to have read your Arthur books', it ended. He fastened it into his diary, writing on the envelope 'Ray's Last Letter'. Eighteen months later he wrote below the envelope:

> I still think of her more than of any other woman. She is as real to me now as if she were alive, and I think she will be till I die. I still puzzle about things she said, regret things that I said, and see her standing with bare feet on the bog, her skirts tucked up, back from some private expedition.

The revised *Witch in the Wood* was published by Collins in April. 'Pretty good in the end' was the best Potts could say for it. White had scamped the revision, because he wanted to get it out of the way. Seeing it in print, he knew it wouldn't do, and began a second revision.

By now he was nearing the end of his third Arthur, *The Ill-Made Knight*, the book Ray Garnett would never read.

June 14th, 1940. To David Garnett
I finished my third volume of Malory a few weeks ago and sent it off to America with an *Ite, missa est*. If it turns out to be a good book, as I suspect it may, it will be due to Ray. Some things she said to me at Sheskin made me think in an improved way, and particularly to settle down to read the Russians. It will be through them, but particularly through

Ray that Guenever has turned out to be a living being. Ray was impatient with me for not attending to my women. I have attended to Guenever with something more than respect. With fear, almost.

Ray Garnett's influence went beyond White's improved way of thinking. In *The Ill-Made Knight* the narrative is barer, there are fewer flourishes, no farce, no extravaganzas. One feels one is reading a true story. At Sheskin, when White was in revolt against her pole star-integrity he complained, 'It is like living with Mrs Be-Done-By-As-You-Did.' But her example silenced the special pleading and the special pleasing and reinforced the example of Malory.

The preliminary notes for *The Ill-Made Knight* which show White still puzzling over Malory's indications were made in October. At the longest estimate, the book took seven months to write. For a quick writer, as he was, this would not be remarkable, if he had worked without distractions. But at Belmullet he went from one distraction to another. He went shooting; he explored the neighbourhood with particular attention to graveyards; he went after geese so inveterately that even the hard winter could not deter him: a Belmullet friend remembers him coming back with icicles tinkling in his beard after lying out on the slob for the dawn flight. He stayed on Inniskea; he pursued the Godstone. And he talked, let loose into male conversation again.

In June he was issued with a card stating that he had been enrolled with the rank of sergeant in the local Security Force for the Belmullet district. An invasion was expected – probably by the traditional foe.

June 18th, 1940
Miss Sheehy dashes in.
   'I've come to hear the news.'
   'I don't think there is any news.'
   'Haven't you heard? The English are invading us.'
   'No!'
   'Yes, I have just heard it from the Super.'
   'Are you sure?'

'It's everywhere. Everybody knows it. Everybody is going to stay up all night.'

It was against this background that he thought about England at war.

June 14th, 1940
Because I came to live in Ireland more than six months before the outbreak of war, I have no English ration card nor identity card and I am probably not on their National Register. When the time comes for my age-group to be conscripted, it is improbable that anybody will know of my existence.

I can either go on living quietly in Ireland, 'on the run'; or I can give notice of my existence to the appropriate registration body, after finding out what body is appropriate. If I give notice of my existence, I can either register myself as a conscientious objector or else accept the fate of a conscript.

Arguments in favour of reporting for duty as a conscript:

(1) England has my bones, etc., and I don't like Hitlerism.
(2) It is the line of least resistance.
(3) Being bombed a bit might do me good, while if you are killed you are dead. I believe I could put up with most forms of maiming except being blind.
(4) It is an attractive way of getting cheap glory. Voluntary Conscription of Famed Writer. Also an excellent tonic for one's self-esteem – pro tem. The last time that I proved to myself that I was brave was by winning a prize for flying in 1934. That proof is getting out of date.
(5) It would be a change. My life is an isolated one, which might renew itself by living in a crowd again.
(6) I would like to. (?)

Arguments for reporting as a conscientious objector were: he would be more valuable as a tax-paying writer than as a combatant; by finishing the Tetralogy he would do more for civilization than by fighting for it; he had already offered his services as a writer and intellectual and been rebuffed; it was the honest course.

Staying on the run would safeguard Brownie and authorship – both jeopardized by possible internment as an objector – and was what almost every Connaught Irishman would recommend.

> There can be no legal proceedings against me if I don't report. Unless I happen to hear it on the wireless, I may never even know the date when my age-group is called to register; and such chance audition by radio could never be put forward as a sufficient notification. This strikes me as a base reflection.

It would have been easier to know his own mind if some other mind he respected had offered opposition. He was afforded nothing but civilized tolerance and broadmindedness. There was no suggestion that he was skulking, there was no call to arms. Garnett, writing in September 1940, reported that there was a general feeling that the Germans would crack up within the next year. White commented, 'I hope you are right.' About the war, he was more realist than his friend. Garnett's realism was more at home in the field of human nature. 'I think it just as well you should spend the war years in your native bog. You are far more likely to work, earn a lot of money and keep the bottle at arm's length.'

But was it his native bog? Was he a bard of Erin or did England command his bones?

June 20th, 1940
The trouble is that my mind does not want to join this war, and is able to face the isolation of not joining it, but my heart floats in the subconscious of my race. The mind seems to be the only part of a person which is individual, ie which does not float in some sort of vast external sea. The heart of a person is only a jelly-fish in the human ocean, and, when the ocean is removed from the jelly-fish, the latter dries up.

So to fight is to kill my mind, everything which I have considered valuable; and not to fight is to kill my heart.

The insecurity of his childhood had rendered him almost incapable of admitting himself to be in the wrong – while at the same time never feeling sure he wasn't in the wrong, that others did not think him in the wrong and that he would not somehow be punished for it. Only a shallow judgment would laugh at his vacillations.

Another thing to debate – though he did not debate it with the same anxiety – was whether or not to become a Roman Catholic. During the previous autumn he had set himself to study the Gospels. This he began to do immediately after analysing Lancelot and Guenever – applying to the Four Evangelists the same methodical scrutiny he had given to the *Morte d' Arthur*; but with less basis of information.

> Note that Luke begins his history long before he could have been an eye-witness of Jesus – indeed before Jesus was conceived: a biographical oddity only to be found elsewhere in *Tristram Shandy*.

After his move to Belmullet the Gospels were put by till after midsummer. By then he knew that Luke was writing from hearsay, and had learned from a footnote in the Douai Testament the tradition that the Gospel of St Mark was dictated by St Peter. This fired him. Peter-Mark became as lively as Lancelot.

> Peter does not even try to understand Jesus nor to establish the human tie of love. He regards him as an act of God. His relation towards him is the same as it would be towards an earthquake or a flood. Peter gives an authentic feeling of impotence before Jesus. Without preliminary conversation Jesus says, Follow me. And the wretched fellow gets up and comes.

He persevered on through Acts and into mid-Galatians. Here he gave up, but not before his dislike of St Paul had prompted a discerning insult: 'His Jesus is simply an antidote.'

White's Jesus was more than that. At one point, indeed, he seems to have been recognized as an *alter ego*.

> Reading between the lines, and noting how he (Peter) refers so distantly to the BVM as 'Mary the mother of James the less and of Joseph' I believe that Jesus was estranged from his mother since the time of his ministry and continued so until his crucifixion. Then he arranged (see John) to have her looked after.

In July White fetched Mrs McDonagh and her sister for the pilgrimage to Croagh Patrick. He was deeply moved and believed himself finally converted. A little later, he went on a Peace Pilgrimage to the shrine at Knock.

> The sermon consisted of raking over old animosities against the English, of implication that war is a punishment for slighting the vested interests of the clergy (synonym: 'turning away from the Catholic Faith'), of dramatic or histrionic clap-trap about the Blessed Virgin and finally of the assumption that the only purpose of the Peace Pilgrimage was to pray for peace in Ireland. This man, this wicked man in priestly garments, did not mention one word of sorrow or commiseration or pity or supplication for all the millions in tormented Europe. Now I think I shall never be a Catholic.

Just as White remarked on the different Jesuses of the Evangelists I was struck when I visited Belmullet in 1965 by the different Whites of his two close friends there, Jack McLaughlin and Harry Cronin.

'I looked after his car, I looked after his dog, I looked after him,' Mr McLaughlin said. Mr McLaughlin's voice was full of affection and pride and entertainment, his stories full of vehemence and calamity. There were always calamities: a forecast of perfect weather brought a storm; the car in perfect order broke down; or White's good humour splintered into sulks and rages.

'One day when we were out, he said to me, "Jack, if I miss a bird, you're not to shoot it." Well, he missed; and the habit was too strong for me, I shot and brought it down. He wouldn't speak to me all that day.' At other times his rage would go off in farce. There was a day when they went fishing the Owenmore from a boat, doing it in style with two boatmen. They fished all day and at intervals filled up with rum. Jack caught one fish, White none. At dusk, the tide changed. The men were too drunk to row, White sat brooding his fury, they were being swept out to sea on one of the fastest currents in Ireland; at last Jack managed to lodge the boat against the bank. By then it was almost dark. White, who had wound up his line and put the reel in his pocket, jumped ashore and stood on the bank casting with a bare rod, making cast after cast and exclaiming, 'That's a good one!' He was mischievous and liked to tease. Once, when they were sitting in the halted car, he challenged Jack to shoot a yellow-hammer on a telegraph wire and joggled the car each time he took aim. Yet he was kind and at everyone's service. He would pluck people off the road and put off his own journey to give them a lift, and on Sundays he got up early to convey parties to Mass. 'Sometimes he would talk to me till I felt afraid – about natural history and foreign countries and history. He was a shy man, you know. That was why he was happy in the west, feeling he was welcome. Everybody knew him and welcomed him. They didn't sponge on him, because they took him as a friend. He was often astray, but always a good heart.'

Harry Cronin's White was a darker and more intricate character – a self-tormentor instead of a schoolboyish tease, an inheritor of calamities instead of their buffoon. When he got badly drunk, it upset him, and he would shut himself up in his room. 'Nobody dared go near him when he had these spells of getting over it. He'd shut himself up for three days on end. It was a way of his.' He thought little of hardship, little of danger, would risk his life; yet he was often afraid – of omens, of a dark night, most of all, afraid of the IRA. When there was an idea that he might buy Sheskin, he consulted Mr Cronin.

Would he be safe there, would Mr Cronin be able to protect him? At a knock on the door, he would look apprehensive, and during some of those three-day spells of locking himself in his room he would not open the door a crack until he was assured that no IRA man stood outside. It was an unaccountable fear, but it was genuine. Mr Cronin's White did not slide so easily into Belmullet's good opinion as did Mr McLaughlin's. He was generous with his money but he put too much faith in it. When he put down a cooked chicken on the floor and said to Brownie, 'Now enjoy yourself,' what could not be forgiven was his assumption that he could put all right by paying for a new carpet: 'That way of thinking doesn't apply in the west.' It is still remembered that at the hotel where he paid £4 a week for his own keep he paid £2 a week for the dog's; that she had the best part of the hamper Mrs Healion had packed for the expedition to Inniskea; that she slept in his bedroom – a thing unheard-of, but consented to because you could see he was set on her, that she was his first thought, was fed before he ate, was dried while the wet was running off him. These were the eccentricities of a rich, childless man, no harm in them. What is remembered with a different authenticity are White's words at the outset of a shooting party. 'I must tell you one thing. If anyone shoots my dog, I shoot him. Shot one. Shot two. Like that – no hesitation.'

Commenting, 'It was no sort of a joke. He meant it. He would have done it', Mr Cronin remembered another example of this flashing fury, which Jack McLaughlin bore out.

The tiercel freed at Sheskin was later caught by a labourer and sold to Mr Cronin, who wintered it for White in his greenhouse. White flew it during the summer, then took it back to Doolistown, meaning to finish its training and give it to Jack as a keepsake. He wrote to say it was ready. Jack drove to Doolistown. He found the door of White's room on the upper floor locked, and was told that White would talk to him out of the window. Speaking from the window, White said: 'I am too unhappy to talk. Your bird was shot this morning. I saw the man, and fired twice at him. He was across the Boyne, too far away and I missed him.'

One way and another, White attracted too much notice in Belmullet. A rumour went round that he was spying for the English. His movements were restricted; he was not allowed on Inniskea. If he hawked, throwing the lure was taken to be semaphoring. The acutest suspicions were fastened on Brownie. She had a close-fitting waterproof coat to protect her from the weather, with spatterdashes to prevent her carrying mud indoors on her leg feathers. Nothing like this had ever been seen in Erris. It was referred to as her 'second skin', and it was between Brownie and her second skin that White was supposed to hide his illicit charts and maps.

His scheme for finding the range of wild hawks by ringing them may have looked suspicious, too. He never knew the result of this experiment, for in October he left the place where everyone made him welcome and some reported him to the police; where, threatening to take their lives, he made friends who still think of him with affection and ponder about him; and drove back to Doolistown.

VIII Doolistown 1940–41

A straight causeway, ditched and hedged on either side, turns off the road between stone gate-posts and is the avenue to Doolistown House, though it appears to lead only to a group of farm buildings. The house stands to one side of these. Derelict, now, and falling to ruin, it asserts its eighteenth-century dignity and composure among its shambling appurtenances like some fine turn of phrase persisting in a dialect.

The hedges would have been discolouring and the leaves dropping into the ditches when White came back 'to settle down for three months to the last volume of Arthur'. The last volume of Arthur was not new ground. It existed already, in the form of a play, called 'The Candle in the Wind'. Noël Coward's letter rejecting it is dated January 27th, 1939.

> I think the play is exquisitely written as I would have expected but theatrically speaking I am not so sure of it. I feel that many of the speeches are too long and I am a little doubtful of its sustaining powers. However, I could easily be wrong about this and I really did enjoy reading it.

This was putting it kindly. Not only are the speeches long; they are lifeless. Past events are related in order to give the action a shove on; coming events are summarized beforehand. When the dialogue escapes from the speeches it is affectedly simple: Arthur, dragging his doom after him, seems to have come in for a cup of tea after tinkering unsuccessfully with the lawn-mower. Only a brilliant producer, given lavish resource and a free hand with the scissors, could have made it into a viable play.*

White set to work to 'produce' it as a novel. As the text of the play grew progressively flimsier and more threadbare he poured more of his developed powers into it. Scene XI of the play consists of Lancelot making a speech to his knights (whom he

---

* He could not relinquish the play. In 1962 a revised version was given to Richard Burton.

addresses as 'gentlemen') in which he briefs them on the state of affairs, tells them his intentions, reads them a long informative letter from Gawaine and closes with:

> Well, gentlemen, there it is. All we can do is to sail for England with all possible speed. De Maris, I shall leave you to arrange the embarkation. Bors will superintend the forage. Gawaine's was a warm heart, gentlemen, and for the rest we can only pray we may get there in time.

Out of this bleak military board-meeting he made Chapter XIII of the book – a demonstration of what, by then, he could do if he put himself to it – though also a demonstration, alas, of how at a finish he could not be trusted to leave well alone.

The end was in sight. Titles for the complete book were turning in his head: *The Dreaming King*, *The Ancient Wrong*, *Arthur Pendragon*. Then, as though recognizing that 'The Candle in the Wind' had not sufficient weight for a full stop, he saw that a Book 5 must follow, and complete the whole. His mind rushed ahead.

November 14th, 1940
Pendragon can still be saved, and elevated into a superb success, by altering the last part of Book 4, and taking Arthur back to his animals. The legend of his going underground at the end, into the badger's sett, where badger, hedgehog, snake, pike (stuffed in case) and all the rest of them can be waiting to talk it over with him. Now, with Merlyn, they must discuss war from the naturalist's point of view, as I have been doing in this diary lately. They must decide to talk thoroughly over, during Arthur's long retirement underground, the relation of Man to the other animals, in the hope of getting a new angle on his problem from this. Such, indeed, was Merlyn's original objective in introducing him to the animals in the first place. Now what can we learn about abolition of war from animals?

In his diary on April 26th, 1939, he had debated whether he should fight or retire into the religious life. A hawk flew across his mind. 'Hawks neither band themselves together in war, nor yet retire from the world of air.' It was a vatic flight, and he had been pondering about it ever since.

It is only in the most highly organized or political creatures (ants, men, microbes) that genuine war is found.

Why?

To most other animals our warfare would seem much more deplorable than civil war seems to us.

I do wish I knew the size of the cerebrum of the ant.

Man's greatest singularity is the size of his cerebrum. What has this to do with his other singularities – warfare, capital? I suppose acquisitiveness is inherent in recognition of personality, and recognition of personality is inherent in the cerebrum's memory.

I wish I could think of some creature, other than man, which owned possessions and did not fight wars. It must be a social animal (squirrels won't do).

Ants and bees. They are fascist, not communist. They are nationalistic. Hives and ant-hills are their nations. They fight wars.

Geese. These are the true communists. They are international. But they have no possessions at all. Neither have they any industry, except eating what they don't grow.

November 15th, 1940
The Candle in the Wind must stop immediately after the boy Hugh – turn him into Tom – Malory? has been sent for the bishop.

One stands outside the work of art, and all is clear. One sees the artist's device, one imagines his private rapture of keeping it up his sleeve till the moment it is needed. In fact, it may just as well have occurred to him at the last moment; and then with a question-mark. 'Turn him into Tom – Malory?' It is a beautiful device, a farewelling obeisance to the old master who had conducted him for so long: but at the time it only rated a question-mark. The diary goes on:

Arthur must droop his head in his arms and begin to cry. All the part discussed in his talk with Rochester must be related in prose by the author, as the reason for the tears. Then it must be Merlyn who comes in, not Rochester, and Arthur must think it is the bishop and not look at him (to hide his face) and look up reluctantly to see why Rochester does not speak, and say in a small voice 'Merlyn?' and then louder 'Merlyn!' Then 'Merlyn, Merlyn, by thunder!' End of book.

On December 6th he wrote to Potts, saying that the American edition of *The Ill-Made Knight* would be sent him.

The next volume is to be called *The Candle in the Wind* (one has to add DV nowadays) and is about the final clash, worked by Mordred. It will end on the night before the last battle, with Arthur absolutely wretched. And after that I am going to add a new 5th volume, in which Arthur rejoins Merlyn underground (it turns out to be the badger's sett of vol 1) and the animals come back again, mainly ants and wild geese. Don't squirm. The inspiration is godsent. You see, I have suddenly discovered that (1) the central theme of *Morte d'Arthur* is to find an antidote to war, (2) that the best way to examine the politics of man is to observe him, with Aristotle, as a political animal. I don't want to go into all this now, it will spoil the freshness of the future book, but I have been thinking a great deal, in a Sam Butlerish way, about man as an animal among animals – his cerebrum, etc. I think I can really make a comment on all these futile isms (communism, fascism, conservativism, etc) by stepping back – right back into the real world, in which man is only one of the innumerable other animals.* So to put my 'moral' across (but I shan't state it), I shall have the marvellous opportunity

---

* Konrad Lorenz in his book *On Aggression* (1966) pursues a similar line of inquiry. It is interesting that he attaches particular importance to the conduct of grey-lag geese, who ritualize their aggressive instincts into ceremonial.

of bringing the wheel full circle, and ending on an animal note like the one I began on. This will turn my completed epic into a perfect fruit, 'rounded off and bright and done'.

'"Merlyn?" asked the king. He did not seem to be surprised.'

Between the excited entry of November 15th and beginning his Book 5 White has meditated on his theme and knew Arthur would be in no condition to exclaim 'Merlyn, by thunder!' or to feel any quickening of emotion. The opening of Book 5 where Merlyn tries to rouse the king from his stupor of misery is a minus opening, like the opening of 'Grief for the Grey Geese';* but in terms of narrative, not description. The pupil–master relationship of *The Sword in the Stone* is recalled as past recall. When Merlyn tries to resume it, Arthur evades his cajoleries as though he were answering the importunities of a child. The pupil has outgrown the master; he has been defeated in the real world while Merlyn sat warming his five wits in a cave. But for White's purpose Merlyn has to be master again and carry the king back among his early friends, Badger, Balin, T natrix, Archimedes, Goat, Cavall and Hedgehog, who are sitting in the Combination Room where an enormous stuffed pike now hangs below the portrait of the founder. They are waiting to talk it over with him, to 'discuss war from the naturalist's point of view, as I have been doing in this diary lately'. White's point of view is discussed through the next fifty close-typed pages. It is as though the last but two chapter of *War and Peace* were to extend over two-thirds of the book.

During the fifty pages where the passages in White's diary about man's place in the animal kingdom (that of a small parvenu), his specialization as property owner, his hubris, ferocity (*homo ferox*), stupidity (*homo impoliticus*) and short-sightedness are canvassed by Merlyn and the animals, Arthur is allowed two educational exeats, one among the ants, the other among the geese. So far, he has been told what is wrong with man, After the second exeat Merlyn preaches on the text of White's 'Now

* p 95.

what can we learn about abolition of war from animals?' To cut a long treatise short, man must forswear frontiers, nationality, territorial claims, must learn to speak a universal tongue, must develop the talent of his species, which is intelligence, and become *homo sapiens* – or perish like the American passenger pigeon.

'It is a straight choice; so all our king will need to do when he returns will be to make their situation obvious.'

The patient Goat returned to an earlier topic.

'He is looking unhappy, whatever you say.'

So they looked at the king, and suddenly all fell silent.

He was watching them with a goose-feather in his hand, wherever he had got hold of it. He kept them off with the feather, his fragment of beauty, as if it were a weapon to hold them back.

'I am not going,' he said. 'You must find another ox to draw. Why have you reminded me of youth and talked about men? Why should I die for them when you speak of them contemptuously yourselves? Do you suppose they would listen to wisdom, that the dullards would understand and throw down their arms? No, they will kill me for it as the ants would have killed an albino. They have killed every peacemaker in history. They even killed their god.

'Why should I go back to man? I was never clever, but I was patient, and even patience goes. Nobody can bear it all his life.'

They did not dare to answer, for they could think of nothing to say.

His feeling of guilt and frustrated love made him wretched, so that now he had to accuse in self-defence.

'Yes, you are clever talkers. You know the long words and how to juggle with them. If the sentence is a pretty one, you laugh and make it. But these are human souls you have been cackling about, and it is my soul, the only one I have, which you have put in the index. I can do this filthy work no longer, trouble with your dreary plans no longer, but I will go away into some quiet place with the goose people, where I can die in peace.'

His voice collapsed into the whine of a beggar, and he threw himself back in the chair, covering his eyes with his hands.

This is as fine as the opening: the goose-feather, a flash of poetic vision. Then the hedgehog leads Arthur away from his tormentors into a spring night; they sit on the tor and as a late moon rises Arthur sees his kingdom, his realm of Grammarye, and his people.

> They were not ferocious now, because they were asleep. All the beauty of his humans came upon him, instead of their horribleness. He saw the vast army of martyrs who were his witnesses: young men who had gone out even in the first joy of marriage to be killed on dirty battlefields like Bedegraine for other men's beliefs – but who had gone out voluntarily, because they thought it was right, although they hated it. They had been ignorant young men, perhaps, and the things they had died for had been useless. But their ignorance had been innocent. They had done something horribly difficult in their ignorant innocence, which was not for themselves.

He goes back to the world, and asks a truce of Mordred. The armies met to see it confirmed by their leaders. A grass-snake moved in the grass, one of Mordred's men took it for a viper, drew his sword to kill it. The sword was drawn, the slaughter began: 'and never stinted, till the noble knights were laid to the cold ground'. But even with Malory's example before him, White allowed Merlyn a previous dissertation of six pages on the pros and cons of war – though he had the grace to score out one of them.

It is difficult to read the fifth Arthur without exasperation. It could have been so good and it is so bad. The fault is not in the choice of theme: abolition of war is an interesting subject; and the idea that man should take a leaf out of the animals' book an idea worth pursuing, since animals are good at avoiding conflict. (Incidentally, White mislaid an argument against the inevitability of war when he omitted to notice that man is so far averse to warring on his kind that war-propaganda has to insinuate that the people to be attacked are in some way non-human: Huns, Reds, Yids, Frogs, Natives, etc.) The fault lies in the book's schizophrenia. Giving the impression of having been written by two different people it does not seem sincere. Written by one man, it seems demented.

Loneliness can become a kind of dementia: it is hermits who start crusades and heresy hunts, simultaneously abhorring mankind and yearning to save it. White had foreseen what isolation might do to him. Lacking

> the encouragement of equal minds, the stimulation from other intellects, isolated from a surrounding war, with letters spied on, journalism censored, wireless stuffed with lies, and ignorance all round one, the writer's life is that of the slaves set to make bricks without straw. It is a form of masturbation or self-massacre. If I contrive to finish Arthur at all, I shall have used up all myself in giving self to him.

He had been working within a scheme of four books; he had not allowed for the drain of Book 2, he had not calculated for a Book 5. He ran out of the self he could give to Arthur soon after the opening of Book 5. After fifty pages a little more had accumulated; he could speak for Arthur and put the goose-feather in his hand. In the interim he fell back on the self which made entries in diaries and was equally sincere, but had been lashing itself into a temper and reading text-books on natural history. White, who was modest about his creative powers, was conceited about his intellect – which was second-rate. When he was giving self to Arthur he resented this cocksure interloper who was a clever talker and knew so many facts. But as though he had to placate his intellect and keep in with the diary fellow – whom he undoubtedly admired – he lent him Merlyn's robes to strut and prate in.

It is sad to look back on the excellence he promised himself, and to have only a goose-feather fragment of the book he intended. Time could have mended it – if he could have taken time off to think, or rather, to feel his way back into creation. Only a little before, he had re-written the play version of 'The Candle in the Wind', and put flesh and shape on it. A re-writing of 'The Book of Merlyn' might have been as transforming. But this was not to happen.

October 24th, 1941
Most of the writing in this journal seems rather unreal to me, since I am returning to England to join the war. I suppose I had to find good reasons against the war, while I was finishing my book. But the book itself, particularly Book 5 Chapter 18, is my reason for going back.*

If you write that and believe it, you must back it up by going.

By going, I am sacrificing everything I have. I never had much. I had no wife, children or home. My friends were only friends, who fade. I did have one thing for seven years, a red setter bitch who went with me everywhere I went, slept on my bed, and lived her life in me, as I in her. If other people, with wives and children, can be said to be clothed in them, as with coat and breeches, I had just this one breech clout. Now I must take her off also, to step quite naked into the remorseless sea. I have, like Abraham slaying his son, to leave her here and go away. I have in cold blood to force my own moral decision upon her confiding mind.

He had planned the parting. As a first step, Brownie now slept alternate nights with the McDonaghs.

Then, when I get a definite letter from England, there will still be necessary formalities with passports, gas masks, ration cards and so on. On the first day I shall go to Dublin on the morning bus, leaving her here, and seeing my bank manager and creditors. Coming back on the evening bus, I

---

* In Chapter 18 of Book 5 Arthur sees his moonlit kingdom and decides to go back to *homo ferox* for the sake of a future *homo sapiens*.

shall leave her to sleep with the McDonaghs. On the second day, going to see consuls, etc, I shall return to let her sleep with me. On the third day I shall not return. On the fourth day, returning, I shall sleep her with the McDonaghs. On the fifth and sixth days I shall stay away. On the seventh, I shall return, have her for one last night on my bed, and then return no more. Meanwhile the packing will have to be done in secrecy, while she is out with Mrs McD upon a walk.

He was above the age for conscription. Having been tuberculous and now with bad eyesight (earlier in the year he had had an attack of near blindness, which impaired the focusing muscles), it was unlikely that he would be passed for use in the ranks. He supposed there might be some use for him, nevertheless: he was able-bodied, educated and, so he believed, of some propaganda value. Over-estimating Garnett's pull and ignorant of the mechanized procedure of a country at war he fixed his hopes on something under Garnett's wing. After a warning 'Do not build too much on me' he suggested he might become a ferry pilot. Garnett replied that he had not enough flying experience, and sent him application forms for a job in the Air Ministry. These were delayed in the post and did not reach him till nine days later. He filled up the forms and sent them off. By then, the post had been filled. It would be easier to pin down a job, wrote Garnett when breaking this news, if White were on the spot: would he come to England? To this moderate request from his overworked friend White replied:

> You ask me to make up my mind whether I really want a job. Well, of course I don't. I never said I did. I am safe, well-fed and surrounded by Brownie. Naturally I don't want to leave here in order to be starved and blown up. But unfortunately I have written an epic about war, one of whose morals is that Hitler is the kind of chap one has to stop. I believe in my book, and, in order to give it a fair start in life, I must show that I am ready to practise what I preach.

In a discarded passage of *The Witch in the Wood*, Morgause consoles herself for the imminent return of her husband by addressing her sons as her Sweet Fatherless Lambkins. The scene has all the actuality of a remembered disgrace; it is patent that during the years when Mrs White was making her son desperately in love with her she must often have addressed him as her penniless lambkin, frightening him into an unreality about money which lasted all his life. His first experience of making a large sum of money had gone to his head. The money meant little to him: the marvel meant everything. He could not understand why there should be this problem of how to fit him into a wartime occupation – a problem intensified, as Cockerell pointed out, by the rarity of hexagonal holes.

> I had thought that as I was a Book of the Month choice, and the author of the next Walt Disney full-length, and was earning £2,000 a year in America (which is high pay for a writer), and as I had also taken First Class Honours in Cambridge, I could do better for the 'war effort' than run about with a bayonet.

It was mortifying to discover that these qualifications were disregarded, perhaps were not even recognized in circles where a Book of the Month choice was something that happened monthly to people who wrote books.

On November 7th, acting for himself, he posted an application to join the Royal Air Force Volunteer Reserve. About the same date he sent a complete typescript of what now had its final title, *The Once and Future King*, to his English publisher.

This version of *The Once and Future King* consisted of five books: *The Sword in the Stone*, *The Witch in the Wood*, *The Ill-Made Knight*, 'The Candle in the Wind' and 'The Book of Merlyn'. Mr Collins was left to discover for himself that the three books already published had been considerably altered to bring them into conformity with "The Book of Merlyn' and White's discovery that 'the central theme of Morte d'Arthur is to find an antidote to war'.

On November 26th, 1941, he wrote:

I am not quite sure from your letter what you want us to do, but it rather seems as if your idea was that we should publish one long new book, to include the two new instalments of the story and the revised scripts of the three books already published. As to whether this would be advisable, requires a great deal of thought; there is also the question of the paper shortage, which prevents us putting out such a long book at the moment.

Mr Collins had made no specific proposal; but White assumed that the proposal would be to publish Books 4 and 5, leaving the other three as they were.

December 8th, 1941

I am afraid that this would not be practical. The last two books are like a hat made to fit on top of the first three as rewritten. They would not fit on the first three as originally published. Anybody who bought the last two after having read the published volumes would be quite puzzled and annoyed. They have not got a unity of their own, suitable for separate publication. What you must do now is to tell me plainly whether or no you can or cannot publish the book as it stands, as a whole.

If you cannot do this, I will ask you very kindly to keep the typescript in your possession while I get into touch with a friend of mine who used to advise for Jonathan Cape.*

There is nothing I would like to do less, Billy, than to leave the house of Collins. You have been very kind to me. Can't you manage somehow to prevent this calamity? I do not fully understand the paper shortage. If you had been intending to publish, say, ten other books besides, could you not make up the paper by publishing only nine others? You publish too much nonsense anyway.

---

* Garnett.

The statement that Books 4 and 5 were 'made to fit on top of the first three as re-written' was disingenuous. When White saw that 'Pendragon can still be saved', he was so much excited by the prospect before him that it would have been odd in the extreme if he had set about interpolating new matter into the earlier volumes before attacking Book 5. But he was protecting his book; one can't blame him for this.

Publishers and authors are conjoined in an unrealistic interdependence. Publishers are experienced in selling books; authors in writing them. The experiences are dissimilar. The conjunction is like that of the two knights in *The Witch in the Wood*:

'I am going to prance and bay tonight, I can tell you,' said Sir Grummore, when he was preparing to be the hindquarters of the bogus Questing Beast.

'You are buttoning yourself to me, Sir Grummore,' expostulated the forequarters. "Those are the wrong buttons.'
'Beg pardon, Palomides.'
'Would it be enough if you were to wave your tail in the air, instead of prancing? There is a certain discomfort for the forequarters during the prance.'
'I shall wave my tail as well as prance,' said Sir Grummore firmly.

Sir Grummore and Sir Palomides were encased in the same purpose as well as in the same canvas overall; they could still behave as courteous knights. Mr Collins had been White's publisher for eight years. If he trusted, like Sir Palomides, that 'a modicum of caution will be exercised in the prance', recollection of earlier prancings must have qualified this trust. He continued to be both patient and polite, while White was already being neither; but he was not going to be taught publishing by an author. Disregarding the prance about Cape, he begged White to come to London to talk things over.

It was always our intention to publish the complete book, and you know we often discussed how this should be illustrated.

But now apparently you have changed the whole idea of the epic and reconstructed the first three books to fit in with your changed outlook …

and he quoted from the firm's reader's report:

The introduction of the animals in the last book suggests *The Sword in the Stone*, but the purpose is sadly different. White has changed into a political moralist. Fun and fancy have abdicated in favour of a purpose. Nor do I see what can be done about it, if the author feels that way.

Unfortunately Mr Collins went on to say, 'I do wish we could get you writing again on your nature subjects.' This was fatal. White was not going to be taught authorship by a publisher.

During the ensuing months of negotiations, interventions, recriminations, invocations of contract, blackmail bargaining on the lines of 'I have two new books but you shan't see them till you have set up Arthur'; 'I am prepared to set up Arthur but first you must send me the two new books', and threatenings of legal action, White's most shrewish resentment centred on that well-meant, ill-timed reference to nature subjects – which was the more galling because on an earlier occasion he had told Mr Collins that he wanted to be the Gilbert White of the twentieth century. He chafed against the suggestion, which bound him to nothing, even more than he chafed at the discovery that his contract with Collins bound him to offer them four more books. Again, though he must be blamed for the shrewishness I do not see how he can be blamed for the resentment. He was defending his integrity; if a creative artist does not keep up to date with himself, he will bore himself and fall from creating to self-faking. White had outgrown his nature subjects.

In the end, the two publishers arranged a partition. Collins kept the three Arthur volumes they had already issued and did not press for the final completion of the contract. Cape added White to their list of authors and published his subsequent books – but not the fourth and fifth Arthurs, which were felt unsuited to stand by themselves. The first four Arthur books were finally published by Collins and then by the Reprint Society in 1958, under the title of *The Once and Future King*. The casualty in all this was 'The Book of Merlyn'. In the course of the shindy White forgot his demand for a set of proofs 'without which I can never properly pull a book together'. By the time he got them, he had lost heart, and was probably out of conceit with the book no one had welcomed. Besides, he had missed the boat. He had written 'The Book of Merlyn' believing that it would influence the way people thought about war and induce them to make a new and more sensible kind of peace; but he had written it as the clinching last section of a very long work, and this was too long to be produced under wartime conditions. Book 5 must have smelled of defeat to him. Written in such haste and with such self-confidence, its faults ran through the whole fabric. It would have needed rethinking as well as rewriting. He put it away. Yet a fivefold *Once and Future King*, with the Aristotelian doom worked out in the three inner volumes and the sadder and wiser Arthur of the fifth volume complementing the growing boy of the first, could have been a substantially rounded structure, which the Tetralogy with its crowded inconclusive conclusion is not.

IX Doolistown 1942–45

By the beginning of 1942 he had heard that his application to the Royal Air Force Volunteer Reserve had been rejected. His qualifications were insufficient.

A proof that when he wrote 'I am returning to England to join the war', he meant and believed it is afforded by the reach-me-down book in which he continued his diary – a second-hand exercise book originally issued to a child at the state school at Trim. The first entry (made in October 1941) is about 'a big, bearded, tweed-cloaked figure, born in the same year as Darwin' – aged, therefore, at the time of writing, 132. 'He calls himself Alpha, but everybody else calls him Sin.' Sin is a misnomer. Alpha has long outgrown such notions. Actuated by the sternest benevolence, he has retired to the island of Rockall whence he intends to destroy the outer world by scientific means in order to preserve the human race.

This global Headmaster, who gets drunk once a month as a relief from the strain of being, is a bleak replacement of Merlyn. What is significant is that White needed another Merlyn and that Alpha was the sort of Merlyn he chose:

> that tweed-cloaked figure standing motionless in the spray of Rockall, propped on the cliff against the storm, almost as mighty as the cliff against the sea, as old and wise as death almost, with its chin in its hand and the hand on the crook of the stick and the stick on the winter stone with the stormy sun sinking in desolation behind.

A few wisps of narrative accompanied Alpha's first appearance, but soon evaporated. The bearded, tweeded figure grew bulkier and more identified. He would keep a Journal whose '15 folio volumes each covering a decade' could include passages from White's own diaries. 'Parts of the Journal would be written in Chinese – or classical Japanese, or Hindustani. Find out about languages.' Another prudent expedient was that Alpha's Journals prior to 1856 could have been destroyed – a date limit which would cut down the number of fifteen folio volumes, and save White from having to imagine himself into decades which didn't interest him while yet allowing Alpha to anticipate *The Origin of Species* by three years. Proverbs for Alpha were invented: 'The ox when weariest treads surest.' 'When a wise man errs, he errs with a vengeance.' 'Many would be cowards, if they had courage enough.' 'If madness were painful, you'd hear cries in every house.'

Alpha accompanied White into the New Year, partaking in many of his experiences – with the absolution of having got over them in the previous century.

> In 1858 or so he must record the symptoms of insanity – low pulse, dejected attitude, furred tongue, constipation, headaches, illusory sounds in ears, insomnia.

And in April 1942 White wrote to Garnett:

> I have been ill for some months with some sort of slow melancholic poisoning.

Apart from ill-health, he had reason to feel dejected; by now he knew that his book was disliked and that its publication would be delayed, that the war would go on and on, that if he were to play a part in it he must begin all over again.

By the end of February even Alpha had failed him, supplanted by the discovery that A R Wallace, 'who anticipated Darwin's theory of the origin of species, should not even be mentioned in the DNB.' White was left to his own company. He forced himself to keep an active mind. The diary is filled with comments on books, current news, talks on the wireless. Everything is seen through and sardonically dismissed. For a time he tried the autobiographical escape: India and his mother, Cheltenham, the few years 'when I was left in glorious happiness with my grandparents'. In one brief entry he returned to his own grown estate, a lonely man in a barren household.

April 19th, 1942
The singularity of turf is that it burns silently. Why have I

never seen this mentioned in a book? Peat's sandalled foot falls noiseless in its rust-coloured ashes. It is the absolute silence.

May 5th, 1942

Within a mile of Doolistown there is a lovely bog, at this season full of interesting insects and nesting birds. This bog is lighted, quite at random and without control, forethought or even definite purpose, every year at mating time. The most beautiful feature of this bog was a grove of about 100 Douglas Firs, more than 100 years old. Because they were mature, beautiful and irreplaceable, they had to be sold. They were sold to some Irish firm which simply slaughtered them. The trees were felled, higgledy-piggledy, like murdering seals: thrown across one another, branches smashed off, felled trees hung suspended in trees yet to be cut. This was my lovely grove, where I had gone on winter walks to hear the sea noise of the wind in their tops, or, in sunny spring, to listen to the fir-cones opening, segment by segment, with sharp clicks.

You burn the bog with random malice and slovenliness. You fell the trees in the same way, leaving a huge dump of sunbaked timber and combustible foliage over which the sappy turpentine, welling up from the trunks in the ground, lies in glistening bubbles. I remarked to Mrs McDonagh three days ago that it only needed a change of wind, and today the wind has changed.

I spent the afternoon sitting beside my poor grove, while the flames roared or boomed around the splintered boles, gushed from the sappy roots, gasped up in red smoky gushes. A bemused yellow-hammer flew agitatedly by a blackened nest. All that hundred-year-old timber first murdered, then through slovenliness made worthless.

During the first half of this destitute year, he wrote a treatise, never published, called 'The Insolence of Man'. Since 'The Book of Merlyn' was held up he compressed its non-Arthurian contents into a tract for the times. The Insolence, Importance, Ferocity, Ingenuity, Problems and Future of Man were severally dealt with as though he were lecturing to a class. The lectures are eloquent and convinced – for they are enlargements of his convictions; but the lecturer's tone of voice is contemptuous and the Jack-of-All-Trades quality of White's mind – which gave *England Have My Bones* and *The Sword in the Stone* their flicker of learning lightly worn – shows as parade and arrogance.

But there is no doubt he was extremely in earnest. With equal earnestness he next determined to examine the ants on the near-by bog, where, four summers back, he had sat with Cressida 'admiring the blue-powdered feathers of her back as she plucked the puffy fur off a light-coloured rabbit'. Warfaring ants afforded a parallel with war-making man. If one could discover what common factor made *messer barbarus* and *homo ferox* fight exterminatory wars against their own species, mankind might yet be educated into renouncing it before wars destroyed the human race.

Warfaring ants are Mediterranean; because of the war he could not import a colony. But ordinary ants might be provoked into proving something. War also made it difficult to get the books he needed. Julian Huxley suggested these might be borrowed from a professor at Cork University. White must have explained too fully what he was up to, for the professor's reply included an *ex cathedra* 'I am convinced that "mentality", "deliberate", and any other words which denote "mind" in the human sense are not applicable to any creature other than man.' Reporting this to Julian Huxley, White complained that even among post-Darwinians 'man is never really admitted into the animal kingdom'.

He began a series of experimental provocations. His equipment consisted of a magnifying glass, some small bottles of diluted red ink to bung observation holes with and a bag. The bag was for conveying groups of ants to other ants' nests; he caught the ants with his fingers. For five weeks he kept seven planted colonies under observation. The ants remained essentially civilian, manifesting dislike and mistrust like residents and evacuees in wartime, but stopping short of slaughter. He noted one instance of collaboration when a resident ant took charge of an evacuee cocoon; but her manner was so half-witted that he had to discount her motives. His observations were impeded by rain and by Brownie being on heat and followed by troops of dogs, but his outdoor spirits bore him away from his first solemn intentions of proving something which would make a great difference to the fate of man. He enjoyed himself and only once was vexed – when one of his bottles of red ink marking the site of a colony was removed by an unknown hand.

I wish I had put some tartar emetic in it.

But imagine him peeping and prying – the nearest hedge from which he could have spied on me was 200 yards away – and then patiently turning over all the stones in that part of the field. And what went on his pig's mind when he found the bottle?

He had fallen out of love with Eire. But he still liked the McDonaghs, and after helping in the harvest he went off with them for a seaside holiday at Bray.

After a long interval he answered a letter from Sydney Cockerell – there had been several others before it.

July 28th, 1942
I am glad you wrote again in spite of my rudeness. I was trying to write myself, and had torn up several attempts. It is difficult to explain what the trouble was, but I have been answering no letters at all from England, except for one person's. It seemed impossible to say truthfully what my attitude to the war was, because I did not understand it myself, so I thought it better to be forgotten than despised for not being in it. But you are kind, and won't forget me, and as it is clearing up, I can write and try to explain now.

He explained at some length – still in the same style of

clearheaded confusion. His next letter answered a series of queries from the faithful old man.

'Hawking, fishing, shooting?' I still keep hawks when I can get hold of them, and probably shall do for many years. But they are difficult to feed in wartime. I still fish for salmon, and shall till I am blind: possibly after. I still shoot, though less and less, and shall probably end by shooting nothing but wild geese, and these seldom. I only kill the things I love very much, and this is one of the reasons why I am not keen on killing human beings. 'Dogs?' I still have my better half, Brownie, whom you met. She is the only hostage I have given to fortune, and I am the only hostage she has given. 'Companions?' Absolutely none, except animals. 'Feminine entanglements?' None. I now suspect that I shall never marry or have children. 'Teetotal propensities?' None left. I am about half a dipsomaniac, perhaps about one third. I can still stop at will, without more than one day's discomfort, but my rule for many months has been to have one very strong drink of Irish whiskey at midnight, which makes me sleep. It is nearly a tumblerful, but it is the only drink I take in the 24 hours. 'Religious ditto?' I have ceased to be a Christian of any sort, though I still go to Mass every Sunday and holiday, pay my dues, and keep Fridays and Lent. This is for the sake of discipline. 'Health and spirits?' Both variable. I have lost my superb eyesight through reading for four years by candlelight, and have to wear reading glasses. I also have slight attacks of melancholia (or bad teeth) in late winter.

Still uneasy at staying out of the war he had applied to the Irish Government for an Exit Permit. Once back in England, Garnett told him, he would find a wartime job. The Irish Government, however, required evidence of employment before granting an Exit Permit. The last entry in the 1941–2 diary is dated October 14th, 1942.

Today I hear with some relief from the Permit Office that I am refused a visa, but I write to Bunny, acquainting him with the facts, in case he feels like doing anything more about it. If he does not, I shall be able to content myself, for several months at least, with having done my best.

So I start a new volume.

He did not.

The one person whose letters he had been answering was Garnett. But after February 1943, when he responded to Garnett's coolish reception of 'The Insolence of Man' by some acidulated pleasantries about his friend's fishing, the correspondence lapsed till the beginning of July.

July 6th, 1943. To David Garnett
Six months ago I suddenly realized the fact (with pleasure) that I was not a normal human being. The great thing about not being normal is that you don't have to do the usual things – go to war, etc. Here had I been forcing myself to be normal for thirty years and more quite unnecessarily and vainly. It was a great relief. I instantly gave up drinking with no ill effects, stopped writing a diary which I had kept for years, improved in health and discovered I was a first-class gardener and carpenter.

He had gardened at the Stowe Ridings cottage; but then he thought in terms of flowers and lawns; now he was under the more powerful spell of vegetables. He sowed Indian corn, celeriac and kohlrabi, made an asparagus-bed, built a green-house, and had

three hotbeds with captive melons and cucumbers in them. I don't know if you have ever kept a tame melon. They are definitely alive but not very intelligent – about half as intelligent as a snake. Next year I intend to stop being a writer and earn my living by growing Iceberg lettuces for the Dublin market. Meanwhile I have had to keep in funds by writing one more book – a novel about Richard II which I am cribbing rather cleverly out of the DNB.

Fragments of the greenhouse remain, with a yellow ceramic butterfly inlaid in its concrete wall. The novel (called 'Beware of the Dogs', and very much an interim performance) must have been given up soon after this mention of it. With his next letter to Garnett ('about September 5th, 1943') he enclosed four extracts from *The Elephant and the Kangaroo* and asked permission to dedicate it to him. 'I think it is one of my better books, but of course I don't know.'

It would be very strange if he hadn't known. This story of how the Holy Ghost* came down the kitchen chimney of Doolistown House to warn the McDonaghs and their lodger that a Flood was coming and an Ark must be built is from the outset one of those well-starred books where everything is in a conspiracy to go well. Its characters are real because they are real characters. By describing himself in the third person, White evades the stickiness of a self-portrait, and as Mr White, applying reason in a supernatural situation which he alone obediently accepts, is sublimely ridiculous; and the theme has the brio of an escapade, since Mr White reversing the Dutch barn into an Ark and deciding what seeds and breeds to people a new earth with is a direct derision of Alpha, that scientific Old Man of the Sea.

Alpha is not the only good riddance. There is no shadow of Constance White, either. White is at ease with both his heroines. In the case of his second heroine, this is not surprising, for she was Brownie. With Mrs O'Callaghan, of whom he says categorically, 'She was a darling', he is on the easy terms of inspiration: unteachable, insuperable and meek, she is at once a ragbag of the Christian virtues and a Noble Savage.

David Garnett was so much excited by the four extracts and the plan of the book that he responded with participation. The barn reversed must be roofed, or it would fill and sink.

> I hope your book does not go beyond the building and stocking of the Ark in the steady rain and stops short of the Flood. In fact I think the end should be the rain coming down softly and steadily and the sun coming out – and NO RAINBOW – and the animals standing about dripping wet and shaking themselves at intervals.

---

* Later modified to the Archangel Michael.

White replied, saying it was an attractive ending but making it plain that he would stick to his own. The Ark was already roofed; the Flood perhaps not quite the sort of Flood Garnett had in mind; but sufficiently universal to carry the chosen as far as Dublin.

> There, under the impression we were parachutists, the Government would have called out the Irish Navy, which consists of two motor-boats, and, after a brisk engagement, they would have succeeded in dragging myself and the McDonaghs out of our tubs. You will think this a tragic conclusion, but no.

After sketching an ending of detailed and lavish extravagance, he added:

> Now the danger of all this is, that the book looks like degenerating into farce. I am not sufficiently grown up myself to be able to write about the real world convincingly. But if I continue to attend to details unremittingly, even during the farce, I might be able to pull it through. And besides, if it is my nature to write farce, I had better accept my nature and do so.

Flown by resignation to his lot (that 'unremittingly' is admirably dutiful), White delivered himself of what was with him a rarity: a sentence of abstract criticism.

> The more I think about it, the more I see that success or failure lies in the description of the event, not in the event itself.

By the end of October he felt another drunken, solitary winter closing round him; and felt it more acutely since he had persuaded himself that Garnett would come on a visit.

> You will see that I am on the booze again. But it is after 6 months abstinence and only out of misery and because you don't come. Nor could any really drunk man write this hand after midnight, miserable and alone.

Indeed, the handwriting is neat and regular as ever. Liquor did not much disguise him. He kept his erratic dignity and his steady industry; he was translating his Roxburgh Bestiary, and by the New Year had begun to write *Mistress Masham's Repose*.

In July 1942 White had told Cockerell:

> My next book after the war is going to be a sumptuous illustrated translation of a Bestiary.

Cockerell, who had viewed White's excursions into natural history and sociology with a Curator's eye, was pleased to see him returning to the right compartment. He advised him to consult the writings of G C Druce, an octogenarian expert, and was so friendly to the project (in which, indeed, he was the prime mover by inviting White to Kew in 1938 and getting him the facsimile), that in 1944 White was emboldened to own up about the Fitzwilliam affair, and sign himself 'Your Cambridge Correspondent'.

He began his translation in October, and soon ran into difficulties. He turned to an acquaintance for help – he turned as naturally as a sunflower for help.

Nov 1943

Dear Henry,

> I am plodding on with the Bestiary, like Captain Scott making for the N Pole. The new scribe* has a Latin of his own, even more peculiar than mine; he is always drunk, or in love with one of the choirboys, in any case his mind is not on his work, for it is packed with slips of the pen, and what with one thing and another I am in despair. I have done about 3 times what you did – in a sort of way – but constantly having to leave out a sentence or two, which I shall have to refer to you. At the present moment I am having a hideous tussle with Canis.

---

* The MS is the work of two hands.

The helpful acquaintance was Henry Wheeler, a boy at Stowe when White was a master there. They had met again in a Dublin bookshop, and White requisitioned his superior Latinity, as well as relying on him for other kindnesses – such as looking things up in Dublin libraries and bringing tubes of oil paint when he came to Doolistown to tussle with Canis. 'Large periods of his time', states Mr Wheeler, 'were spent as a virtual recluse at Doolistown.'

By 1943 there was no petrol in Eire for private cars; trains, fuelled with slack, ran twice a week. White was too large to fit commodiously into a crowded bus, but probably his main reason for being a recluse was that Brownie was liable to small heart-attacks and he did not like leaving her. Doubtless she did not like being left. She had become rather autocratic. She used to kidnap chickens and small animals and keep them as pets, and insisted on taking her pet rabbit to bed with her – in White's bed. The rabbit bit him freely, but he submitted. She had geological interests, too, and collected stones which she kept under the kitchen table. Whatever her vagaries, Mrs McDonagh smiled on them and said she was 'so loverlie' – making 'lovely' a trisyllable as an emphasis of affection.

February 18th, 1944. To L J Potts
I have written to you so often for help that I don't see why I shouldn't write to you once in a while for friendship's sake.

The first thing to tell you is that I am in the seventh heaven with my Bestiary, etc. I was always intended to be a scholar – thwarted by buggers like you – and now I am being one at last, off my own bat. My preface to my Bestiary is going to put Sir James Frazer in the ice box, and will quote from 43 authorities beginning with the letter A alone. (This is true. They begin: 'a-Costa, ab Hurto, Aber-Ezra (Hispanus), Absyrtus, Acius, Aegineta, Aelian, Aesop, etc,' ending with 'Ausonius, Austin, Augustinus, Averroes and Avicena'.) If anybody in the world knows more about whether a Camel copulates backwards, I should be glad of an introduction. The fact is that I have got so far into the subject that I really and truly know the name of the only other living person I need consider, and that is a man called G C Druce. But I am stalking up on him fast, and soon he will be saying 'That's Tim, that was' as I whistle past into a knighthood and the Order of Merit.

Dear Pottës, I really must stop this drumming on my breast – you know it is only in fun. Yet I am honestly delighted with it, all the same. It is so nice to strike an unworked vein, worth working, and to go ahead for nothing but the nettle reputation in the bubble's mouth. My incentive will be that one day Pottés will say 'I taught him.'

White did not receive the Order of Merit, but an unexpected distinction was on its way to Doolistown House.

February 18th (sic), 1944. To L J Potts
Today there has come a grand sort of unilluminated address, which informs me that I have grown up and become an MA of Cambridge University. I feel quite different already – more portly. I waddle a bit as I walk, and have decided to wear boots in future instead of shoes. Well, it was very kind of you to take the trouble, but I don't think I can very well let you give it to me for Christmas, as I have an idea it costs several pounds. Also I am working out a scheme for getting money from here to England, by means of a fish with a waterproof bag tied to its tail and directed by wireless. I shall use an electric eel. So will you tell me how much it costs to be an Artis Magister, in case I can perfect this invention? I shall feel just as grateful if you will let me pay for it, as I would rather not sponge on people until I have to, when I intend to do so with a vengeance.

Do you know, it strikes me we have lost touch too much. There you are in a sort of enormous office at Queens', lined with card indices of all the Christian names of all the little boys of 19 since the days of Erasmus, and I suppose you shuffle them about, and play Happy Families with them, and wonder whether it would be better to buy two asps or open your veins in a bath. Here am I, sitting in a vast barrack with a leaking roof and nobody to talk to who can pronounce words of more than one syllable, and wondering whether it is not an expensive form of suicide to do it with Irish whiskey. Can't you put aside the bundles of *exeat, nihil obstat, sciant presentes et futuri, excommunico, nolle prosequi*, etc, and write to me sometimes? It would be a charity to me at any rate if we could only work up a correspondence about something that wasn't just gossip. What are you thinking about? Would it bore you to hear what I am thinking about? I sometimes feel like putting a message in a bottle and floating it down the Boyne: 'I am alive. T White, 1944. Is anybody else?'

'Would it bore you to hear what I am thinking about?' It seems an idle question in this long friendship of kindred minds. But White, whose good conceit of himself was the protective deposit of his insecurity, had by now been forced to admit that people might not want to hear what he was thinking about. The years of exile during which he expanded so many provocative ideas had somehow rendered him parochial; the war had somehow imposed a corresponding parochialism on his friends, who disregarded his challenges; on his publisher, who jibbed at the new Arthur and begged him to write about nature; on the official experts who turned down his suggestions for a revolving Lewis gun, an improved method of laying smoke-screens. His instinct to renew a correspondence 'about something that wasn't just gossip' was sound, but came too late. He did not realize the cramping scuffle of daily life in England, nor that to Potts a vast barrack with no interruption except some rain through the roof must have sounded like the courts of heaven. If White sometimes seemed insultingly ignorant of what his friends were enduring it must be granted that he wasn't given much opportunity to know better. The double censorship of a country at war which would let nothing out and a country in neutrality which would let nothing in was reinforced by the mumness of correspondents who by now were so bored by their deprivations that they wouldn't mention them.

He consoled himself with the gossip of more leisured minds. Thumbing the DNB, recalling Stowe and Blenheim for purposes of Malplaquet (the stately background of *Mistress Masham's Repose*) he planned a book about eighteenth-century characters and went to sales and Dublin bookshops for material. Among these purchases was a *George Selwyn and his Contemporaries* of 1844, in the fourth volume of which he noted: 'This volume uncut when I got it in 1944. Just a hundred years to lose its virginity.'

Another interest of this period was painting. He wrote to Garnett in September:

> I have been painting without stopping for breath since January, and am beginning to know my own mind about it. I am fixing glass eyes on my canvas with putty, and eyelashes made of salmon-fly silver tinsel.

His career as an artist (beginning with a Drawing Prize at Cheltenham) included the pen-and-ink drawings in *Burke's Steerage* and the head- and tail-pieces in *The Sword in the Stone* and *The Witch in the Wood*. The 1938–41 diaries contain many portraits of his hawks and of Brownie. I say portraits advisedly, for photographs of Brownie make it clear that he had a good eye for the individual as well as for the type. The 'Biography of Brownie' which he wrote in 1943 for his godson, William Potts, has a frontispiece of her, in coloured chalks, which is obviously a true likeness as well as a portrayal of the slight shabbiness, the relaxation and marks of wear, of an ageing animal in comfortable circumstances.

All these drawings are orthodox and would not be out of place – though above the ordinary – in *Field* or *Country Life*. Not so the oil-paintings of 1944. Of one of these he wrote 'Guests scream when they see it.' A non-screaming guest was Maurice Craig, who recalls

> his fantastic (and I think almost totally worthless) paintings, with glass eyes stuck into the oil paint, bits of silver paper and so on. These I think were therapy, as I don't remember being asked to admire them more than perfunctorily.

On April 1st he began another six months of sobriety (the date was chosen to discourage any misunderstandings of motive), and as usual began to feel unwell. In August he went to Dublin to have his tonsils cut out. 'There are no modern refinements. A rusty guillotine is used, with half its parts missing, and your first meal is tough beef.' White could genuinely make light of this; he had remarkable physical fortitude. He never made light of death. When he was going under the anaesthetic he set himself to measure by the clock how long the loss of consciousness took, how long the sensation of dying might last.

In September he had to consider death in another aspect. David Garnett was going into hospital for a spinal operation – and after years of overworking and months of being in pain, he was in poor condition for it. Since White could not travel to England to visit him, he wrote a succession of those sickbed letters which are so difficult to write – as one aims them at a person already slightly unknown because one does not know whether he is to live or die, as one's own health abashes one with its rudeness, as one has no means of judging whether one's attempt to be diverting allays or grates, as in all such letters one is forced back on what cheerfulness one can supply from one's own resources and therefore must seem egoistic, fortunate and unconcerned.

White had a further handicap: the time-lag of wartime posts between London and Co Meath. For some time he had to write without knowing whether the operation had been done or how Garnett had come through it.

> When you feel well enough to write, you must boast your fill about the operation. You will find it is an immense pleasure. Say how brave you were, and what you thought about so coolly. Give all the ghastly details. Don't be modest or afraid of boring. I shall hang on every word. Besides, when I publish your correspondence in nine volumes, ten years after both our deaths, think how interesting it will be for posterity.

The same letter concludes (as if the writer were offsetting his rude health by an admission of his reduced circumstances):

Brownie and I shall visit the local wise woman after lunch, where we will arrange to have everything done that can be done: blessing stones turned clockwise, red flannel tied to scapegoats, and the rest. For miles around, until we hear again, everybody will be hopping up and down, gathering dew, reciting spells, standing on one leg with our fingers in our ears.

It can't fail to be a success.

In a subsequent letter the reduced circumstances serve to lighten the texture of a letter which was becoming rather too much like an article (indeed, it afterwards provided the theme of an essay, 'Tears', in his *Age of Scandal*).

Here we are, two literary men (pauses to catch flea on waistcoat: throws it into the fire) with the unbounded influence of our pens. Can't we start a Lachrymose Revival?

The device was good enough for a second appearance.

Bunny, when you feel like writing, will you tell me all you know about that great house at which you were staying when you told me the story about the *variorum* edition of the Pentateuch (or Septuagint)? It was either Penshurst or the other one beginning with P – Petworth? (Catches second flea on sleeve.) I am passionately addicted to places like Knole and deeply regret never having cultivated enough dukes to be a constant guest in such.

The letter is full of spirit and cajoleries. It is almost celebratory; for when he began it he had convinced himself that the operation was over. Then –

On the whole, after looking through this, it does not seem a very wise letter to send without being certain that your operation is over, I mean with all that about ether and hurting when you move, so I will keep it and write another. I see how mannered and laboured it is, but it is bricks without straw, and all it can do is to cover its paper as best it can, to show that it is concerned about you, which is what it is for.

And the next day the other letter was written. It is about Peacock and Don Quixote.

> If Cervantes had not killed him so utterly at the end I would have half a mind to write a continuation, just for the pleasure of taking him out of the box again and loving him.

He wrote every second or third day – ten letters in all. The last is dated October 30th, when Garnett was over his operation and recovering. White had begun to think about another book. It was to be called 'Extinct Family', and would tell the fortunes of a family that established itself under Richard II (it would be a pity to waste all that research in the DNB) and come to an end when the last earl was shot down in aerial combat over Hamburg. A draft of a final chapter headed 'Chapter Nought' is in the folio notebook which contains *The Elephant and the Kangaroo*, part of 'The Insolence of Man', the beginning of 'Beware of the Dogs', and some preliminaries to *The Age of Scandal*. Chapter Nought of 'Extinct Family' is unpromising – a prance among White's *bétes noires* – but the theme would have suited him, for by this time he had sweated out his enthusiasm for Parables from Nature and his feeling for period was at work again. He was a lightweight historian, but he had one essential for this projected book: a good ear. His Puritans would not have talked like the Clapham Sect. With 'Extinct Family' and the unhurried Bestiary and *The Age of Scandal* ahead, the winter looked to be provided for. Before he settled to a duration of work he had to send *The Elephant and The Kangaroo* to America. This entailed going to Dublin. That evening, Mr McDonagh met him at the bus-stop. He said, 'Mr White, I'm afraid I have bad news for you.' His voice was solemn, and White with jesting gravity replied, 'I hope I haven't been arrested as a spy?'

'Brownie is dead.'

White's entry in the folio notebook was probably written in the early morning of November 26th. (The date refers to the day of her death.)

> Brownie is dead. 25.xi.xliv.
> She had a happy life, probably happier than most setters,

except that the happier you are the more you want to be happy, so it evens out, Her major troubles were only being allowed to sit in my lap for 6 hours a day, and things like that.

She lived fairly long for a working setter. I can't be sure if she was 12 or 14, but could make a good guess if I had a copy of *England Have My Bones*.

She could have lived longer, but for the filthy piece of work that I was on one of my bi-annual trips (for 9 hours) to Dublin at the time she had one of her annual attacks. I could have saved her, perhaps. The people here didn't understand her. But it was impossible not to go to Dublin sometimes, since I had our living to earn. This trip was about getting *The Elephant and the Kangaroo* to America. I had to leave her for a few hours every year, or we shouldn't have earned a living at all.

All the same, I let her down in the end: she had trusted her whole life to me always, and I was not there to save it.

I had saved it at least twice before, which is something.

The dead body by my side is not Brownie. But what is?

She was a sprite who danced before me through 12 perfect years of love. But she is not that now. It is gone. And the poor dead face is not it either. I have an actual physical feeling in my heart – muscular, not emotional – as if it were going to burst.

It means that I died last night. All that me is dead, because it was half her.

It is useless and ignoble to repine about one's lot. Is it any use repining about hers? Whose? The dead body's? The sprite's?

Might-have-beens are too agonizing, and not practical.

She was the central fact of my life.

It is only me who has lost anything. Brownie has lost nothing. For when the self itself is lost, that self cannot lose anything.

The handwriting is perfectly steady till the last paragraph where it slightly wavers. On the next page, written in a large stumbling, childish hand, as though by someone illiterate or almost blind, comes:

Brownie, I am free of you,
Who ruled my heart for 14 years!
O Freedom, all begun anew,
O iceblock heart, O tears!

My gentleness, my trustfulness,
My looker-up, my life,
My coward who leaned on my care
In vain, my child and wife,

My mother with the golden pelt,
Myself with melting eye,
My Brownie, rooted in the core,
My hoping lover-lie.

Then the steady handwriting resumes:

I must make myself realize that she is now entirely a thing of the past. It is rather an effort not to follow her into it myself, as I have always followed her everywhere else. But I must not, and I must face this, a little at a time.

He sat up with her corpse for two nights and buried her in the grounds of Doolistown House. A lock of copper-red hair, tied very neatly with a strand of blue silk, is fastened in the large diary, on a page where he had stuck some photographs of her taken at Belmullet. It is still glowing, silken and pliable, as though cut from a living head. With her death, he lost the only being he dared to love, the only being who found security in his insecurity. The trust she fixed on the handsome, rather showy, not very attentive young man with a beautiful top hat, who accepted her dependence as an embellishment – like a rich tassel – had become the thing he depended on.

For three consecutive days after Brownie's death he wrote to Garnett. The language of total bereavement can be heard as heartless, because it is so practical. There is not much else it can be. Bereavement impales one on practical considerations. They are all that is left to think about.

> Please do not write to me at all about her for a very long time, but tell me if I ought to buy another bitch or not, as I do not know what to think about anything. I might live another 30 years, which would be two dog's lifetimes at this, but of course they hamper one very much when one loves them so desperately.

Her body was beside him as he wrote that. Then, after her burial:

> Now I am to begin a new life and it is important to begin it right, but I find it difficult to think straight. It is about whether I am to get another dog or not. I am good to dogs, so from their point of view I suppose I ought. But I might not survive another bereavement like this in 12 years' time, and dread to put myself in the way of it. Or I could get two dogs and breed up vast families of puppies, but what would be the good of that? It would only be an occupation. Brownie was my life and I am lonely for just such another reservoir for my love – not for an occupation. But if I did get such a reservoir it would die in about 12 years and at present I feel I couldn't face that. Do people get used to being bereaved? This is my first time.

Garnett replied:

> You ask should you buy another bitch. One can only speak for oneself, but I think the best antidote to the numbing obsession of grief is having responsibility to a living creature. So I would say Yes: you should. But not just any bitch. A gun-dog preferably as all the job of training will be good for you. Often it will hurt you – but you will realize you cannot dodge the responsibility.

It was the thought that by going to Dublin he had dodged his responsibility to Brownie – the only responsibility he had – which caused White his sharpest torment. He was to blame.

And at the same time his complicated conscience told him that he was more likely to be blamed for having fixed his heart on a mere dog. Suddenly, in the third letter, he regained himself.

> The whole and single unnaturalness of the position is that dogs and men have incompatible longevities. Everything else is perfectly natural and I would not have it altered in any respect. I regret nothing about Brownie, except the bitter difference of age.

Towards the end of December he wrote again:

> I stayed with the grave for a week, so that I could go out twice a day and say, 'Good girl: sleepy girl: go to sleep, Brownie.' It was a saying she understood. I said it steadily. I suppose the chance of consciousness persisting for a week is several million to one, but that was the kind of chance I had to provide for. Then I went to Dublin, against my will, and kept myself as drunk as possible for nine days, and came back feeling more alive than dead.
>
> I have done what you said I was to do, or at any rate I have bought a puppy bitch. Brownie had taught me so much about setters that it seemed silly to waste the education, so I stuck to them. No setter could ever remind me of her any more than one woman would remind you of another, except in general terms.
>
> The new arrangement looks like the foetus of a rat, but she has a pedigree rather longer than the Emperor of Japan's. She nibbles for fleas in my whiskers.

The new arrangement was named Killie. Presently there was another puppy; Garnett wanted a gun-dog – by 1945 a rational desire – and asked White to find and train a pointer for him. But Killie and Prince (revised by his prospective owner to Quince) did not keep White from going to Dublin. Maurice Craig remembers him

> holding court in O'Meara's pub on Aston's Quay or in the

United Arts Club which he took to staying in after Brownie's death. He sat there looking benevolent, sometimes talking brilliantly but not selfishly.

On March 12th he sent typescripts of *The Elephant and the Kangaroo* and of *Mistress Masham's Repose* to Garnett – the latter with a dedication to Garnett's infant daughter.

> Would it be too much to ask you to blue-pencil these books as you read them? I don't think you will need to rewrite them. The structure seems sound, and if you scratched out the places where the tone is false or forced, and altered a few clumsy expressions, you could probably improve them without too much trouble. You may leave out whole chapters if you like, for I trust your taste implicitly and my own not at all. I will accept every alteration you make unseen.
>
> Is it too much to ask you to do this? I feel awkward about it. But I thought that if they were dedicated to you and yours, you would like them to be as good as they could be in the circumstances.

Garnett replied that White must see the alterations. White held out.

> I haven't the least desire to see the alterations you are likely to make. I know they will be right. If you send the MS back to me with a lot of suggestions, I shall only become re-entangled with the post office and censorship and the books will never get to America at all. Structurally speaking, the Lilliput book is sound and the Burkestown book is unsound but past mending. There is a chasm or fault running right down the middle of the latter, between the impossibility of the Holy Ghost and the possibility of the rest, which I can't see any help for. It is the last chapter of the Holy Ghost book which I suspect you may omit.

In the event, the last chapter was omitted. But it was one of the chief characters that Garnett took most exception to.

March 28th, 1945
I think you should change the Holy Ghost for an angel. Angels are the traditional messengers who are always sent on such occasions. It is a pity to start the book by being too outrageous: an angel is not outrageous and for that reason seems far more probable.

This is followed by a statement of interest to theologians:

Also an angel would have to come down the chimney. The HG can materialize inside a room as easily as on the roof.

On surer ground, he pointed out the danger of libel actions, and added:

I should either omit the reference to plating Churchill or else change it to Stalin.

White replied:

I agree most gratefully to all your alterations and think it very clever of you to have thought of changing the Holy Ghost into an angel. But can you do this yourself? Please don't despise me too much, but I don't feel quite equal to looking at the book for some time yet, because of Brownie.

If the painfulness of reading about the living Brownie so soon after her death lay at the root of White's insistence that he would accept every alteration unseen, visible alterations found him less complying. After that first admiring embrace of Garnett's angel, he fought a spirited retreating action on behalf of the Holy Ghost, ingeniously suggesting that the angelic visitant who came down the chimney and looked like a mop might later have doubts thrown on its character and be the Holy Ghost after all; pointing out that for the hymn 'Come, Holy Ghost, our souls inspire' it would be necessary to 'substitute some Protestant hymn about angels or archangels, if you can find any in the prayer-book', and playing on human weakness by 'it does seem a shame that you will have to alter the word wherever it appears, which practically means rereading the book, as I shan't see proofs before publication.' Garnett won: the Holy Ghost became the Archangel Michael. (This really imposes a further improbability on a story which is already improbable; no variety of angel coming down the kitchen chimney would have reduced Mrs O'Callaghan to invoking Mr White's superior presence of mind: reared in the Faith, she would have taken an angel in her stride.) But no victory is total. By the time the Ark has sunk it is the Holy Ghost, *Columba oenas*, who broods on the face of the waters. And author and critic alike overlooked the desirability of replacing Churchill by Stalin. It is still the former whose features must be raised out of the electrolytic tank after, say, fifteen minutes.

'Structurally speaking, the Lilliput book is sound' … It must have been a surprise to White to find *Mistress Masham's Repose* being so sternly received.

> You have stumbled upon a most beautiful subject and you have the opportunity of writing a masterpiece. But you have not stopped to think, and instead of writing a masterpiece you have filled it up with a lot of twaddle about Miss Pribble and the Vicar, those stock clowns.

White had not stopped to think about *The Elephant and the Kangaroo*, either. As he told Garnett:

> One day Mrs McDonagh was explaining the nature of the Trinity to me, and I thought: I wonder what you would really do if the Holy Ghost suddenly put its head down the chimney? So I got involved in working it out, and then I began putting it in a book. The Holy Ghost had to have some object in coming down the chimney, so I made it come to warn us that there was going to be a second flood, and that we were to build an Ark. After that I became involved in the problems of building an Ark …

Not a moment for thought, in fact. But in the Lilliput book he was working with an idea; and other ideas rushed in: the endangered intrepidity of a child alone in a grown-up world, the charm of incompetent elderly scholars, the inherent good-heartedness of foxhunters. It is not the stock clowns but the stock prejudices that derail the masterpiece. He replied that he would attend to Garnett's advice, and rewrite. 'Are you at all pleased with me for being so meek?'

Industry was no pain to White, who would rather write than not. Meekness was not so easy, and so he looked to earn a kind word by it.

It was April – the cruellest month. He added a note beneath the entry of Brownie's death.

April 19th, 1945
The swallows have come back, and last week the sand-martins did. Last year my sweetheart used to dig out their nests, feeling guilty about it a little, but longing for the babies she never had. The sand-martins are back, but she never more. If there are any animals with no memory they may be happy, but even the swallows remember last year's nest. All mine are torture. So I get on very well by being careful to remember nothing, and my life is nothing, my darling, without you. And I cannot tell you so.

The end of the war was in sight. The difficulties of returning to England: permits to sail, visas to re-enter, transport of books and belongings, two dogs who would probably be sick on the crossing and the certainty that he would be sick himself, together with the peculiar heartbreak of leaving places endeared by sorrow, the fields where Brownie had quartered before him, the hearth where she lay groaning at the typewriter which kept her off his lap, the bed they had shared, might well have induced him to put off his departure. But the McDonaghs were proposing to sell the farm. Even if the newcomers were prepared to keep him, they would be strangers, the house would not be the same. Garnett had promised him a cottage in Yorkshire to live in. It was not so clear what he would live on. He had his car – which would sell for twice the money in England. He had his gold watch. He had two novels on their way to the United States. They would pay later (one of them was to pay very well), but not yet. He had the half-finished Bestiary, and what he referred to as the Horry Walpole book – essays that might be sold separately. Against these assets were debts which he must settle before he left Ireland, the cost of removal and the fact that once in England he would be liable for UK Income Tax.

He sat typing the Horry Walpole *Age of Scandal* book while possible buyers inspected the farm. No offer was high enough, the sale was put back. In August he went to Co Mayo, for the puppies' education to be enlarged on a grouse moor. It was as though the west of Ireland were making a last assault on his feelings: Glenturk Lodge was Sheskin in the bewitching madness of a dream.

> Built c 1860 by a gentleman who was under the influence of Ruskin and Morris. All the furniture is of the period – Gothic bookcases and carved cupboards hanging on the walls like cathedrals built by swallows. Everything has been cracked, shrunk, deliquesced, peeled or warped. The ivory keys have fallen off the piano like visiting cards. The owners have not visited it for 40 years.

The spell did not work. He had no money – and he was practical in such matters. He made the most of what Glenturk Lodge offered and afterwards put it into *The Godstone and the Blackymor*, where it is called Glenafron. The letter to Garnett about it ended:

> I have left no address except with you. Consequently since August 12th I have had no letters or newspapers, and your statement that the Japs have surrendered is the first I've heard. This it is, to pay no attention to the present day. It is the happiest fortnight I have had since Brownie died.

It was the fortnight when the first realization of the Atom Bomb was making Victory an outdated word. But as Garnett's letter made no mention of it, White was free to go on paying no attention to the present day.

After a turmoil of delays and formalities he left Dublin. His departure is said to have caused considerable relief at the British Embassy.

X Duke Mary's 1945–46

October 6th, 1945

Bunny brought me to Duke Mary's on the evening of October 4th. We made up the beds, had a tin of pork and beans for supper and talked. Next morning I got up at 7, de-rusted frying-pan, made breakfast, and he left on the 9.30 bus. After Bunny had left, I made up the beds, laid a fire in my bedroom in case I should get 'flu or break a limb, sorted linen, unpacked, tidied upstairs, took stock of rationed larder, swept out house, washed up, pumped water, put a red tablecloth with fans on it on the kitchen table and cooked dinner. After dinner went up the fell. The dogs caught a rabbit. Went to bed before eleven, first locking the out-door. For a moment it felt strange to be quite alone in the converted outhouses, in the dark, a thousand feet above Swaledale.

The last time he had been quite alone was on Inniskea. All that was behind him. His future was vague. Meanwhile, he was in Garnett's cottage, a 'two up and one down' dwelling with the haybarn extending on either side, where in the previous century Mary the daughter of Marmaduke had lived alone and reared two bastards. He had two dogs with him – for Quince had come too.

A correspondence kept up over a length of years with never a meeting is a bridge which with every letter seems more elastically reliable. But it is a bridge that only carries the weight of one person at a time. When the correspondents meet it collapses and they have to flounder their way to the footing of actuality. When White reached Hilton Hall on the evening of September 25th he and Garnett met with affection; for six years the bridge had carried a traffic of sympathy, advice, enlivening nonsense, exasperations, understanding and misunderstanding, dependence and assurance. It could have been the happy reunion they had earned by remaining alive to each other if the dogs had not added their overwhelming goodwill. Garnett was irked by the noise and physical presence of Quince, who stood four foot six on his pads and knocked everything off any table with his amiable tail and Killie, bouncing, ingratiating and all too female.

White sensed this, fled into the defensive (his flight may have been hastened by remembering that he had been asked to get a small working pointer not a show-bench bullcalf), decided that Garnett knew nothing about dogs and trailed his petticoat about the war. Worse was to come. Garnett had acquired a rough shooting in Northumberland, called Ridley Stokoe – which White had annoyingly professed to believe was called Ridley Stokehole. Ridley Stokoe was Garnett's reason for wanting a pointer, though perhaps he would not have wanted one from Ireland if he had not thought that training it might help to distract White from his desolation after Brownie's death. Quince was taken to Ridley Stokoe to show his worth. The Ridley Stokoe Game Book records that he made exemplary points – but without discrimination, as they included a frog, a pipit, and a flock of sheep.

White knew enough about shooting to realize that Quince was not doing him credit. However, it was Killie who set off the quarrel. Quince put up a grey hen and chased it. White, who was using William Garnett's gun, slipped it through Killie's leash to act as a clog, and went after Quince

leaving Killie to drag William's gun, with the breech open, over the moor. I rushed to grab her, and Tim in a fury exclaimed: 'Kindly refrain from beating my dog.' I replied: 'I should be much obliged if you would refrain from smashing William's gun.'

Tim went off with gun and bitch (she is on heat) and twenty minutes later we met at the farm. By the stable door he poured out a long catalogue of my crimes. First had an inexplicable hostility to Killie. My other crimes were that I laid down the law about shooting. 'You can lay down the law about courage and bombs, but you have no business to talk about shooting.' I was also reproached because I believed that courage existed but in a discussion with William said I did not believe in absolute justice. Finally I was told that for several days Tim had made all allowances for the effects of buzz-bombs and so on which accounted for my bad temper.

In the afternoon he went on to the moor with both dogs during which time he shot a rabbit. When I got back to the inn, Tim asked me whether his fits of ungovernable rage were due to his falling on his head. I said I did not know and perhaps we had better say no more about it.

Next day – the last at Ridley Stokoe –

Tim was most amiable the whole day and I do not think it was an effort for him. I told him that I did not want Quince. He would be practically useless on this moor.

Two days later White was spreading the red tablecloth on the kitchen table at Duke Mary's and planning a rule of life. From nine to eleven he would breakfast, put the house in order and prepare dinner. From eleven to one he would translate the Bestiary. Dinner and reading would occupy him till two, when he would take the dogs for a walk. From four to six he would feed the dogs and potter. From seven to nine, after an hour for tea and reading, he would 'write the Walpole or any other book'. At eleven, after reading and writing up his diary, he would go to bed 'and go to sleep'. These last words show his resolved mind; he did not fall asleep easily. After laying down Mondays and Thursdays for going to the village to shop, the rule of life concludes:

No work on Sundays, except writing letters.
   Always make coffee the last thing at night and leave it in Thermos, to expedite breakfast. Smore fire, as it can be kept just alive till morning.

October 9th, 1945. To Sydney Cockerell
Here I am on the top of an alp in Yorkshire, living alone in a stone haybarn with two dogs and having to carry our rations over stone walls up 1,000 feet in ¼ mile, because there is no

road. I am really a sort of Quasimodo, a gargoyle brooding over Swaledale, and the freedom and altitude are giving me delusions of grandeur. I do all the housework and cooking and washing myself, which only leaves me four hours a day for writing. It is lovely. My only neighbours are grouse, of which there are some 2,400. I speak once a day for 10 minutes to the woman who supplies me with milk from a farmhouse several hundred feet lower down, but have to go a four-mile walk down the precipice twice a week for shopping, which I carry back in a sack on my back.

I can no longer exist without being a member of the London Library, reading so many expensive books for the Bestiary and other work. Will you introduce or sponsor me, whatever is necessary, and put in a good word for me with the Librarian? I have another string to my bow, Garnett, and can ask him to do the sponsoring if it is troublesome for you. The only reason why I didn't ask him first was that I have lately been taking so much advantage of his kindness that I am a little shy. This shyness can easily be conquered if you are not feeling up to the mark.

I am collecting my own books here, from Ireland and Buckinghamshire, and shall have to drag them up the crag with a horse and sledge!

For purposes of the Bestiary, he had ordered an Aldrovandus *Historia*. It cost £41 and would come in nine parcels, each weighing fifteen pounds. Meanwhile, he found plenty of things to do.

Mended striped bedspread with a patch. It would be a good idea to mend one thing every day.

There is a fine rusty grate which lights quickly, gives good heat and is not hard on coal. I can make do with one bucket a day. The oven door won't shut unless you press it with a brass candlestick and hammer it with a hammer.

Abandoned by Bunny and Angelica when they left this cottage 12 months ago, there lay on the shelves of the larder a small medicine bottle of fermenting orange juice and a marmalade pot containing between quarter and half a pound of deliquescent sugar, partly petrified, with six clothes moths in it. I peeled the two grapefruits and cut the peel into slices, broke the marmalade pot with a hammer to get the sugar out, and boiled the whole caboodle for ¾ of an hour. Also I added a sliced apple. The resulting marmalade is excellent.

Spent all evening patching a flannel shirt and making it a new collar from a pair of Bunny's torn pyjamas. I wish I had a sewing-machine, an auto-giro and the Oxford English Dictionary.

White's intentions were always directed towards happiness. His approaches were practical, for he saw it as a commodity within his powers. At Duke Mary's he would use his strength and physical versatility, make do and mend, carry loads up a mountainside, outwit the difficulties of food, clothes and fuel rationing, be asleep before midnight, find the fire alive in the morning, potter legitimately within his time-table, translate the Bestiary and be happy in his lot. His solitude did not intimidate him: the fire was laid in the bedroom in case of influenza or accident. And though his riches had melted and he was poor again, and out of the contemporary market, thrift had charms and he was prepared for honest poverty.

He wrote to Cockerell:

So far I am simply ravished with joy at being Robinson Crusoe at last. It takes 80 minutes to walk to the village and back. On Saturday I carried home, in one load on my back, 2 gallons paraffin, 3 lb paint, 5 loaves bread, 1 cauliflower, 1 box groceries and one chamberpot.

He carried home no bottles. Drinking had lost what few associations with happiness it might have had. It got in his way, it thieved his time, there was no pleasure in it and it was extremely expensive. But it seeped into his rule of life like rising damp in a wall.

October 10th, 1945
In the afternoon I walked down to the post-office, then some devil led me to the local pub, the Punch Bowl. They were hospitable, invited me to tea, tried to give me one pound of filleted plaice, 1lb Swaledale cheese, 2 grapefruit, 1lb dripping. I insisted on paying for these. Drank two double gins. Arranged to have lunch there on Mondays and Thursdays, as it is more convenient to shop in the morning. But I must, must, must regard this as opportunity for food only. If I start boozing, I shall never get any writing done. I consider this has been a wasted day. I hate pubs, I hate fiction, I hate gin, I hate people and I hate myself. No, I don't hate myself. The fact is that when I am alone with my books and dogs we are the best company in the world, and, if it were not for shopping, I would stay up here all day and every day and be content.

In fact, he did not hate people. He did not run after them – to that extent he was a solitary. But if they came his way and liked him and were the sort of people he liked being liked by he was gratified. Swaledale did not charm him as Doolistown on first acquaintance had done; but the locals were kind and generous with gifts to help out his housekeeping, and their speech was full of words he didn't know and they remembered a great deal about Duke's Mary – a formidable shepherdess who had carried ten stone of flour up to the cottage on her back and the baby, born while she was cutting peats on the moor, down to the cottage in her apron. Even the keeper, who had looked askance at the stranger who walked among the grouse with a setter and a pointer, thawed, told him stories about floods, grouse-disease, adders and Lord Halifax, and gave him rabbits for the dogs. The rabbits were welcome; it was a problem how to support himself and two large vigorous dogs on a single meat ration. There would presently be a further problem. He had been careless about Killie, and Quince had got her in whelp.

I can drown all but two at birth without feeling a murderer, but I suppose two will have to be kept, to draw her milk.

After their eyes are open I cannot drown them. I cannot keep them, for my rations are hard stretched as it is. I cannot bear to give them away, to be tied up as yard dogs.

October 21st, 1945
An immoral evening at the Punch Bowl last night. I suffer from this hideous failing of setting out to charm strangers, at which I always succeed. Last night played bar billiards and drank with all the locals, leg-pulled, paid for drinks, got people laughing and generally swaggered about, adored by all. This is hateful. Everybody behaved as if I were the games mistress and they at a boarding-school, and it was my fault. I behave like a tart.

October 25th, 1945
In one month from today I shall no longer be able to say, Brownie was alive a year ago. It seems a lifetime.

October 30th, 1945
Still raining. Lunched at the Punch Bowl. Stayed to tea and drank 4 pints in all. Going down this morning I caught myself looking back with affection at my little home, to see it still there safe, like a bitch looking at her puppies. It is a simple pleasure to know that one has left everything washed and swept and laid, so that on coming back in the dark, there is only a match to strike, to fire and the oil lamp, for it to be a going concern.

My partner at bar billiards was a doctor and I asked him if mild concussion could produce causeless rages afterwards. He said it could. When I had my 'American wake' on leaving Dublin I fell down a long flight of wooden stairs on my head when drunk, and I have had two rages since – one with Bunny. I don't usually have them.

October 31st, 1945
A mild blowy day, very lovely, and in the afternoon we walked over the fell into Wensleydale. Coming home, on the very top of the watershed, a vast aeroplane came bee-lining

along the boundary fence, only fifty feet up. It was within a hundred yards of me, and must have seen us, for it gravely, slowly, courteously dipped its starboard wing as it passed.

In the shortening daylight he must have found Duke Mary's a dusky dwelling, the more so since he came to it after the well-windowed Georgian Doolistown. He began to lay on the three pounds of paint he had carried up with the cauliflower and the chamberpot. On November 3rd he noted that he had finished painting both bedrooms and the stairs, that Aldrovandus had arrived, that he had made something 'out of own head, which may turn out to be chocolate fudge, chocolate toffee, chocolate butter, or almost anything'.

> *November 4th, 1945*
> Sydney Cockerell sent me his 'Friends of a Lifetime'. Burned mutton chops for dinner. The chocolate toffee is horrible.

That evening he began a long conversational letter to Cockerell, which breaks off with an 'Excuse me, I'll be back later', and is taken up again at 12.15am, and goes on, commenting and itemizing, until he interrupts himself with 'The fire is out, so I shall take the book to bed', and begins again the next day with a 'Well, Sydney, I don't thank you for sending me this book. It has kept me awake till I was too tired to look at my watch, and I didn't wake up till 12.50 this morning.' It is the kind of letter written by the happily married, running on through this and that, beginning anew for the pleasure of not letting go. Written by a middle-aged man of letters to an elderly one, it is curiously moving. One has the feeling that they are conversing in the Duke Mary's kitchen, the fire subsiding, the rain falling; sometimes White gets up and does something about the house, then comes back to Cockerell with something else he wants to say.

> What an absolute treasure house of unpublished letters you still have. I beg and implore you not to destroy any syllable which you may consider indiscreet in any one of them, as you most wickedly seem to have done in one of Ruskin's. I have

kept all Siegfried's letters to me and they wear wonderfully. One of them, or perhaps two, I can't remember, is about you. Will you be pleased to hear it is a glowing tribute? He says in effect that what he admires is your insistence on truth and the unexpected intransigence of your opinions. At the same time he pulls your leg most charmingly, about your habit of burying the great. 'Ah, yes, dear old Milton. I wrapped him up in some spare proofs of *Paradise Lost* and buried him on the top of Ben Nevis in a snow storm.' That wasn't Siegfried's phrase, which was much funnier, but I have invented it because I can't remember what he really wrote, and my papers are in Ireland.

Evening. Mrs Hardy's mention of Walter de la Mare makes me think of him and gives me the idea that perhaps you would like to perform one of your habitual good offices. I know he is old now and probably would not care to be bothered by a letter from me, a total stranger and junior to his world. But if you are writing to him ever, or should meet him, will you tell him that an anonymous young friend of yours has written him 3 letters in the past seven years, and torn them up, to tell him that he is an immortal. I do feel this deeply, but the tenuity of his supreme mental delicacy might be bruised or whatever the word is by my clumsy bounces. I wish I could have known him. I would tire him now.

Proofs of *The Elephant and the Kangaroo* and of *Mistress Masham's Repose* were now arriving from New York. 'Looked through Tempest and Midsummer Night's Dream vainly for ideas on titles for the Lilliput book.'

'Mistress Masham's Repose' was already its working title, but he was in two minds about it and thought of many alternatives. Those ticked for consideration were: 'No Masters, No Slaves'; 'Lilliput in Exile'; 'Lie Low, Lilliput'; 'Through the Minifying Glass'; 'Canaries Never Shall Be Slaves'; 'As Yahoos Like It'. The last of these emphasizes an aspect of the book which many of the book's admirers don't notice, or prefer not to: that Maria's first reaction to the exquisite orderly society of the Lilliputians is that of a young female Yahoo. She steals the baby because it pleases her, man-handles the baby's mother when she opposes the theft. White seldom relinquished his ideas. Three years before *Mistress Masham's Repose* he was writing 'The Insolence of Man'. There, man is the Yahoo among the animals; and Lilliput is what the Yahoos would like – to exploit for profit, if Miss Brown and the Vicar; to delight in and despoil, if Maria.

> *November 11th, 1945*
> Scrubbed upstairs floors and landings. Put candlesticks in hot water to get off the grease and polished them. Finished extensive patching of pyjamas. Went to bed with a gargle, knowing I was in for a dose of 'flu, after carrying up the dog's bread, paraffin, Brussels sprouts and 4 kippers.

He was accustomed to getting influenza and had allowed for it. The dogs had to be fed and he continued to fetch the milk; for the rest, he stayed in bed and let his thoughts have their way with him. The entries for November 12th and 13th are entirely given over to recollections of Brownie, their love and her death.

> 25.xi.1945 was spent alone, in silence, bitterly.

It was the first anniversary of Brownie's death, the day after which he would no longer be able to say, A year ago, she was alive.

Garnett, offering Duke Mary's as a home if White came to England, had remarked: 'It is probably rather bleak after the end of November.' On December 15th 'a little powder of snow still lay' when he let Killie out early in the morning. She had woken him by panting, and when he had twice let her out, and twice she had rushed back and been sick, he struggled out of sleepiness and realized she was about to whelp. She was before her time; he had nothing ready nor had he decided what to do about the puppies.

I stumbled about, trying to organize things, trying to make up my mind. When four had come I began stealing them and spiriting them out, to drown horribly in a bucket in the stable.

He kept one puppy, a female.

December 20th, 1945
Emptied bucket of dead puppies – seven dead ones. Horrible sense of guilt and shame. I ought to have kept them alive, and might have done so if I had tried very hard to get masters for them, by advertisement, etc. I now see that any kind of life, with any master, would have been better than death. Strange that life should be valuable when men and nature are cruel. I won't exorcize this shame with words, but feel it.

One feels winter taking possession of the diary. There are no more records of household exploits. When he had finished a consignment of books from the London Library he began to read 'all the dud plays of Shakespeare'.

Pericles is perfectly cinematic, if only Hollywood knew: ie it is practically a cinema script as it stands and would make a superb film, with its gruesome start in the voodoo-house of the dead suitors and its procession of sea storms.

Titus Andronicus stinks of Marlowe.

The Shakespeare Head 'Works' in one volume purports to give the latest low-down on the assumed order of the plays. If one puts 'Very Good', 'Good', 'Bad' and 'Very Bad' against the plays in that order, one can make a sort of graph of Shakespeare's state of health during his writing days.

He had resigned himself at last to Shakespeare's authorship. But the conviction expressed in a letter reproaching Potts for misapprehending a term in falconry: 'You carpet critics ought to go into the world and *do* the things as Shakespeare did before James cut his head off' was maintained till at least the June of 1942, when his diary for two successive days was taken up with tabulating the dates of the plays against the events of Raleigh's career.

December 22nd, 1945
It is the Year's midnight, and it is the Day's – Lucie's who scarce seven hours herself unmasks. And at midnight, the puppy unmasked the faintest slit of one eye, the left one. That is, at midnight on the 21st. Today both eyes can open halfway, like a child peeping at hide-and-seek, but they are quickly tired, and do not stay open for more than a few seconds.

Killie has a tapeworm.

NB Titus Andronicus is far worse than anything in Marlowe, or perhaps anywhere else. It needs to be acted by the Marx brothers.

There, except for a pencilled 'Killie wormed 30th', the Duke Mary's diary ends.

January 16th, 1946. To Sydney Cockerell
My hand and brain are frozen solid but I must try to write to you before my letter debts get out of control. These Yorkshire fells are all as white as snow in the frost-moon-light and the Swale itself looks like being frozen tomorrow, as the pipes in the kitchen where I sit already are in spite of the fire. So you must think of us poor bumpkins starving here, while you sit in knightly coziness at Kew, toasting your monogrammed slippers at the gas-fire designed by W Morris.

My bombshell about getting married has failed to go off. The parents or she or somebody took out the fuse, so I am still alive. It is a merciful release. I never wanted to be married, but was too polite to say so.

The bombshell had been suavely introduced at the close of a preceding letter of condolence on the death of Cockerell's brother.

There are hundreds of people who still love you for yourself, and I am making arrangements for two things (1) next summer I intend to arrange that Siegfried shall let me and my dogs sleep in one of his loose-boxes in order to meet you, (2) next autumn I am arranging for you to meet my wife in the Yorkshire dales.

After the paragraph dismissing the bombshell White continued with a request – and this can have been no surprise to Cockerell – for guidance about his gold watch:

a full hunter, repeater, stop-watch and timepiece with second hand, but it also tells the phase of the moon, the name of the month, the day of the month and the day of the week. As I am now penniless I want to sell it for £200 – but I don't know how to set about it. In the first place the machine has stopped.

The watch was not sold. Though he was no richer, he had prospects. Writing to Potts on January 23rd, after taking brisk exception to a recent Cambridge appointment he continued:

I am full of gin and news. The American Book of the Month Club is a touchy body which does not like to have its choices revealed in advance. Consequently, the only living person to whom T H White mentions that he is likely to earn £9,000 next summer is the debased and humiliated Pottës, once his guru but now a mere university politician.

February 28th, 1946. To Sydney Cockerell
I shall get about £9,000 next summer, but the Americans will steal £3,000 and the English another £3,000, which seems a little unfair on a poor author. I am rather thinking of emigrating to America, to avoid double taxation.

Now that I am a plutocrat I would like to establish my lineage. My father, who was divorced by my atrocious mother, died last month. All I know about the paternal line, and I don't care about the distaff side, is what sometimes dropped from my mother's lips in unguarded moments, and she is an incurable liar. The romancing kind. From these hints I suppose him to have been an elder son in the direct line from

Lamb's friend who wrote 'Falstaff's Letters' and hence from the publisher Benjamin White, and hence to my adored field-naturalist Gilbert White, who was Benjamin's bachelor brother. There is also an admirable pirate knocking about in the 17th century whose name was Samuel and who became a mandarin of two buttons. I should much like to include him. Do you happen to know of anybody who undertakes these commissions at so much per grandfather?

I have written to Quaritch for a set of the OED, that's all I've done with my future so far.

On March 4th he confided that the novel was *Mistress Masham's Repose*.

Now that I am getting the OED I think I may say that I shall have the beginnings of a reference library, as I already have the Enc Brit and the DNB. Some of my books have arrived already and here I sit most happy in Duke Mary's kitchen in the middle of the Pennine Chain, with books all round the walls, 2 dogs asleep by the bright fire, and a snow blizzard outside. If I look out of the window I can see your friends the human race like small black fleas in the valley snow. How lovely to have them at such an arm's length.

If I went to America it would not be to the parts frequented by you. It would be to some log cabin in the State of Washington, near the Columbia river, where I could catch fish and shoot pine grouse and be snowed up in winter or mosquito-bitten in summer. I should like to find a haven still remoter than this. The only thing I should miss would be the London Library.

April 19th, 1946
Do you remember that I told you a couple of months ago that I nearly became engaged? Well, I've given in at last, so you must write me one of your loving letters to say it will work. Nothing could be less likely to work.

It did not work. By midsummer she had broken off the engagement. During that interval White's immunized attitude to marriage (though he had sometimes thought he would be happy as a family man: at Stowe a young widow with four small children drew the admission, 'When I have drunk two bottles of port I feel like marrying Celia') broke down. A note-book of this date contains drafts of letters in which he pleaded, argued, reasoned with the girl to change her mind. To draft love-letters may seem a cool-headed proceeding, but the reality of his torment in so desperately wanting something he had no inclination for is unmistakable, 'I love you so painfully' – the conclusion of one letter – summarizes them all. On the heels of the last letter he began to write, flowingly and almost without erasures, a version of the story of Troilus and Cressida. A writer's remedy, it enabled him to dwell on the past and at the same time to put it at a remove. It breaks off before Diomed.

There would be no marriage; by the final estimate, his earnings by the Book of the Month choice would be about £15,000; a proposed May visit to Cambridge had been postponed till early autumn; nothing else in his future was settled. He played with the idea that he would go to Cambridge to study natural history, letting double taxation do its worst. He went to London and applied at the American Embassy for a passage which would get him to the States in time to avoid paying UK tax. The lists were full, he applied in vain. He had considered Mexico; but as he would be taking Killie he would have to stay there till she died, for he could not sentence her to six months' quarantine. It was Garnett who recommended the Channel Islands, where there was neither quarantine nor Surtax and Income Tax was four shillings in the pound. He consulted a chartered accountant who said he could remain in England till the end of November. So, returning to Duke Mary's, he set about preparing to leave it. Quince and the puppy went to new owners. As he did not know where he would live next, the best he could do was to leave his belongings in some sort of marching order. The crates which had come from Buckinghamshire and Ireland were left in an outhouse, needing only to be re-addressed and sent after him. There they remained during the severe winter of 1946–7. The gales drove the freezing snow among the slates. When the thaw came it melted and dripped. It was the crate containing his Cambridge diaries and notebooks which suffered most. On top of the diaries was a ten years' run of letters from Potts. The sodden mass fell to pieces in his hands when he unpacked the crate over a twelvemonth later. Unlike the frayed twine and the strawberry netting and Killie's rape, this calamity was not really his fault.

While in London he met a friend who had known him at Stowe. The friend was shocked – disillusioned, too – to find him so much changed. He had thought of White in Ireland maintaining his stand as a conscientious objector; it was disconcerting to hear him insisting on all his efforts 'to join the war'. But to Potts and Mary, he was the same Tim, 'no more changed', according to Mary Potts,

> than we would have expected him to be after six years, the same dear entertaining person in 1946 as he was in 1935, and fifty per cent more alive than anybody else I have ever met.
>
> Our life together was very simple and family. There was no entertainment going on so soon after the war, and though Tim went out to the pubs this wasn't LJ's way, and so we didn't observe his attempts to conform and to understand post-war England. He was horrified to find Canon Raven, Master of Christ's, washing up at the Lodge.
>
> Ellen Wilkinson was his symbol for all that was bad in England. He burned her in effigy on Guy Fawkes' night in the allotment garden we had in the Botanics. He was a wonderful Guy Fawkes maker, and that was a wonderful bonfire. Fireworks were still unobtainable, but who needed fireworks with Tim there?

XI Alderney 1946–57

After the Channel Islands were surrendered by Germany in 1944 they resumed their traditional role of sanctuaries where British subjects can retire from the taxes of real life. Writing to Potts soon after his arrival in Jersey, White remarked on the quantity of colonels.

> The hotel where I am staying has no less than four – it is a small hotel – and each colonel is worse than the other. They play golf all day. I need never meet such people if I build.

Having spent two days being driven round the island in a taxi he had seen how thickly populated it was, but his instinct to settle was automatically at work.

> On the whole, I think I will buy an acre or two in one of the few desolate places and build on it. If I do not spend my money like this, I shall only spend it on drink.

At Doolistown his self-imposed rule of drinking by the half-year made drinking a seasonal habit. The pattern broke down when he began to drink in order not to be sober, as he did after Brownie's death and as, companionless, at a loose end and still smarting from that painful love-affair, he was doing now. Fortunately, he met some horsy people who asked him to exercise a steeplechaser, and he rode himself sober again.

In the New Year he decided to have a look at Guernsey.

> He arrived early in the morning by mailboat with his setter bitch and went to the Royal Hotel which is near the White Rock pier for breakfast. He settled in at the table with the dog and had not been there long when the manager and head waiter arrived and told him dogs were not allowed in the dining-room. After some furious altercation Tim left the hotel purple in the face saying he would not stay another moment in a hotel that refused to have his dog. He picked up his suitcase and strode the length of the pier to the end

from where the Sark and Alderney boats left. He decided on the spur of the moment that he would go and live in Sark only to be told that no bitches are allowed in Sark. He then furiously drove up to the airport and managed to get a ticket to Alderney, again to be told that no dogs were allowed on the plane, whereupon he tore his ticket up and returned to the White Rock where a miserable little boat was about to take off for Alderney. He embarked.

Lady Sherwill, who was to become a good friend to him, narrates the departure. Lt-Commander Harry Griffiths, also to become a good friend, remembers the arrival. There was a strong north-west gale and a heavy sea. The boat was long overdue, and a crowd had gathered to see if she could make the harbour. The first thing across the gangway was a drenched frantic dog. After the dog came a large, drenched man, water streaming from his beard. A voice from the crowd commented, "The boat must have gone deep. They've fetched up Father Neptune.'

He was still dripping when he stood in the doorway of Grosnez House, the hotel kept by Archie and Maisie Allen, and asked if he and his dog could have a bed for the night. He stayed on for a second night, a third night. 'He liked Alderney because his dog could run free.' He continued to stay on. The process of settling had begun. The remaining sixteen years of his life were spent in Alderney because he had stayed a night and ensuing nights at Grosnez House, where Maisie Allen's welcome perpetuated itself like those legendary peat fires on Dartmoor hearths which never go out. People of old-fashioned piety used to assert in their difficulties that the Lord would undertake for them. White had the same comfortable faith in Maisie Allen. Though he later set up a house of his own, Grosnez House remained his shelter. He went there for his meals; he took his visitors there to regale on her renowned cookery. When his cistern froze and his pipes burst, when he fell and fractured his skull, he went there to stay and be undertaken for. 'My dear benefactress, Maisie Allen' – so he wrote of her to Cockerell. The adjective is the significant word: not all benefactresses endear themselves.

May 2nd, 1947. To David Garnett
It must be about time I reported progress. Well, my latest vagary is that I have become an old salt. All that about being seasick turns out to have been just a fad, and ever since I last wrote I have been ranting and roaring all o'er the wide Channel Islands in a succession of hurricanes and horrid little boats. Probably I shall settle down in Alderney where I now am, and buy a yacht. These are horribly dangerous coasts, packed with jagged pinnacles of granite rock and raving with currents. Alderney is quite the worst. North-west we have a race called the Swinge which runs at a maximum of nine knots and south-east we have a kind of Edgar Allan Poe maelstrom called the Race which also goes at nine knots. They say that seven tides meet there, and you can actually see seven waves whacking together from different directions.

Alderney calls itself the Cinderella of the Channel Islands, and, though a cliché, it is a fairly good description. It is the poorest, least visited. It is windswept and treeless. The streets are cobbled. The architecture is a cross between Cornish fishing village and Horry Walpole Gothick – very attractive.

I have an awful feeling that I am going to buy an enormous castle or fortress in Alderney, which covers about an acre. It is totally inconvenient, but so gloriously situated, half in the sea, and so dramatic and sun-drenched and lonely, and still in working order as a fortress because the Germans used it.

The other thing is to buy some tiny Walpole cottage in one of the cobbled squares of the town.

In the upshot White chose neither a fortress in working order nor a tiny Walpole cottage. 5 Connaught Square, where he lived for the rest of his life, is a three-storeyed house in the polite quarter of Alderney's one small town, St Anne.

June 6th, 1947. To David Garnett
I have bought, but solely as an investment, for about £800, a delicious little Frenchified house in the main place of Alderney. I would date it about 1850, but of course fashions

took longer to reach these outposts: consequently it is of a better and (then) old-fashioned period. Say, 1790. It has two immense greenhouses (broken) but with the vines in them. Also orchard, garage space, main drain, cobbled square – almost everything the heart could desire.

He had kept no diary since that year's midnight at Duke Mary's, when the puppy unmasked its left eye; but on July 2nd, 1947, he wrote a short summary:

> I stayed in Jersey for five months, then in Guernsey, and now have bought a house in Alderney.
>
> I have been drinking much too much.
>
> My book about Eire, *The Elephant and the Kangaroo*, has raised a scream of rage from one side of America to the other.
>
> I have refused £1,000 for an option of 120 days on *Mistress Masham's Repose** in advance of £15,000 if accepted.
>
> On examining the above, I feel faintly guilty, I don't know which about.

> *July 3rd, 1947*
> Wrote yesterday to Cape to see if it was too late to tone down *The Elephant and the Kangaroo* for the English market. That was what I was feeling guilty about.

The USA publication of *The Elephant and the Kangaroo* (March 1947) roused fierce reactions among Irish-Americans,** incensed by a book which laughed both at the Irish Republic and at Holy Ireland. At Doolistown it had seemed inconceivable that he would ever be read in Co Meath. When Garnett warned him of the possibility of libel actions, he replied, 'I shan't let

* Film rights.

** Some very eloquent: 'We ask our readers to condemn *The Elephant and the Kangaroo* in no uncertain terms, and to regard it as just another typical English stab in the back which will only prove a boomerang'. (*The Irish Echo*, New York, NY, May 1947.)

it be published or sold in Ireland.' White had a fine, arrogant disregard for legal proceedings – what did one have a literary agent for, if not to dispose of such matters? – but he felt protective about the McDonaghs. His conscience worked too late. A copy of the American edition had somehow got to Trim and the unfailing provincial readiness to bear ill news and ram it home with condolences had seen to it that Lena McDonagh learned what her dirty, drinking Mr White had said about her husband and her religion. There were no more letters with the closing formula of 'I must now ring off joined by Paddy' after July 1947. Of course, he should have gone to see her. Rushed on by new projects, he didn't.

December 31st, 1947. To L J Potts
I spend my time like this – half the day mixing concrete, half the day writing books, half the day abusing plumbers, half the day writing to people in Italy or Sweden, half the day taking Killie for walks and half the day getting drunk. You may think there are not so many halves, but in my day there are.

He could have added, half the day planning how the Potts family would travel to Alderney; there are seven letters about this, detailing all possible routes, all probable mishaps – though not all contingencies. These were covered in a postcard which arrived on the eve of their departure by air in August 1948.

Yes, I will be there to meet you at 6.50. Bring furs, tarpaulin jackets, heavy overcoats, ear muffs, electric heaters, parkas, balaclava helmets, ski gauntlets, ankle warmers, snow glasses, skates, toboggans, fog-horns, umbrellas, hail-proof goggles, hurricane tent, suntan oil and bathing trunks.

His letters were so filled with inducements to visit Alderney – lobsters, ormers (a local kind of clam: 'It is well known that archangels live on them almost exclusively'), sandy beaches, dangerous bathing, double cognacs at 2s, desert islands with puffins – that one gets an impression that he had forgotten his friends might wish to visit him for his own sake. It was for his own sake and his own good that he was visited in October by Garnett, who told him to drink less and get on with his writing. White then had three books on hand: the Bestiary, *The Age of Scandal* and its sequel *The Scandalmonger*.

'Your visit stimulated me so much', he wrote in November, 'that I accepted the two days' hell of sobering up, and I have been too busy rewriting the final Arthur book to write letters.' In this rewriting, *The Once and Future King* began to take its ultimate form. "The Book of Merlyn' was discarded, but its chapter about the ants replaced Chapter XIII of *The Sword in the Stone* and the chapter about the geese replaced the visit to Athene. The geese were travelled birds; they had first appeared in the novel he left unfinished when he moved to Ireland, which, with its theme of the killer who renounces killing, engendered the argument of *The Once and Future King*.

Echoes of the row with Collins soured White's earlier letters to his new publishers, but when Wren Howard of Jonathan Cape visited him in March 1949 they immediately liked each other. During this visit Wren Howard, finding himself incommoded by a bulky object beneath a settee cushion, abstracted it. It was the typescript of *The Goshawk*. He read it in bed and insisted on taking it back with him next day in spite of White's vehement resistance. From London he wrote:

> We also want to publish the falconry book, manuscript of which I brought back with me. Heaven knows what the public will say, but it will be fun to find out what they think. Anyway, it is so good that it certainly must be printed.

White disagreed. The manuscript was then read by Garnett, who also thought it should be printed.

April 15th, 1949. To Wren Howard
If Bunny Garnett says that the Hawk book is really good, I will consent to publishing. I have not read it since I wrote it, long before the war.

My shyness about it is personal.

You see, apart from not wanting to spread one's personality naked before the public, I have become a much better falconer since then – even an authority on the matter.

I know just how bad the falconry in that book is, if I recollect it.

It is like asking a grown-up to sanction the publication of his adolescent diaries, or like asking Sir Donald Bradman to publish his earlier thoughts on French Cricket.

However, if Bunny says so, it is so.

This touching *Fiat mihi* with a closing 'I am heartbroken that you should want to publish it' was submitted to Garnett. Publishers seldom want to break an author's heart. But there were indications that the heart might get over it. At the end of the letter, White mentioned that if pictures were wanted, he might be able to find photographs of his lost oil-paintings of the bird. Garnett gave a written opinion:

I think this is really Tim's best book – an opinion which is perhaps not very flattering when analysed. For Tim is not a lover of humanity or human beings and when he writes he usually writes partly for them, and the wish to please is a pretence. Here he only lapses occasionally into awareness of other people and is writing privately. He is therefore more exact, more honest, more interesting. The battle between Tim and Gos is a masterpiece. I have scarcely ever known an agony so prolonged without insensibility setting in. One cries with relief when Gos goes off with his broken string to hang himself.

Tim's reputation will not suffer among falconers. They will love him for having once been more ignorant than he is now. It will be an intensely popular book among all thirty British and American austringers and falconers.

This opinion was sent on to White – a hazardous proceeding, for that last paragraph's implication that he had not attained total omniscience as a falconer might have displeased.

May 21st, 1949. To David Garnett

For about the hundredth time you have saved my life. I have been on the water-wagon for weeks, plodding around the island on my afternoon walks, battering my head against the problem of what to write next. I had got as far as realizing that I was not fundamentally interested in character – could I say, not even in my own? But I was trying and trying to think of some way of getting interested in it, so that I could write novels. Then at lunch today came your enclosure to Cape, saying that I was essentially –

The next page is missing. It must have conveyed a decision to write a day-to-day journal.

I see it as a sort of Woodforde diary. I will put in prices and what I had for dinner. Even if nobody reads it nowadays, it will be priceless 200 years hence. No, I won't make any plans about it at all. I will enjoy it, and write about what I enjoy (instead of these dreadful humans – I won't even write *for* them or expect them to read it) and then it will be good.

And the same day, he began it. Naturally, it is not in the least like Woodforde: White was not; but it is not like White either. It is long-winded and stiflingly detailed. After a week he gave it up.

The Age of Scandal – the first of the two volumes of eighteenth-century studies he worked on while possible bidders for Doolistown trampled through the house – came out in June 1950. Sending a copy to Garnett, he wrote:

Here is this thing, which I post with more than a lot of misgiving. For some reason which I don't fathom – it is something like whirling things round in a centrifuge – all the cruel and sadistic bits have settled in vol I, while the kind bits about country life, Parson Woodforde, Palladian architecture, General Ponsonby, etc., have all been put off to vol II. Anyway, don't be cross about all the birching and head-chopping – which they did do – until you have seen the sequel.

The give-away was in the choice, not in the treatment, for the cruel and sadistic bits are written with decency and reserve. With one exception, the essays in *The Age of Scandal* and its sequel, *The Scandalmonger*, have the impersonality of a well-informed spectator. It was not for nothing that he called them the Horry Walpole book; they have an affinity with Walpole's *nil admirari* mind; they are sensible as well as entertaining. The exception occurs in the second volume where, at the opening of 'A Struggle of Sentiment', White's self-identification with Lord Camelford is like a spurt of blood.

The Goshawk was published in 1951; but the Mondays and Tuesdays of the diary narrative were Mondays and Tuesdays in the autumn of 1936, when White had reverted to a feral state, and was living in the Stowe Ridings cottage and making notes for the book he proposed to call 'A Sort of Mania'. Its safeguarding postscript was included at his insistence. It weakens the book; but like Lord Camelford who, 'born to the purple tried to win esteem by being a good carpenter', White was bent on winning esteem as a good falconer.

The Scandalmonger (1952) was followed in October 1954 by *The Book of Beasts*.

Four books within five years suggests an active authorship. In fact, all four came out of his larder. There was a substratum of larder in a project which he was working at by 1950; but the treatment was to be a new departure. The theme of 'Dry Blood and Distant Thunder' comes from an essay in *The Scandalmonger* about Caroline Matilda, sister to George III, great-aunt to Queen Victoria, whose marriage to Christian VII of Denmark was only one degree less scandalous than her adultery with the Court Physician, Dr Struensee, her divorce and his execution. The story has the 'horrid' violence of a puppet-play, and in *The Scandalmonger* White treated it as such and in a rather *de haut en bas* manner. But the ghosts wouldn't be laid. Four years later, he went back to the subject, re-read and reconsidered the sources more extensively, and filled a notebook with preliminaries. As with Guenever and Lancelot, it was the characters he wanted to make out; and for a man who had blithely agreed that he was not interested in character he went about it with remarkable thoroughness. 'She was extremely fair with the characteristic flaxen hair of her family, which in some places was nearly white,' he copied into the notebook; and interpolated 'Like a pig's eyelashes'. The notebook gives one the feeling that once more his stars were in a fortunate conjunction, as they had been for *The Elephant and the Kangaroo*. He was still near enough to his eighteenth-century reading to be at home in the date; the puppet King and Queen were both very young; only a little older than Heneage Lloyd and his sister in the conversation piece which was his favourite picture in the Fitzwilliam Museum. The enlightened Struensee, so busy abolishing social abuses that he set every class of society against him, was material for another self-portrait; he was safeguarded against being nauseated by Christian because Christian as a child had been flogged into fits, and against being sexually antagonized by Caroline because she was fat, and the calves of her legs 'of a surprising circumference'. All this portended a good novel. But it was not to be a novel. He was tired of writing novels. 'Dry Blood and Distant Thunder' was to be a film- script.

As I know as little about film-scripts as White did, I cannot pronounce on it. It is full of visual inventiveness: the shot of the ruffles and ringed hands moving among the chessmen; of Christian's delirium: 'serfs mopping and mowing at him in the snow, and writhing saints and corkscrew steeples turning round like screws'; of his madness: 'The King is sitting on the floor wearing a large Gainsborough hat for ladies, playing with his dolls'; of the crowd on the quay, dark and motionless, with the fishwives' head-dresses flapping in the wind; of the very high scaffold, seen from below, with blood beginning to run through the seams between the planks. In one sequence, where Caroline and Struensee, who have been following a stag-hunt, get left behind, dismount, 'and are as it were silently swept into each other's arms', the final shot goes beyond invention and is poetry. 'The two horses move off unnoticed, stumbling a little on their reins.' But the dialogue is lifeless, the action is clogged with chatter, and Struensee is a bore. 'All this must somehow be put into words,' he commented in the preliminary notebook – a death-sentence.

Little of the film can have been written when he wrote to Lady Sherwill about casting it.

January 1950
As there is not going to be a single Hollywood Hug in the whole film, and as the heroine of it is fat, the thing is obviously unproduceable. In fact, it is a character play – a vehicle for some talented character actress who is not afraid to play the pathos of being fat.

If only I could think of a few such people who were already famous, I would send copies of the script to them, telling each that it was specially written for them, and they might be able to influence Mr Goldbumstein in its favour.

Can you help me to think of some? Do your children go to films enough to know who acts in them? I never go.

This doomed project lingered on into 1952, when John Wyllie, author of *The Goodly Seed*, was living in Alderney. White showed him the unfinished script and asked his advice. Wyllie recommended cuts and began a shooting script. The two men saw quite different films and both gave up.

Alderney, alone of the Channel Islands, was evacuated by the British. From June 1940 it became a detention camp for Russian and French-Jewish political prisoners whose forced labour was used in converting the ten nineteenth-century forts – built as a counter-threat to Louis Philippe's naval base at Cherbourg – into underground strongholds and ammunition stores. When the islanders returned in the late winter of 1945 they found their houses in ruins, their land gone back to the wild, their boundaries effaced – and three burial-grounds and a piped water-supply added to the island's amenities. The island became a Home Office responsibility. Its constitution was brought up to date. White, feeling that the hated Welfare State had caught up with him, thought of buying the island of Jethou (he cannot have known about the Prince Blücher who had lived on the island of Herm naturalizing kangaroos: the challenge would have proved irresistible) and composed some Johnsonian letters of protest. His most arresting intervention took place during the ceremonial opening of the new Court of Alderney. Harry Griffiths, just sworn in as a jurat, saw him, considerably drunk, ricochetting down from the public gallery. Approaching under the cold eye of Mr Chuter Ede, then Home Secretary, White produced a dirty pound note and flourished it into Harry Griffiths's hand, saying, loud and plain (drink did not impede his utterance), 'I begin with the law as I intend to go on.' The note was afterwards reclaimed.

Realizing that it takes more than an Act of Parliament to change an island's character, he found that Alderney was where he wanted to be.

Alderney – which is also Aurigny, and geographically pertains to France – began with the law as it intended to go on, doing a little friendly smuggling again, making as few changes as possible and adapting newcomers to itself, rather than itself to newcomers. The fortifications served a new purpose: summer visitors explored them. John Betjeman who, with his family, stayed with White in 1950, recalling 'an impression of laughter, high seas, steep cliffs, empty beaches out of the wind, and a sense of home in that house in Connaught Square', particularly remembers how 'we all used to enjoy exploring the sinister remains of Nazi occupation – underground forts with German notices in them, and remnants of offices underground and electric light fittings.'

The Betjeman visit was a success. Others were not. Asked if White was good at giving parties a discerning friend of his replied with emphasis: 'No! He dragooned them.'

After settling in Alderney he developed – perhaps because he had lived so much alone – a sense of social responsibility. At a time when he was drinking only moderately himself it struck him that a friend was drinking dangerously. He challenged him to a match of abstention till an agreed date and kept him to it. When he enlarged his property by buying a cottage next door, he added tenants to his responsibilities. A rowdy young couple had almost exhausted his patience when, news of their goings-on having reached the mainland, an anxious relative came to ask him the truth. He instantly perjured himself in their defence. He wrote to Lady Sherwill:

> I have done the best I could about all this, so don't be too critical. It would have been so easy to make worse worse.

On another occasion he installed a newly widowed neighbour 'because she adored her husband and cannot be left to despair in the wintry flat he died in'. He refused to be resigned to the woes of others. 'I go away and bite God,' he explained.

Inevitably, he took up the cause of every under-privileged dog on the island, though sometimes to his own hindrance.

> About a year ago [he wrote to Lady Sherwill] some foul stoker in a cross-channel boat kidnapped a female greyhound, brought her to Alderney, and sold her to the next comer for a couple of quid. Well, this very beautiful brindled greyhound bitch has been knocked round the island ever since: she does not know whether she is on her head or her heels; she is lame in one foot, but that will clear up: she is as gentle as a mouse, but not very sensible, so that she bites me a good deal – about five times a day – and why shouldn't she? I bought her out of sheer rage, because she was not being fed or loved enough. Obviously this is most unfair to Killie, and I have had to divide the house into two bits. The greyhound has the ground floor and Killie has the *piano nobile*. Killie never stops telling me that I am keeping a MISTRESS. I will love her if I am forced to it, but it makes Killie so miserable that I don't know what to do.

In the same hospitable if rather fatalistic spirit, he prepared to receive Ylla – whose animal photographs he should have known about, but didn't. She had been heralded but not explained in a telegram from Garnett: SENDING YLLA BY SATURDAY PLANE. In case this unknown animal proved savage, he went to the airfield wearing heavy gauntlet gloves. It was foggy; no plane landed. Later an unknown lady, elegant and deliciously perfumed, rang his door bell and was Ylla.*

In December 1952 he went hurriedly to England, where his mother was in a nursing-home with a coronary thrombosis. He stayed with her till her death a week later.

Time and absence had calmed his animosity. Since his father's death he had been helping her with money. Some of us find it easier to forgive those who drink the champagne we send them; some do not. The former is the nobler class, and White belonged to it.

May 10th, 1953. To Lady Sherwill

Dearest May,

> I thought perhaps you hadn't written to me because you had heard rumours of my abandoned behaviour since we last met. I had a beautiful debutante to stay for six weeks in January and fell madly in love with her. No decent people speak to me now. She has gone away but swears she will come back in September. I shall be five years older than twice her age this month, so it is all very baffling and for some weeks after she left was painful too. Don't be afraid. I will *not* be a dotard.

In Lady Sherwill, White found a point of stability. She was a woman of the world, a wit and a grandmother. He liked her the more for her position (Sir Ambrose Sherwill was Bailiff of Guernsey); not from snobbishness, for no snobbery could exist in her atmosphere, but because of his regard for hierarchies,

---

* She wanted an Introduction to a book of her photographs. Garnett thought White might supply it.

ceremonials and the top-hat side of English life; but when he sent her account of the Coronation to Sydney Cockerell it was the woman he boasted about.

The writer is a person of immense charm, vitality, intelligence, fun. She's ageless, though a grandmother, and has been married three times. It's impossible to keep her single.

The surmise that she had not written because of rumours about his behaviour was indiscerning; but it was also a tribute. He would have been very sorry to lose her good opinion. It was the girl he lost.

While he still hoped, he tried to get himself included in a parachuting course, but was pronounced too old to essay that method of rejuvenation. He received the news – so he told Garnett – with disappointment and relief. This tentative love-affair did not scar him as the affair in 1947 had done, but it drove him to a spell of heavy drinking.

August 8th, 1953. To David Garnett
I had a fight with a sailor in a pub (nobody won: we kept on missing each other) and did my best to destroy myself with liquor. Then the little men in my subconscious mind had a committee meeting and, being averse to being destroyed by their raving chairman, decided to immobilize me. I woke up at 4 am in a mysterious agony of cramp which lasted for eight hours solid and was kept in bed by the doctor for three weeks. One of my legs had seized up. I am back on the water-waggon again now, walking, having discovered that broken hearts can be situated in the calf of the leg.

It was the first occurrence of the interrupted circulation which ultimately caused his death.

In October, he learned that Cockerell proposed to include some of his letters in a sequel volume to *Friends of a Lifetime*. The compliment fell on him like a last straw.

I really can't let the whole of these letters go into print during my lifetime, or that of some others. Evidently I am a sort of Boswell, boasting, indiscreet, ranting, rather pathetic, but even Boswell would not have liked to see his London Journal printed while he was alive. That long ranting letter about Malory's *Morte d'Arthur* makes me blush all over. I don't want to tell the world that I spent 6 months in the Brompton Hospital for consumptives. Finally, there is all the war stuff. I seem to have written to you only when I was feeling pacific and with an intention of bravado. It's this cursed trick of mine of trying to shock people.

This seems like Lord Camelford trying to win esteem by being a modest violet; but though White was careless of the public eye he retained – it was part of his old-fashionedness – a respect for his private dignity.

It was during the preliminaries to *The Book of Beasts* that Michael Howard, then a junior member of the firm of Jonathan Cape, having to query some of White's spelling, received the endearing reply: 'You mention my spelling. Well, I never could spell. On "Isiah" and "diminuitive" I have no opinions. What is wrong with them?' In the spring of 1954 Howard flew to Alderney to help in the preparation of an index.

The large scarlet-sweatered bearded man waiting to greet me looked fairly ferocious, but fun; he bore me off in a flesh-coloured, sagging war-surplus van full of odds and ends and Killie, an excited, adoring red setter bitch. At the house he moved about – with extraordinarily small-footed neatness for so big a man – preparing Killie's food, stoking the stove, glancing at the post, and all the while interrogating me sternly on publishing and personal matters. Suddenly he discovered that I too could fly an aeroplane, and my immediate acceptance was accomplished. We went to work.

That index took far longer than was needed. At any unusual reference, Tim would sit back, gazing for a moment with that piercing blue stare which could soften suddenly to a twinkle, and then musingly begin some outrageous anecdote prompted by his researches into medieval notions of natural history. The fund seemed endless, and we 'worked' together, with a good deal of brandy, far into the night. During those few days we took each meal in a different room, so that the occasional help could clear them all away at once when she came in.

The Book of Beasts was an exceedingly difficult book to put into print. Since February 1952, letters had gone between London and Alderney with suggestions and counter-suggestions, problems, second-thoughts and last-minute alarms – as when the printer 'by a stroke of his own genius stuck nearly a whole page of Lions into Panthers'. At one point a parcel containing one third of White's one and only manuscript disappeared between Alderney and London (it had been pouched by the Customs). Its arrival was announced by a godlike telegram:

FOURTH PARCEL NOW SAFELY RECEIVED ALSO SEVERAL
POSTCARDS STOP AM NOW RETURNED WREN.

Throughout these preliminaries both parties behaved with exemplary consideration and White did not once lose his temper, though his feelings were passionately engaged; for it was by this book, he considered, that his name would endure.

It had been a long ambition. The assignation was made as far back as 1938, in that freezing Norfolk December when he sat reading by the fire in the intervals of goose-shooting – a blind assignation, since at that time the thought of translating the Roxburgh MS had not occurred to him: it was difficult enough to make out its Latin for his own purpose. Then the idea crept into his study of imagination. Puzzling over contractions, tussling with *canis*, invoking Henry Wheeler's Latinity and Cockerell's specialist knowledge (he was always good at knowing what door to knock at: the Greek of the mermaid's expostulation in *Gone to Ground* was supplied by Tillyard), consulting the ancients, comparing Aldrovandus with Pliny and tempering them with applications of Aristotle, stretching his memory, restraining his conjectures ('I have always suffered from conjectures'), he worked on, confident of recognition, both for himself and for the Bestiarist who in his mid-twelfth century had also worked with so much scholarship and application.

> *November 5th, 1954. To L J Potts*
> Well, it is about 17 years' work and it seems to have dropped still-born from the press. Only one big paper reviewed it, the TLS, in which a wretched young fellow busily reviewed himself and misrepresented me. A few minor papers have given short paragraphs saying how funny the book is, in spite of my desperate efforts in the appendix to explain that it was not.

Later, he said that the book would have been better understood if he had turned the appendix into a preface. But the word 'Beasts' carries overtones of facetiousness: the title, combined with the mildly earnest expressions of the animals in the twelfth-century pictures misled people into thinking it a funny book. Afterwards it found readers who could distinguish between amusement and delight, and who were well-read enough to appreciate the wide and unforeseeable range of his annotations. The best summary he wrote himself, in an earlier letter to Cockerell.

> Please help me in this, Sydney, because it is a genuine, though unimportant little bit of useless scholarship on which I have now spent in a scatterbrained way twelve years of love.

'The best thing for being sad is to learn something.' Cast down by the reception of *The Book of Beasts*, White followed Merlyn's advice and began listening to music. He had an ear for tunes, he could play the penny whistle, and soon after coming to Alderney he had bought a harmonium at a sale ('The point', he imparted to Potts, 'is to pump like mad with your feet, but to snatch your fingers off the ivory as quick as possible.') Now he bought a long-playing radiogram – the precursor of the many scientific contraptions, cine-cameras, underwater cameras, recording-machines, washing-machines ('I have bought a new washing-machine and a great many mineral nightshirts to wash in it') which alternately embellished and embittered his later years.

March 20th, 1955. To Lady Sherwill
A most humiliating situation has arisen. It says on the cover that Haydn made a loud noise in the middle of his 'Surprise' symphony to wake up the ladies, but however much I play it I can't find where it is. It all seems equally tedious to me, but I intend to be surprised sooner or later, if it kills me. Could you bring a little gong with you when you come in May, or one of those uncurling things with a feather at the end of it which you blow out at parties, and blow it at the correct moment?

In the main, he liked his music hot and strong, but a letter to Mary Potts ends: 'and slowly, but slowly but slowly I am beginning to listen to the calm mathematics of gentle music. It is like this and like that.' He was lucky with words; but sensibility as well as luck went to that seven-word summary of contrapuntal style.

During that summer he took up snorkel swimming ('an enchanting rockfish lay on its side beneath me, to look up, just like those cheery people on Etruscan tombs – I don't try to kill or catch the creatures, merely to consort with them'); he made cine-films – the first essay at what later became a passion; and when an Admiralty diving vessel came into Alderney harbour, he had a try at diving.

April 18th, 1956. To Mary Potts
Did I tell you that last year an Admiralty diving vessel turned up to amuse itself in our harbour? I got them to let me go down in the whole paraphernalia. It is agony. You know when you see a film of divers they always seem to move slowly, like

old, old men. No wonder. They are carrying about 140 lb of metal – 30 lb of lead, for instance, on each foot and 60 lb round their necks. The deck is strewn with ropes and cords and to step over each one is like jumping a high hurdle. I met another diver at the bottom and we leaned against each other like two amorous manatees, making faces through our glass plates, and when at last I dragged my dropsical body to the top of the ladder my nose was bleeding. One is too old at 50 for these low jinks. On the other hand, it is good for one's soul to put one's life *in other people's hands* once every few years. It was enchanting to be mothered by these tough, tender, bronzed young men. The diver whom they are dressing and whose life depends on their efficiency is always addressed by his title – 'Diver'. 'Sit here, Diver.' 'Now your left foot, Diver.' 'Stand up, Diver.'

I loved being a titled, important person – like being called 'Master' or 'President' at a College – a sort of knight in armour with his attendant, faithful squires.

The assumption of old age seems premature – the more so since a few days after this he fought violently in a public house with one of the vessel's officers. But White habitually overdid his age, and just now he had the incentive of an identification. He had been associating with the same elderly mentor he walked out with in the winter of 1941–2 – that 'tweed-cloaked figure standing motionless in the spray of Rockall'. Alpha, now aged 157, still on Rockall, with his finger on the determining button and Mr and Mrs Charles Darwin's yellowing visiting card on his hall-table, is the hero of *The Master, an Adventure Story*. 'My *Treasure Island* Story', White called it, and dedicated it to Robert Louis Stevenson. It is a *Treasure Island* story to the extent that it is an author's idea of a story he would have enjoyed when he was young. *Treasure Island* was written to please a spirited extrovert, tingling with ballads and romances, socketed in a devoted family. *The Master* was written for a highly-strung introvert, ill-read, insecure, much more of a Shorter Catechist than the Scotch boy, and combating his fears by inventing terrors. But its texture is not adjusted to its terrors; it is too slight to carry the weight of Alpha, and his thunderbolts.

On November 18th Garnett sent White a copy of *Aspects of Love*, his first novel since 1933. The accompanying letter, about Italy, *The Prisoner of Zenda* and the Orient Express, ended:

Well, do get better, rouse, rouse, shake out the great pinions and laugh. I am sending you my little novel. You won't care much for it, I think, but I like it myself.

[On January 1st, 1956 White wrote to Sydney Cockerell:]

I feel dreadful about having been so long in thanking you for *The Best of Friends*. I doubt if you will believe my excuse – it sounds such an eccentric one. About two months ago, David Garnett sent me a present of his new novel called *Aspects of Love*. I am very, very fond of Bunny, but I did not like the book. How was I to write and thank him, while admitting this?

The admission had already been made, but was not yet posted:

November 24th, 1955. To David Garnett

Dearest Bunny,

This is a hateful and stupid letter, but I must face it and write it, otherwise I shall never be able to look you in the face again. First of all, the letter you sent with *Aspects of Love* filled me with such pride and pleasure that I could hardly sleep all night, I was so happy. But second, as you predicted, I *don't* like *Aspects of Love*. I kept fidgeting about and putting it down and starting again, it was only at the bottom of page 144 that light suddenly dawned on me like an atomic flash. You like cats and I loathe them. This is not a *rational* criticism, and God knows I don't claim to be *right* in loathing cats or that you are *wrong* in loving them. It is just an allergy or a misfortune or a numb place in my mind. You must not forget that you were really beautifully educated by loving, intelligent, unconventional geniuses, who were accustomed to move in the highest ranks, while I was brought up by middle-class, conventional people who had been in the Indian Civil Service since time immemorial. I was being caned all the time and made to roll about in the mud with a leather ball, and this, by now, is *ingrained*. The heritage of this is – you will think it quite dotty – but I can't help it – that I believe human beings ought to be monogamous, like those glorious creatures, ravens, swans, eagles, etc – that if they consciously take a solemn vow in public they should stick to it – or not take it – and that women should not behave like head-strong babies. Consequently, to begin at the wrong end first, I see no reason why Alexis should not (at 34) have married Jenny (at 14–15) – provided he meant to marry her and nobody else. As a historian, you know quite well that almost every genius noted by man has, at the age of 99, married a girl of 9 or 10, and made her very happy. Try Napoleon. Then start at the other end. I hate Rose, like a cat, for going to bed with Alexis first, then tossing him over for Sir George, and then taking him and other lovers. Surely women are dependable people as well as men? My adored grandfather on my mother's side was a judge, but not a hanging judge. He would have simply (like old Sir Sydney) have answered your various dilemmas in two ways. He would have said: Number One (a Victorian One): it is unfair to ask one male to spend the money to educate the children of a different male. Number Two: if a woman cannot behave herself according to the laws I have given all my career to, as an Indian Civil Servant – the laws of honour – then take down her crenellated, lace, Victorian pants, and give her one resounding blow with the flat of the hand on the buttocks. In short, I think your Rose is a selfish, short-sighted, self-admirer and a bore. Obviously you don't think so, and neither of us is right. It is the dog and the cat.

Before I end this letter – which is bound to wound you – I must make one other confession. I was truly delighted a week or two ago to learn that Princess Margaret had decided not to marry Group Captain Townsend.

On January 4th, he wrote an alternative letter:

> For the last two months I have been in a kind of trance –
> paying no bills, answering no letters, sending no Xmas cards
> or presents and not even thanking people for theirs. It was a
> mental log-jam, with all my projects at cross-purposes.
>
> One of the first logs in the jam was how to thank you
> for *Aspects of Love* while admitting that I did not enjoy it
> as much as *Flowers of the Forest*. If love is the lineaments
> of gratified desire, where do you fit in the fact that for the
> last 24 years I have loved 2 setters without gratifying any
> desires or feeling any? Yet I have been faithful to them, often
> at inconvenience to myself, and it has been a satisfactory
> relationship of importance to all 3 of us. You see, I am old-
> fashioned. I was brought up in a different background from
> yours. My childhood was spent with Indian Civil Servants
> who had a tremendous sense of duty and fidelity, and it was
> also poisoned by my mother divorcing my father with every
> circumstance of squalor and ferocity. The result is that my
> reaction to your heroine is that she is simply a wilful, selfish,
> promiscuous, empty-headed bitch. No, not bitch. Cow.
> Bitches are faithful creatures like Killie and Brownie.

He then posted both letters together.

January 10th, 1956. From David Garnett

Dear Tim,

> There is indeed a profound difference between us. Your letter
> reveals a medieval monkish attitude. I believe that the sexual
> instinct in normal people is good: possibly the highest good.
> You can find out what I think about fidelity in several of my
> books. It is a large part of the subject of *Lady into Fox* and of
> *The Sailor's Return*. My experience is that an exclusive passion
> as a first love is extremely unusual; most young people are
> more likely to mate well if they experiment a good deal.
> Naturally this was impossible at a time when a different
> standard of sexual morals was expected from women than

from men, and when a high value was set upon virginity and when honour (in women only) was considered synonymous with chastity. This was almost inevitable until the discovery of birth-control. That discovery has liberated women and made them the equal partners of men. It has made love a matter of delight and not of terror.

I intensely dislike the whole Christian attitude to sex and marriage. If the first mating is a success as often happens all is well. But if the partners fall out of love they are penalized by the Church and, in the case of Royalty, by society and if they accept the religious bunkum, they torture themselves and each other. Your remarks about taking down a woman's drawers and beating her smack of flagellation – a perversion which, as you know, is frequent among those who are much caned as small boys, among schoolmasters and judges who have been able to inflict corporal punishment with impunity. But the corporal punishment of women though pleasant for its addicts will not make them live with men they dislike, or give up lovers whom they do. That is over thanks to the Married Women's Property Act.

I have replied to your letter because you might have misinterpreted silence. But I don't intend to discuss the subject further. I have been twice married, have had six children and been the lover of an enormous number of other women, so that my views are founded on a greater variety of experience which you have avoided. Your experience with one human and two canine bitches does not lead me to treat your views seriously. This is not written in ill-temper. Indeed I wish I could come and see you. I would like to convert you to drinking claret, a more important matter than dragging you out of the Middle Ages and the company of the Fathers of the Church.

Unfortunately for such hopes, White had a high opinion of the Middle Ages and did not care for claret. He did not answer Garnett's letter, but referred to it in an invitation of 1957, with 'and bring several of your wives and children', and again in a letter of 1960, telling Garnett: 'Tony Walton read your *Aspects of Love* and the cross letter you wrote to me about it. He agrees with you, not me.'

January 12th, 1956. To Sydney Cockerell
I managed to write to Bunny Garnett about his novel the day I wrote to you – only to get, this morning, a furious letter denouncing me for being a medieval moralist, etc. It has made me feel quite ill. How restful it would be if there were no human beings on the world at all. If there was only a religious order which not only took a vow of perpetual silence but also decided to go to bed for ever, how gladly I would join it.

The aspiration was partially gratified.

March 7th, 1956. To Lady Sherwill
I dived head first down the granite steps in my garden about sixteen days ago, off a piece of ice, and have been in hospital for nine days with a suspected broken neck. All nonsense of course, but I still have a capeline bandage to keep the remains of my skull together and my dear benefactress Maisie Allen has had me to stay with her at Grosnez House since leaving hospital as I am not considered compos yet. It has all been a splendid holiday.

While in hospital, he had thought of the things he had left undone, and set one right by buying a sailing dinghy. This, as he told Cockerell, added a new dimension to his life – the tide.

You cease to be your own master, as you become a waiter-on upon the moon and sun, whose tides take no account of mealtimes or bedtime or times to get up. I am supposed at this very minute to be writing the leading article for the TLS.

This was his review of the first volume of Churchill's *History of the English–Speaking Peoples* – which gave him, he remarked, 'a much worse time than breaking my neck' since it set the problem of how to be civil about a second-rate book by a great man. He felt easier in reviewing Julian Huxley's *Kingdom of the Beasts.* In Huxley's assertion that man is the mammal 'most successful at living' White heard something akin to the accents of that Professor from Cork University (170). Man, he pointed out, has only his own word to go on, and to be most successful at what you happen to be best at doing does not constitute an absolute superiority over the rest of the animal kingdom. With the opening sentence of the review: 'God made man in his own image one Saturday in the year 4004 BC, according to the chronology of Archbishop Usher', the tip of the lever was artfully inserted. Others than Archbishops may turn out to be mistaken. Archbishop Usher was also used to open the review of Dr Gartman's *Man Unlimited*, where White seriously expressed the same mistrust of *homo sapiens*, whose ingenuity at living successfully as a scientist might end with making the world too hot to hold him. This review brought a postcard from Garnett.

> Do you know who wrote that wonderful first article in the TLS this week? It is most admirable; in fact no words can say how good and in some way it reminded me of you.

It could have reminded Garnett of 'The Insolence of Man'. White had come a long way since writing that intemperate treatise, and on the way had learned a great deal; but the journey was consecutive.

It was to Cockerell that he confided that reviewing Churchill had been worse than breaking his neck – a breath of heresy which Cockerell, who after Queen Elizabeth's visit to Alderney inquired with goblin glee in a postscript: 'Was the Queen's visit a flop?', must have enjoyed.

Cockerell now lived in his bed. His precise handwriting grew smaller and smaller. He was fading, but not failing. In the summer of 1956 White had the pleasure of being able to offer him a new item for his collection: G L Cheshire, VC, whom White remembered, though not very distinctly, as a boy at Stowe called Cheese. Cheshire was visiting Alderney. White, in addition to entertaining Jimmy Blaize and the eighty-six-year-old Flodie, Potts and Mary, Michael Howard and Michael's wife Pat, found himself swept into the chairmanship of a local committee to start a Cheshire Home for Incurables in Alderney. 'He has all the characteristics necessary for a saint – obstinacy, fanaticism, charm,' was his comment. Later it was found that Alderney had none of the characteristics necessary for a Home for Incurables, being

at the back of beyond, where none of the essential things like massage and crutches and invalid appliances and hospital apparatus are obtainable and where the cost of living is higher and where the patients don't want to come because their relatives can't visit them.

The alarming vision flickered out. White, pursuing a vision of his own, learned the deaf-and-dumb alphabet. This, fingered on the hand, can also be used for the deaf and blind.

There was a television set at Grosnez House, and White had watched a group of deaf people conversing with their fingers. Of the calamities that come singly he believed that blindness was the worst. But as a child he had observed that at the moment when the guide to the Hastings Caves put out his candle everyone fell silent, intimidated by the total unresonant dark. This recollection came back to him and he began to think what it would be like to live, day after day, neither seeing nor hearing. It became what the Society of Friends calls a concern, what he referred to as 'one of my usual crazes'. He got the address of the Association in Aid of the Deaf/Blind, and sent his invitation.

A Miss Collier, travelling with a guide, came for a week's stay. She had lost her sight and hearing in her teens, but never her interest in life. She had a nickname, Puck.

September 6th, 1956. To Sydney Cockerell
In about a fortnight I will be able to write you a proper letter. At present I am living in an absolute whirl of pleasure or excitement or something, as it turns out that my deaf/ blind friend is an enchantress. We talk together all day on our fingers, as happy as two babies in a bath, and I am determined to learn Braille too. She is in her fifties – but

has remembered colour and music and the lovely sun all that time, and she fills me with such a sense of the wonderful endurance of pitiful man – she is without a morsel of self-pity and makes no parade of her ghastly situation, but is of course rather wistful in an absolutely natural way – a child isolated in the dark for forty years and behaving just as such a child would behave, but with glorious dauntlessness – that as I converse with her on indifferent topics my eyes are pouring with tears, which of course she does not know. But come, I must lay off the sob-stuff. I will tell you all about her in my next letter. Meanwhile I must not waste her short time here doing anything except for her.

To him, finger-talking was a novelty; but as a host he had to provide fresher entertainment. His guest recalls:

As soon as I arrived in Alderney, Tim asked if I liked bathing. I said, yes, very much and I had bought a swimsuit on my way to Croydon but could not swim as I had never had a guide who would do more than paddle. Tim immediately said he would teach me and we started right away and I never gave a thought to being afraid. Tim was a strong swimmer so naturally I left it at that. At first he kept his hand on my head, then, as I got accustomed to the movements, he just turned my head at longer and longer intervals and then only had to turn me around when necessary. We climbed the rocks and did everything.

[On October 12th, 1956 White wrote to Sydney Cockerell:]

I write in great haste and glee to tell you that the deaf/ blind visit was a wild success from start to finish. Fortunately there are some enchanting children who come to Alderney for summer holidays, and I had interested them in finger-writing, so Miss Collier was met at the airport not by one boring old novelist but by 5 children, who seized her hands at once and positively queued to write on them. She told me later it was the first time she had ever been met by children, or almost known children who were not scared of her. We took her sailing in quite a breeze and she personally caught 4 fish, never having been in a boat or touched a live fish before. We taught her to swim! She was avid for sensation of any sort, utterly dauntless, liked the bigger waves, insisted on running on the sand. Try running with your eyes shut and no hearing. Perhaps the highlight of the week – in which everything turned into a series of miracles, in spite of the rain – was a visit we paid to one of the German underground ammunition stores, while her guide was away picking wild flowers. It dawned on me just in time that this was a heaven-sent opportunity to reverse our roles. Quite dark and windowless, here was a chance for her to lead me.

'This must last me for the rest of my life,' she had said, in the bleached voice of the long-deaf. As she was getting into the plane he put a letter – the first he had ever written in Braille – into her hand. He saw her read it, flourish it; it was an invitation to come next summer.

In the first week of the new year, 1957, he wrote to John Verney, whom he had met through the Howards:

I am enchanted with the preview which you have been so kind as to write of *The Master*. It makes me feel it was worthwhile writing the book. Don't you feel, as an author, as if you were quite mad, talking to yourself in a dark room, without knowing that anybody is listening? Now I know that the book has one listener anyway which puts me in great heart.

White had never been good at presenting himself as an author, even to himself. Falconer, sportsman, naturalist, biologist, scholar – his enthusiasms whirled him away from being creative into assumptions of being authoritative. The better informed dismissed him as a smatterer; the uninformed supposed him an expert. In fact, he was neither: he was a man whose enthusiasm had an unusually low flashpoint. Few of his friends had been discerning enough to see, as John Moore did, that he was 'a dead serious writer'. His seriousness was so chemical, so nearly an appetite, that it was barely articulate except when it exploded, as in the fury of his row with Collins or the arrogance of some of the letters with which he flailed his devoted literary agent, David Higham. It was after the row with Collins and the frustration of a fivefold Arthur that Alpha was conjured up, a remedy and a receptacle. It was after the poor reception of *The Book of Beasts* that he reappeared. White's larder was not so bare that Alpha was all he could fetch out of it – it contained, among other things, "The Merlins', an unfinished sequel to *The Goshawk*. If he recalled Alpha it was probably because he needed him. (This is borne out by the extreme concern he showed over the portrait of Alpha which was under consideration for the book's jacket, whereas he had accepted cuts and alterations in the text without boggling.) But in this second identification Alpha is a sadder character and wears his infallibility with a difference; one feels that White resorted to him for some reason less immediate than rage or sense of injury – as if he had recognized a decline of his powers and thought that an identification with Alpha, austere and companionless on Rockall, might rescue him from being that familiar eccentric on Alderney with his old dog and his old car.

XII Alderney 1957–60

In March 1957 he once more began to keep a diary. It afforded companionship; and as he wasn't drinking, or writing, and had got into the winter habit of thinking, he felt the need for a blank page to talk to. But a blank page cannot answer back; it is merely what you make of it. And the resources of his own mind, the inventiveness and prancing exaggerations, were running out. Six months in a desert or a foreign capital could have renewed them; but Killie was old, he could not leave her. Till she died he was irreparably domiciled in Alderney.

Alderney had enforced on him the penalty for being more remarkable than anything he wrote. He had become remarkable for being remarkable – a distinction bound to subside into being got used to. He cared very little for public opinion but acutely about keeping his good opinion of himself. At the thought that he might cease to be unforeseen and surprising to himself, he took alarm, and turned to his natural panacea: he must write. The second entry in the diary is about a possible construction for a book which might be about dogs, or a love-story, or a good thriller – and goes on:

> One of my troubles about writing books – which I loathe doing – is that practically nothing I want to say can be said. Anything I want to discuss in a novel, anything of real interest, confronts me with a sort of introductory course of lecturing about biology or morals or religion.

He had confronted and yielded to the same challenge when writing 'The Book of Merlyn'. There, his heart was engaged as well as his wrong-headedness. Here it was not. But determined to keep his mind in working order, he continued to fill the pages which could not answer back, to question and speculate and be pleased when he learned something new to him, to satirize ('In the 18th century a member of Parliament openly bought votes. So they still do. But in the 18th century they paid the money out of their own pockets, and now they promise it out of mine'), to air his grudges and to disagree. He had plenty to disagree with, as he was living at Grosnez House while his own house was being done up and had the television to fall out with. He was particularly exasperated by scientific Panglosses, who explained how nuclear fission would make the world a happier place as well as a launching-pad from which to hurry to other worlds.

> They are mad to establish satellites or to get to the moon or become masters of outer space, and when you ask them why, why the satellite, why go to the moon, they look mysterious and explain that it will help the motor industry.

On March 20th he 'Got up with the idea of repolishing *The Once and Future King*.' Instead, he went to see how the re-decorating was getting on, watered the greenhouse, bought an old map of the Channel Islands and read Suetonius after tea. 'Augustus wore woolly gaiters, underpants, shirt, four tunics, a woollen gown and a broad-brimmed hat.' The soothing factuality of Suetonius prevailed. The diary grew less acrimonious. On the 26th he noted: 'Back home, cleaning the spring-cleaning.'

March 31st, 1957
The scullery, kitchen and refrigerator passage are spick and span now. All the floors are black rubberoid tiles with a few scarlet squares at random. The walls and ceilings are scarlet, the doors and wall-cupboard a deeper pillar-box red. The stoves, shelves, tables, chairs, movable cupboards and window frames are white enamel. It is like living inside a Guards Sergeant Major, and two polished brass tankards on the mantlepiece give a flash of gold for his buttons.

White was given to scarlet. He wore a scarlet jersey, a red cummerbund, a cassock of scarlet towelling. He filled his garden (and much of his correspondence with Wren Howard) with geraniums: 'Nothing can exceed the *devilry* of Mephistopheles, who leaps out of his trap door in a blaze of scarlet, singing Gounod like mad.' In winter he spent many evenings in his scarlet kitchen, sitting in a battered black horse-hair chair with a writing board on his knee. Though he was house and garden proud, liked things to be handsome and welcoming, bought antique furniture and modern equipment, his improving hand stopped short at his apparatus as a writer. The mean little writing table in his library was of the kind supplied in 'spare-room suites' for guests who take themselves upstairs to write a few letters and be out of the way.

The four Arthur books were going to be published as an omnibus in England and the USA. It was an opportunity for a further revision, and for a change of title (*The Queen of Air and Darkness* had already been substituted for *The Witch in the Wood*).

April 8th, 1957
If I took another dexedrine tablet tomorrow morning, it would stimulate me into setting about The Matter of Britain, but on the other hand I suspect that it would blunt or confuse my sensibilities. You have to be acutely poised and healthy – sort of Inner Cleanliness Comes First – to write well, and I have a deep distrust of artificial stimulants. You feel better, as from drink, but are you better? It is quite a good idea, even for absolute agnostics, to recite the better prayers in the C of E prayer book, before writing. The Matter of Britain will have to be my chef d'œuvre, so I need to be at the top of training for it. The best psychiatrist in the world can't beat the Book of Common Prayer. The only prayer I know which comes up to the Common Prayer Book is the poem in *Under Milk Wood* which mentions 'all poor creatures born to die'. When I say my prayers, I add this one in. I say them as a spiritual exercise, which is possible without believing in God.

April 9th, 1957
Killie did not wake me till nearly 5 am, whereupon I got up, made coffee, said the General Confession and set about The Matter of Britain.

April 17th, 1957
Today, the seventeenth of April 1957, I finished what I hope is my final revision of *The Once and Future King*, about twenty years after I started it, and I believe and hope it is

a great book. It sounds presumptuous to say so, but on a great subject, which is the epic of Britain, you have to write downright badly to make a mess of it.

It must be twenty years since I started off with Arthur, because I began writing the summer after I left Stowe, at the gamekeeper's cottage in the Ridings, which must have been 1937. Or could it have been 1936? It was a very happy summer, and I was a happy man. I had escaped from being a schoolmaster with £100 in the bank and a promise of something like £300 a year for two years. I was free, like a loose hawk at last, *ferae naturae*. I was training a goshawk.

I have been a free man for twenty years. People don't realize this when they see me in the streets. They don't know what a rarity they are meeting. I have been free to get up when I want to and eat when I like and live where I like. I could at this moment get into an aeroplane and set up house tomorrow in Timbuctoo. In theory, in theory, in theory. In fact, I am bound hand and foot like everybody else by taxes and passports and sterling areas and immigration quotas and God knows what other filthy bureaucracies. But so is the Archbishop of Canterbury, and than him [sic], who must breakfast at such a time to open that bazaar and be at such another place to attend this or that diocesan conference, I am at least more free.

On April 23rd he 'staggered out three times, half dead with exhaustion, to see if I could see the comet. I saw Halley's when I was little and want to keep a date with this one.' The next night, he saw it – 'just a smear or brush stroke of the pollen of light across a faint dot of the same. It seemed as if the tail were in front as well as behind.'

April 26th, 1957
How difficult it is for us humans to see things – to use our eyes impartially and affirm what they see. Describing that comet, I had the greatest difficulty in writing that the spot was not at the end of the tail. I knew that comets ought to be stars with horse-tails streaming after them, so I could not

'believe my eyes' that this smear of light had the dot in the middle of it. In drawing the picture of it, I even cheated a bit, putting it so low on the page that the dot could not be in the middle. An impenetrable wall of what I thought I ought to be seeing stood between me and it.

May 17th, 1957
I got up at 6 and by midday had paid all my bills, answered all my letters, including two not quite fatuous fan-mail ones which had been knocking about for more than a year, and sent off the parcel containing the Arthur typescripts. Thus for a few hours I am absolutely level with myself – an extraordinary experience like being a schoolboy again with no taxes to pay, no decisions to make and no debts to anybody.

One obligation was constant. The diary began with:

When Killie dies, don't go on the booze straight away. Go at once to the Battersea Home to investigate that, and try to find out everything possible about laboratory animals.

Killie was thirteen. Her muzzle was frosty, and she could no longer jump on to his bed (he sold it and bought a divan). She was not Brownie, but he was deeply attached to her and as she grew older he fitted his days and nights to her requirements. 'Like Jimmie Blaize with his old Flodie, I try to keep her on the trot till she drops of her own accord.'

He had a particular affection for the old. Of the distinguished people he met at Heytesbury, it was Cockerell he clove to. At Doolistown there was Old Farran, whom he redeemed from the poorhouse, paying the relations a subsidy for his keep at home. On Alderney there was Bender.

He was a Frenchman by birth, and had the peasant's grasping fist. He owned eight houses and two stores before he died, as well as his fishing-boat – a gaff-rigged lugger called the Constar – but to the end of his life he was sailing visitors round the island for money. His detractors said he sailed because he grudged the money to use the petrol in his engine which was untrue. He loved sailing for its own sake. He knew every rock, every eddy, every permutation of wind and wave. He could take you to the cork of a lobster-pot in dense fog, by listening and knowing the time and tide.

And all trades, their gear and tackle and trim.

White was so much of Hopkins's mind that if he had frequented, say, grocers, he would have been enthralled by the skill that knows almost to a grain how much rice to pour into the bowl of the weighing-machine and ties a parcel with the flick of a finger. When he bought the *Popsie*, it was not only to possess a boat. It was to possess himself of a technique and to be closer to the fishermen he admired so observantly.

> What colours sea-fishermen have! In summer their leathery jowls glow to a wonderful chestnut – but in winter, in the icy, briny, finger-numbing sea-toil, their running noses and rheumy eyes and thin-freezing ears and chapped, unhealing, battered hands have all the carmines and ivery yellows and bone blues and colours of the oyster.
>
> The temperature of the lobes of the ears falls to about 68.

On July 6th White, after a careful study of tides and currents, circumnavigated Alderney in the *Popsie*:

> but I wouldn't have done it if I hadn't taken Bender, because at Coque Lihou the outboard engine went to the bottom of the sea. It was a thundery day, and a squall helped us to sail nicely in quite a chop from Coque Lihou to Les Bonfresses before it died away to a flat calm. This left Bender to row with infinite cunning inshore along the Bonfresses and under the lee of Brinchetais round Quenard, cheating the tide, the ground swell gnashing at the jagged rocks and bursting and sucking away from them within feet of us, until we picked up a land wind and the last of the ebb tide somewhere near Sanquet Rock and came fairly spanking home with them.

The summer children of the year before were back again to greet Puck when she arrived on August 6th. She and White had kept up a steady correspondence in Braille. After her departure came a couple called Pat and Queenie. 'Queenie can see just a tiny bit,' he told Cockerell.

> She once owned a house in which they both lived, but she decided she was too handicapped to look after him properly – so she sold the house cheap to some people she thought would look after him better and voluntarily put herself into a home. But they were both so miserable separated that she came out again and they set up together in a new house. They were absolute *darlings*. Very under-educated, and when you are deaf/blind you are liable to get stupider, but they had golden hearts and enjoyed every moment and invited themselves back for next year with determination.

During their stay there was a violent gale. They sat unconscious of the tumult, telling White laborious funny stories.

> The other couple were tragic. It was a mother who brought her deaf/blind son. The mother took one look at me, saw she could shove everything on to me, and retired to bed after vomiting all down the stairs. So I was left to do everything for the youth, who is 21 and has only been deaf/blind for five years. It is said to take about eight years before you accept your fate, and he was still waking up with a shriek in the night, thinking he had gone deaf and blind and finding that he had.

Cockerell took a warm interest in White's deaf/blind, sent money to be distributed anonymously among them, and added Puck to his protégés. His interest was realistic enough to foresee a danger that Puck would fall in love with White. White also had considered this.

> It is a danger which must be accepted as a calculated risk, as it is the least of two evils. The important thing is to give her air in her dreadful predicament, and cross other rivers when we come to them.

Another warning was received more evasively.

> About spoiling these children – please don't forbid. They
> have their parents to keep them in order – and really I don't
> believe that love ever spoiled anything much. Besides, on
> holidays you ought to be spoiled. They have the terms and
> their home-life to get steam-rollered in, and this house is
> to them a place of joy, as they make it for me for these few
> weeks.
>
> Don't forget I am also good for these children. How many
> 12-year-olds do you know who have of their own accord
> learned to write Braille, and deaf-and-dumb and who will
> waste their time on mad-looking old ladies being washed
> about in the sea?

This year, as well as entertaining three lots of deaf-and-blind
visitors, he was housing an overflow of summer children.

September 17th, 1957
Tomorrow my enchanting brace of boys, who have filled
this house with noise, vulgarity, Gilbert and Sullivan and
pure happiness for three weeks, go home to London. It has
been my happiest summer since I don't remember when.
Happiness is a dangerous thing to play with.

September 18th, 1957
I can't write about the important part of this summer,
because I have fallen in love with Zed. On Braye Beach with
Killie I waved and waved to the aircraft till it was out of
sight – my wild geese all gone and me a lonely old Charlie
on the sands who had waddled down to the water's edge but
couldn't fly. It would be unthinkable to make Zed unhappy
with the weight of this impractical, unsuitable love. It would
be against his human dignity. Besides, I love him for being
happy and innocent, so it would be destroying what I loved.
He could not stand the weight of the world against such
feelings – not that they are bad in themselves. It is the public
opinion which makes them so. In any case, on every score

of his happiness, not my safety, the whole situation is an impossible one. All I can do is to behave like a gentleman. It has been my hideous fate to be born with an infinite capacity for love and joy with no hope of using them.

I do not believe that some sort of sexual relations with Zed would do him harm – he would probably think and call them t'rific. I do not think I could hurt him spiritually or mentally. I do not believe that perverts are made so by seduction. I do not think that sex is evil, except when it is cruel or degrading, as in rape, sodomy, etc, or that I am evil or that he could be. But the practical facts of life are an impenetrable barrier – the laws of God, the laws of Man.* His age, his parents, his self-esteem, his self-reliance, the process of his development in a social system hostile to the heart, the brightness of his being which has made this what a home should be for three whole weeks of utter holiday, the fact that the old exist for the benefit of the young, not vice versa, the factual impossibilities set up by law and custom, the unthinkableness of turning him into a lonely or sad or eclipsed or furtive person – every possible detail of what is expedient, not what is moral, offers the fox to my bosom, and I must let it gnaw.

They say they are coming again next summer, to stay in my house all the time this time, which seems terribly unwise. If I can still my heart between now and then, it may be safe.

He could not still his heart. During the next four years he was to live at the mercy of a love which could only be expressed in falsities, which he dared not let out of his sight, which he could not trust, could not renounce, could not forego without sinning against his own nature, could not secure. He was totally involved: his best and his worst, his solicitude for what was young and wild and dauntless and dependent and had to be fed on the best beefsteak, his passion to impart and educate and oversee, his craving which thirty years earlier it had been so

* A. E. Housman, Last Poems, xii.

247

easy to voice in that inquiry to Potts: 'How is Mary? Has she had any of those children yet – of which she promised me one for immoral purposes?' His life on Alderney with its ownerships and neighbourlinesses, above all his success with the deaf/blind, had almost abolished his sense of insecurity. Now it was back, with every ingenuity of suspicion and self-pity, and became paranoia.

Meanwhile, he was only at the beginning, thinking he could reason himself into some sort of order and hoping for a letter.

September 27th, 1957
Went for a spin in *Popsie*, a nice westerly breeze and lovely, blue autumn day, the sea still heaving a little, like somebody after they have been crying. I must get on with the Churchill review, powder Killie, begin fixing geraniums for winter.

The powder was for the canker in Killie's ear. She had an old person's cough and perhaps the delusions of senility. 'She is restless and snaps at nothing in the air above her head.' He took her for patient daily walks, brushed her every night because she enjoyed the feeling, tried to persuade her to eat. When she would not eat the meat he stewed down for her, he ate it himself. He preferred to live as a vegetarian, but when an animal has been slaughtered for food you have a duty not to waste its flesh. He dared not leave her behind, he would not crate her in an aeroplane: Lady Sherwill in Guernsey was asked to put them up for a night before they caught the boat to Southampton. He was going to London to see his analyst and to spend Christmas at the boy's home.

November 6th, 1957
I tried in tears tonight to say the General Confession, but it stuck in my throat. My Father may be Almighty, but he is not most merciful. I may have erred and strayed like a lost sheep, and may have left undone those things which I ought to have done and done those things which I ought not to have done, but I have never known what they were. If there is no health in me, it is not for lack of trying. I am only too

anxious to confess the fault if I can discover it. I cannot be restored to what I have never had, or be penitent for what I don't know I have done. I try to be righteous, I am sober and I am willing to be obedient – but I don't know what to obey.

The analyst told him his case was not extraordinary and put him on a course of hormones. After a brief flare of joy, the Christmas visit fell to pieces. He ran a fever, began drinking again, finally swept out of the house in a rage. Before then, and while he was still his own man, he had been to see Cockerell, and Puck. From London he went to visit some old friends with whom he had a reputation for conviviality to keep up, and from them to the Howards, where he was put to bed and medicined with books and quiet.

March 12th, 1958. To Pat Howard

Dearest Pat,

Thank you for saving my life and curing me of pleurisy and helping me back on the water-waggon and restoring me to some measure of sanity. Last night, all alone here and looking wretchedly at the pile of bills and correspondence, I thought to myself, Oh, let it slide. You are miserable enough already. Let's go out and get drunk. But I remembered the sort of expression you used to put on when you said 'Are you sure you are not slipping?' and was able to stick it out, so I think I am pretty safe on the waggon now, with a little mercy from Fate.

April 1st, 1958. To Pat Howard

My new camera has arrived and I have gone stark staring mad. I put it up on its tripod in the music room and kneel before it actually with trembling hands and worship it and pray to it to be a kind master to me and not to go wrong too often.

I did entertain the mad idea that I might be able to enthuse Zed about it, because thrills are catching, but in calmer moments I see I must not make him a burnt sacrifice to it.

We are going to Burhou to camp there and do as much of the bird film as possible, but if I bore and exhaust him I will let up and bring him back and do the film as best I can myself later alone.

The boy comes from the 19th to the 30th of this month.

Burhou is the main island of an archipelago lying north-west of Alderney. It is uninhabited and in some weathers inaccessible because of the violence with which the Swinge beats in and out of its rocky creeks. It has a seasonal population of puffins who breed in underground colonies. There is a hut for visiting ornithologists or castaways. White had been in an ecstasy of preparation, writing scripts, making lists, checking his equipment, being beforehanded with emergencies, hanging on the weather and tying up parcels. The boy did not catch his enthusiasm. There was a great deal to carry about, long waits for the puffins and the camera to coincide. After a couple of nights they went back to Alderney.

The filming was unsuccessful too. White might pray to his Bolex to be a kind master to him, but he was incapable of being a good servant to anything mechanical. 'The Emitape was making miserable recordings because something had gone wrong, spontaneously, with the engine' are the words of a naturalist, not a technician. But he was bent on completing this film, and returned to Burhou with Killie for sole companion; and except for being unhappy was probably a great deal happier.

May 19th, 1958

The hut, whose lock turned easily this time, was swept and stowed and shipshape, just as we'd left it. It greeted me like home, loved and neat and nothing amiss, a faithful waiter-for-us. Dinner was a fine meal of bread and butter and four hard-boiled eggs and tea with a drop of rum in it. On desert islands you may drink rum. Water is the most precious thing on Burhou. I have one churn of it, to last four days. After that, if we are trapped here, we shall have to filter the green slime and eat gulls' eggs. Hurrah!

The last time I lived alone on an island was on Inniskea. I loved that holy solitude as I love this now. Poor old man, you have to wear spectacles now, to write by the same candlelight as you had in those bright days, to write your poem to the goose-god.

At the beginning of June the first of his deaf/blind guests arrived – the uncongenial couple of the spotted boy and his mother. She had her sight and hearing, but she did not notice that Killie was dying. After they had gone, he had three days more for the last kindnesses.

After her death he did not go on the booze or to the Dogs' Home in Battersea, but to Burhou, where he was honest with his grief.

I did not love her like Brownie. Dear Brownie, you were and still are the most loved thing in my life. When you died, too soon, in my absence, I swore to your dead body that I would buy a second setter bitch as an actual memorial to you. I swore that I would have learned by our mistakes – yours and mine, Brownie –and that I would not make a single one of them with the new puppy and that I would keep her alive to an infinite age and that she should die in my arms. I have kept my promise.

July 30th, 1958. From Sydney Cockerell

Dearest Tim,

Thank you for the greetings telegram you sent me on my ninety-first birthday – it was very kind of you.

I feel I am going steadily downhill. My chief solace during spells of sleeplessness at night is to think of the many friends, men and women, with whom my long life has been blessed. You are in the front rank of these. Let me thank you from my heart for all you have meant to me.

I should like a little news of you.

Yours always,
SYDNEY

White did not answer, though later he sent messages via Puck. He too had been sleepless. Killie was dead and neither Zed nor Zed's mother had sent a word of condolence. 'I try not to think badly of them, but the warm-heartedness of Pat and Queenie and everybody else makes it show.' During Pat and Queenie's stay (they arrived loaded with presents for him) their happiness kept him going; but after they had gone, and still no word of sympathy had come, he brooded and raged and starved and lay awake, noting in his diary that since Killie's death he had lost a stone in weight.

In August Puck came for her third visit, and the summer children were back, filling the house with noise, vulgarity, and a precarious happiness, laughing at the battered old car so that a new one was hurriedly ordered – but did not come in time, since the boy it was to please had to go away early. He was sad to part with his old car, of which Puck had said, after he had apologized for its age and infirmities and the door tied up with string, 'Never mind. It's had a happy life.'

The Godstone and the Blackymor, the last of his books, was to be published the following year. Based on his Belmullet diaries, it was to be illustrated by Ardizzone, who was going to Co Mayo to see for himself. 'How I wish I were going with him,' White wrote to Wren Howard, 'and how I would interfere if I did.' It was planned he should visit the Howards and meet Ardizzone in October. While he was packing, he was felled by an implacable pain. He recognized it. It was stone in the kidneys, which he had had once before. He was taken to hospital and put under morphia.

October 15th, 1958. To Pat Howard
I got your telegram this morning, with much relief. I was afraid you would think I had let you down, or that the usual good-natured friend would have told you I had collapsed with DTs or something.

Being in hospital is a splendid change now and then. It is lovely to be organized by quantities of kind-hearted females in a clean, sterile place – it is our new hospital, the one the Queen came to lay the stone of, and I am one of the earliest patients. We play with the mod cons and long to have a chance to chop somebody up in the operating theatre, which at present still has its maidenhead. Another funny thing is the visitors you get. Tommy Rose I would have expected, because I knew already he was a man of secret good works and perhaps an angel in disguise, which would account for his flying so well, but how was I to know that the laundryman was fond enough of me to come with a jar of apple jelly?

He wasn't likely to know because, as George Rudé noticed at Stowe, he was modest before his social inferiors and did not take it for granted that they would like him. Mrs Herivel, his charwoman, talking to me after his death, said, 'He was well thought of on the island.' It was a commendation he would have valued – and probably never looked for since it would not have occurred to him that esteem could be won by having good manners.

If he wanted esteem for being a successful writer, the summer of 1958 should have gratified him. *The Once and Future King* had been acclaimed on both sides of the Atlantic. In the United States it was on the Ten Bestsellers List for three weeks running. The BBC asked him to write a play for them. He was only perfunctorily elated. It was not till he saw that a play about Mark and Tristram could be a means of analysing his relations with Zed that he began to work on it. His ambition had fastened on films about birds. Summarizing a November visit to England, he wrote in his diary:

Stayed first with the Howards, feeling a bit shaken from the short convalescence but dashing up to London almost every day to see people at the BBC and to try to market the puffin film.

White's cinematography was a classical case of the nay-saying interpolation from the fairy who was not invited to the christening. 'The loud scratchy shambling way a shag moves on the rocks and the distinct rustle of thick, dry plumage with which it takes to the air,' he noted on Burhou, and went on 'like a Victorian mourner at a funeral shaking out her black brolly.' He had a kind of animal sympathy with the animal creation, and with it the sweep of mind, the pounce on the unexpected analogy, which gathered the Victorian mourner into his animal kingdom. (With another such pounce he said when being driven along a lane which, tunnelled under the leafy overhang of hazelwoods, that it was 'like bicycling up the inside of a snake'.) His quickness to see and to transcend what he saw was not confined to the naturalist's territory. His vision fired whatever it rested on; he could have been inventive about a broomstick. He wrote once to John Wyllie:

> Remember Housman's poem 'West and away the wheels of darkness roll'? I must station myself on a sunny day opposite the town clock and take stills every half minute for six hours. Then you would get the shade of the buttress swinging round under the clockface like a pendulum.

He had invention, perseverance, enthusiasm, the means to buy his very expensive equipment. He was neat-fingered. All these gifts were stultified by his inability to come to terms with anything mechanical.

He failed to market the puffin films – there was a plethora of films about puffins, so he was told.

He spent Christmas in bed, running a fever and wretchedly hiccoughing. Sonia Wyllie (John Wyllie's wife), who was staying in his cottage, nursed him. It was she who found him his third red setter bitch, Jenny, whom he did his best to welcome but was careful not to love.

January 22nd, 1959
Began work at last on Sir Tristram and King Mark. May as well keep notes here. What start in all literature could be more terrific than the start of Malory's 8th book? 'It was a king that hight Melodias ...'

This study of Malory's narrative, with its casual 'May as well', is White's last attempt at creative writing. It can justly be called creative. After the first self-regarding impulses to fit himself into the story – 'was it that the peacemaker generally gets it in the neck from both parties, as I have done from X and Y?', to identify the young Tristram who 'came into the field as it had been a bright angel' with Zed and King Mark with himself and to establish a love-hate relationship between them ('Had he been deeply in love with the boy and never forgiven him for growing up?') – he gave his mind to the analytical collaboration with Malory which had shaped *The Once and Future King*. There was the character of King Anguish to determine: 'A bit of a pander. Easygoing? A bon vivant? A Dublin type?'; and the age of Sir Palomides and why King Mark should choose black armour and a black horse when he wanted to be secret on a moonlight night. There were problems: 'If Palomides was in armour when he had the fall in the river, why didn't he drown?' and awkward passages: 'Isould la Blanch Mains was Tristram's step-aunt.' There is an unmistakable creative fling in his 'NB And so must Alice la Beale Pilgrim be cut. It is, as Malory would say, "Overmuch to rehearse". Let them go off to their country of Benoye, and live there in great joy.' The escape and exhilaration of this is like a changed wind rising.

As usual, he worked as fast as a greyhound.

February 20th, 1959
I begin to feel today that I know how to handle the Tristram story, and even felt that I was beginning to feel well enough to want to write it. Perhaps it ought to be in three books – the first ending with the forgiveness of the step-mother, the second ending with the imprisonment of King Mark and the third ending the whole thing. The overall title of the 3 books, which will eventually have to be published in an omnibus volume like *The Once and Future King*, might be called *The Sad One*.

He had quite forgotten the play for the BBC.

But play or trilogy, "The Sad One' ended there. The seed had fallen on a sick mind. Weeds sprang up and choked it.

Under the same date, though in a different volume, he wrote:

Today the Lit Editor of the *Sunday Dispatch* flew over to interview me about the Lerner and Loewe rumour. Everybody seems to think it will make me a millionaire.

This was the musical, *Camelot*. He had known for some months that Lerner and Loewe were considering following *My Fair Lady*, their Broadway wonder based on Shaw's *Pygmalion*, by a musical deriving from *The Once and Future King*. This had made so little impression on him that 'Lerner and Loewe' is interlined above a crossed-out 'Rogers and Hammerstein'.

News of *Camelot* poked up the comatose Disney project to make a cartoon version out of *The Sword in the Stone*, and this poked up White's resentment at the twenty years' inertia since the screen rights had been bought. When the *Camelot* contract arrived he read it censoriously, misunderstood a restrictive clause and refused to sign. His agent David Higham flew to Alderney to reason with him.

April 10th, 1959

He told me that their previous musical of Shaw's *Pygmalion* had made for Shaw about $400,000 already, and was expected to make another $400,000. He said I was getting the same terms.

It feels strange to be the possible earner of $800,000 – but there's many a slip. I refuse to be elated until I have it and when I do have it (if) it will probably be a nuisance and a danger.

At about half-past six I suddenly began to feel excited – as if I might rush out and celebrate with a drink. But what on earth about? As the owner of a quarter of a million pounds, I would only have a great many more forms to fill up.

As the owner of a quarter of a million pounds he would still have been destitute.

March 1st, 1959
If I had no insight into my condition, really I would say I was insane. I am in a sort of whirlpool which goes round and round, thinking all day and half the night about a small boy – whom I don't need sexually, whose personality I disapprove of intellectually, but to whom I am committed emotionally, against my will. The whole of my brain tells me the situation is impossible, while the whole of my heart nags on. It is like having a husband and wife inside myself, who can't agree and quarrel all day. What do I want of Zed? – Not his body, merely the whole of him all the time. It's equivalent to a confession of murder.

April 12th, 1959
David [Higham] rang up in the evening, asking if I would go to London to discuss the new wording of the contract if they sent a charter plane to fetch me and bring me home. I said no. I am being bloody.

The next day, however, he consented, signed the contract, and was flown to Southampton to make his affidavit before the American Consul. 'The nicest thing about today was that the Dove, on taking off, lifted her wheels very stylishly when she was only a couple of feet up … the lovely legs folding into the tail, just as a gull does.' The succeeding entry begins: 'A busy day doing sensible things with all this fantasy of money put away.'

C Northcote Parkinson, who was on Alderney at this time, relates in *A Law Unto Themselves* an incident not recorded elsewhere:

He had the bachelor's confidence where children are concerned, and once offered to adopt my son, Charles, whose parents, he felt, were unequal to the task of playing Merlin to Charles's Arthur. Our unvoiced objections to this plan included a doubt as to whether the ideal guardian should be alternatively marooned on a rock or drunk in his studio.

257

With no child to spend them on, White's riches taunted him. His character was immediate, he had to see to things himself; large donations to the NSPCC were no answer.

The Godstone and the Blackymor (titled in the USA *A Western Wind*) was published in June. His original suggestion for the title was 'Portrait of White as a Confused Person', but this was when he contemplated enlarging the book by other pieces of autobiography. In the end, it was decided to keep it Irish. Some of the material comes from his diaries, some, like 'The Fairy Fire', from recollection. The first story, 'Losing a Falcon', is recollection embellished. Fraoch is Sheskin, where the defeat of his ambitions was so mortifying that at the time he gave it little more than a bitter mention. He had been led to expect a great many grouse. There were very few. The dearth of the grouse becomes:

> At Fraoch, where the rare, crafty and ancient grouse used to hobble about on crutches or sit before their heather cottages smoking broken clay pipes, with steel-rimmed spectacles over their rheumy eyes, spitting in the turf ashes and exchanging folklore about Niall of the Nine Hostages …

It is an instance of how by grace of technique wrongs will repent to diadems. It is also an instance of that *holde Leichtsinn* which Goethe said was given in compensation to mankind. White, for all his emotional turmoils, was always capable of being surprised by joy. He did not make it a matter of conscience to hoard old misfortunes.

Potts, writing to praise, remarked that the book was carelessly printed and gave a list of errors. He also gave a list of Irish words and place-names whose exact pronunciation he wished to know. Later in the letter he mentioned that he had had a heart attack.

> I don't mind dying, and I can put up with pain; but I have a distaste for the idea of pain for the rest of one's life. Oddly enough, I never thought of that.

White commented in reply:

As I get older myself, bits keep falling off, like an old car, but one can't do much about it. In some ways it will be a relief to be dead – no more spare parts to fuss about, and think what a rest too! Curse you for sending me this list of pronunciations.

He then obediently supplied them. It was the last exchange of letters between them.

The deaf-blind visitors came: first the boy and his mother, which was hard going, then Pat and Queenie. They hugged him, they caught fish with shrieks of joy, they went round the town buying presents for all their friends. His fingers grew so tired with talking that by the evening he could scarcely hold a pen. After he had got these grey-haired children to bed, he read Josephus. 'It is a pleasant fact that the Holy of Holies in the Temple contained absolutely nothing.'

July 13th, 1959
Got to the airport just in time to hug Puck out of the aeroplane. Spent the whole afternoon on the beach with her, telling her the news. Came home to show her Hadrian's Temple and the swimming pool. I told her the Hadrian story, rather expurgated. Now she is busily writing it home on my Braille machine, while I cook Jenny's supper.

At intervals in his private desperation he had admonished himself with the example of Puck, so infinitely more deprived than he and never dramatizing her lonely, cheerful self-sufficiency. Not till the next day, when all the other news had been imparted, did she tell him she could no longer see even the glimmer that had been her sun. His condolence was practical: he fed her up. With Maisie Allen's cooking, and sea air and kindness, her health improved and by the end of her visit she could distinguish the glimmer again. It proves how unaffectedly he fitted himself to her infirmity, that he could 'show' her the temple and the swimming pool.

These embellishments to the garden had been started the autumn before. The temple, with its columned front and small-scale grand manner, made an acknowledgment to Stowe. It was nameless in its newness and whiteness till June 6th.

> At night in bed, in the intervals to myself, I have been reading Marguerite Yourcenar's superb book about Hadrian. Last night, in floods of tears, I got through her version of the Antinous tragedy. I shall dedicate the temple we are building in the back garden to Hadrian.

The ceremony of dedication took place in August, when the habitual summer holiday visit was being paid.

> To the arches lighted dimly blue Zed entered alone in my red bathrobe which made him look tall and stately. He did the whole thing alone, I being only in charge of the lights. He bowed first to the star Antinous in Aquila, then brought out the vessels of Greek honey, Samian wine, salt, unleavened bread, and with these anointed the name **AΔPIANO** in its large, Britannic, copper letters on the floor. He prostrated himself. The bust of Hadrian, under a black velvet cloth, was hidden behind its hollow plinth. He put the vessels and Yourcenar's book and the sestertius into the plinth, put on the coping stone, hoisted the bust into place, unveiled it, put one rose before it, stood back with grace and gravity and dignity and said the Greek words τωι θηωι αδριανωι αγαπητωι και αειμνηστωι [sic] in a loud slow firm voice. Meanwhile the blue light had been growing and increasing through all the columns till the whole temple was a blaze of light, and so he bowed, and all the lights went out except a candle in front of the bust, and we all jumped into the swimming pool.

White was a tall man. The red bathrobe would have looked grotesquely ample and trailing on the 'small boy' whose image had obsessed him for the last two years. In rational moments, White renounced the dream of being an all-provider to a fledgling tiercel and looked forward to paying his fees at Cambridge.

The summer, the long flawless summer of 1959, drifted to an end. In his empty house White drank in order not to be sober.

October 28th, 1959

My leg is beginning to pack up, as it does in autumn and spring. I begin to regard myself as a sort of old bore I live with. He has handicaps and hobbies.

In September he had had to pull himself together and exhibit the old bore and his habits for a television interview in the BBC 'Monitor' series. Though he commonly called television 'The Idiot's Lantern', he cannot altogether have disliked this, for he accepted an invitation to appear in the televised *Julie Andrews Show* on November 11th, when he would meet the chosen leading lady for *Camelot*.

After his return to Alderney he wrote in his diary:

I arrived most dubious, and breathing fire against all 'theatricals', 'cue-merchants' and other artificial people. Also I arrived believing I could ad-lib till the cows came home and need have no more to fear than I had from 'Monitor'. Quite soon, it became evident that I was going to be part of a highly artificial piece of genuine workmanship and would smash the whole lot – including all the other performers – unless I adapted myself to them. When I realized this I was more terrified than I have ever been in my life. I had a piece of business in which I had to snatch the long woolly pants off a clown. On cue for this, I found my heart was literally thundering at my ribs, enough to shake down the studio.

Besides, Julie was plainly a darling person.

One thing that began to save me was watching while the clown and Julie rehearsed their dialogue with professional skill. I saw that it was just another technique – another thing to learn. I have always adored learning techniques.

Julie and her husband [Tony Walton] want to adopt me as a son – my age is equivalent to both theirs put together – and I am to spend Christmas with her and they are to stay here when they want a rest.

It was his first experience (he really had led a singularly secluded life) of stage people and the camaraderie which flowers from their dedicated lives. Delighted to have something he could safely brag about, he wrote to Garnett:

> I bet I had a better Christmas morning than you did. I spent it with Julie and her husband the impresario, opening the various tiaras, Cadillacs, etc, which we had put in each other's stockings.

(She had put red tights in his.) He was still under the spell when he got home and set about preparing for their visit.

February 11th, 1960
A general clean-up. It feels strange to be in a warm, dry, tidy house with everything up to date for the time being, solvent.

He was certainly solvent.

White's finances baffle inquiry. This is not because he did not refer to them. But his references are no real guide because he had no consistency about figures: £200 will re-appear as £300 or £100, and all his figures are round. (In his last years he carried this into his payments by cheque, reckoning to the nearest nought: a bill for £27-odd would be paid as £30, a bill for £24 19s 6d as £20.) Nor are his expenditures much guide to his means. He bought extravagantly, as for his Stowe Ridings garden, when a cabbage was making him a good dinner. This makes it impossible to conjecture, for instance, what a legacy of £1,000 from two old ladies who saw him as a boy at St Leonards was spent on, whether he bought a car with it or a horse, spent it on books, firearms or settling his debts; for that matter, it may just as well have been £100. His one mention of it is retrospective, in a diary of the 'fifties. One can only say that for the first thirty years of his life he was poor, that his first Book of the Month award made him temporarily rich, that in the interval between that and the next he grew poor again and that a few years after the second enrichment he observed that he must somehow make enough money to pay his Income Tax – a statement which usually indicates some degree of wealth. He was an easy spender and not purse-proud; but he was retentive of what he considered his own and righteously indignant about a taxation system which extorts the full tax on the earnings of a fat year regardless of the lean years that preceded and might follow it. It was to evade this (when he had already paid the USA tax on *Mistress Masham's Repose*) that he moved to the Channel Islands.

In 1959 the impending profitability of *Camelot* threw him into a fever of contrivance: he planned against it as Mr White of Burkestown planned against the Flood. His first thought was to become a company situated in the Channel Islands. But there was a flaw. The reciprocal treaty between Great Britain and the United States under which, if he had remained in England, he would not have had to pay USA tax, did not, by some maladroit oversight, extend to the Channel Islands. His next idea was to sell the *Camelot* rights to an English company, 'which I would form. I would be the director and chief shareholder of the English company, with one other nominal shareholder.' Counsel's opinion was taken on this, and was adverse. 'He expressed the fear that – in view of the large amount of money possibly involved – the Inland Revenue might try to attack it.' After further legal and expert opinion (one of the experts met White, in true *Elephant and Kangaroo* style, 'quite by chance on a remote cliff in Alderney') there was a new plan.

> White is about to form a company in Liechtenstein which will become the owner of all his works. All monies from the States will be channelled through an organization in Switzerland. This is a company set up some time ago to take care of just this sort of thing.

In the end, the company in Liechtenstein was thought superfluous and the ownership of White's works passed into the hands of the organization in Switzerland, which itself was dependent on a company registered in Curaçao. Peace of mind was secured and the Inland Revenue foiled; but at a price. White's earnings being channelled into Switzerland they had to be channelled out again before he could enjoy them. In October 1960, shortly before the Boston opening of *Camelot*, his literary agent confided to his publisher: 'Tim's desperate for money in order to go across.'

This was not all that resulted from *Camelot*.

The Christmas hospitalities, the theatre-goings and parties, had been enlarged to take in Zed, whose dazzled enjoyment made him thank White for 'the most wonderful holidays I have ever had'. His father took alarm. He wrote to White, asking him to be more circumspect about exposing Zed to the limelight of *Camelot* pre-publicity, and stipulated that at future meetings a third person should always be present. White wrote back agreeing. He knew that the decision would rest with Zed. Whatever the decision, his love would still be thwarted. What he wanted was that equivalent to a confession of murder, 'merely the whole of him all the time'. He felt no guilt; the relation had been a gay, shameless consent in enjoyment.

> The love part, the emotional bond, is the agonizing one – and this I have spared him. I never told him I loved him, or worked on his emotions or made any appeals or forced the strain on him.

The boy would come in August. Pat and Queenie were due in July. A few days before their arrival White had a bout of pain which was thought to be gall-stones. It was the oncome of an attack of shingles – an affliction which Dante took seriously enough to include eternal shingles among the pains of hell. White did not take it seriously enough to put off Pat and Queenie.

July 12th, 1960
There are far too few discriminating words for the kinds of pain like ache, twinge, etc. Your teeth and perhaps your head ache – slowly, unvaryingly, on rather a high pitch. The pain of stone in the kidneys is a tremendous one, but heavy, deep, massive like lead, dull, total and again unvarying. There are no stabs about it. It is there steadily, like a cannon-ball in your belly. The pain of beating (on the buttocks) flames and shrivels and leaps in crescendos. It fills you and dies down. *Tic douloureux* stabs. Broken limbs ache unbearably but vary in waves. You can have waves of pain or stabs of pain or stolid pains that never alter. You can have location pains, deep or

superficial or sub-surface or all of these. There are flashing ones which strike you down with a fulmination. There are slow aches which you only recognize by time. There are pervasive ones and local ones. The pain of shingles is a penetrating or convecting mixture of aches or soreness. It is a nagging pain, not noble like kidney stone or leaping like a beating or searing like fire or life-killing like bad toothache or shooting like the touched-nerve stab of a tooth, but petty and altering and unrelenting though moving from one situation to another, like a woman scolding all night. Also it has several sometimes simultaneous kinds, an ache, a discomfort, a twitch, an irritation, all very subfusc and variable and rising and falling (the ache increases or diminishes) and ignoble. Kidney stone is a steady, quiet Colossus – you can almost love him, certainly give him homage and respect. Fire, cane, touched-tooth nerves and others certainly make you jump to attention. They are great as far as that goes, at all events they have authority. But this bloody ceaseless shingles is a petty torturer who goes from here to there with mean variations, never a great tyrant or ruler, but a hired assistant (3rd murderer in plays) who slinks about with his ceaseless, varying, mean repertoire of torments. Stab? yes. Twinge? yes. Ache? yes. Even itch. And he goes on all night.

It is 6 am and soon I can get up and take the d/b some morning tea.

He was not properly recovered when Zed and his train arrived, but he resolved to put his best foot foremost. There was a great deal of junketing and outlay and ceremonial revelling, an entertainment in the temple of Hadrian, the largesse to be expected from a host so much richer than before. Perhaps the fact that everyone was a year older provoked comparisons with previous summers. After spasmodic illusions of happiness as usual White realized that he no longer had the same power to please.

A young girl, Tony Walton's sister, Carol, was invited, to supply Zed with a companion of his own age. She arrived after the others and was still there when they left. To amuse her, he took her for a trip to Cherbourg. On their return he found a letter from Mary Potts which began: 'Almost the last thing James said to me was, The thing I really wanted to do on this holiday was to write to Tim.' He held out the letter, and asked her to read him the rest. It was her first encounter with an adult grief.

The tenth item of the entertainment in Hadrian's temple was: 'Scene from *Macbeth*, Lady Sherwill, Tim.' This was so outstanding, if only because both actors knew their words and were sober enough to speak them, that it was decided that a production of *Macbeth* must be the feature of August 1961 (the visitors took it for granted that having come so often they would come again: a flattering testimony to White's hospitality though he once confided to his diary that he was tired of being treated as a bathing-machine attendant). When Puck, his final visitor, had gone he combated his autumnal melancholy by writing 'Macbeth the Knife', an adaptation condensed for a small cast and an audience who wouldn't want to sit out the whole thing. He was full of excitement. After failing with puffins on Burhou, filming, English literature, it seemed that with theatricals he had at last found something where Zed would share his enthusiasm.

October 22nd, 1960
If Zed is not allowed to come and help with this major undertaking, which is for him, for at least a week at Christmas and at Easter – it is impossible to do without proper rehearsals – I shall tell them not to come in the summer either, not at all.

Paranoia cheats its harbourer by all the times it has cried, 'Wolf, Wolf!' White had long suspected Zed's parents of plotting against him. He saw that Zed, growing older, was growing away from him. Yet when Zed wrote that he could not promise for Christmas and Easter, White replied, 'Then I'm afraid you had better stay away for good.' Trusting in his blackmail he went to London. At his hotel he found a letter from the boy who agreed that it would be better to stay away for good.

XIII Alderney, Florence, Naples: 1961–63

On November 21st he flew to Boston.

After rehearsals in New York – in course of which Julie Andrews wrote propitiatingly: 'You'll love King Pellinore's dog – a marvellous red-eyed sloppy basset-hound – called "Horrid". And even she has an understudy!' – *Camelot* was taken to Toronto and then to Boston to be tried out before opening on Broadway. Bob Downing, production stage-manager, remembers that painful time.

> Our behind-the-scenes troubles started with our concern for Bob Loewe, who had suffered a heart attack not long before rehearsals began in the summer. Alan Jay Lerner fell ill early in the engagement in Toronto, suffering dangerously from internal bleeding caused by ulcers. No sooner was Alan somewhat stronger than Moss Hart was stricken with an almost-fatal heart attack, which took him away from us as director for the rest of the out-of-town try-out. In Toronto, lacking the artistic directors of our project, we simply played and played the hulking show, which lasted more than three hours and must have bored the pants off our viewers. It was simply frightful to play that long, unsatisfactory behemoth of a show week after week – with none of the rehearsals a company expects out of town, because there was no one to rehearse them. There were peripheral disasters. Our wardrobe mistress's husband died; our chief electrician was stricken almost fatally with some sort of internal ailment and rushed to hospital; another electrician was bashed on the head by a falling plugging-box and nearly killed; a dancer ran a needle through her foot and almost died of blood-poisoning. Had it not been for the fact that Julie Andrews and Richard Burton understood (thanks to their British theatre training) the importance of stars behaving as 'heads' of a company, we might have suffered complete demoralization. The arrival of Timmy White in Boston was the turning-point.

Even when paced and trimmed down, *Camelot* did not have the first night that had been hoped for. There was too much of it, and too many things had been aimed at. The critic of the *New York Post* wrote:

> It was the ambitious endeavour of *Camelot* to be at once a musical romance, a satire, a fantasy and the wistful tale of an idealistic young king whose dream of bringing about a wiser and better world is shattered by mankind's frailty and stubbornness. All of its elements contain lovely and imaginative things, but they are seldom fused successfully, and it often seems that several fine musical plays are fighting for recognition, interrupting and getting in each other's way.

It is an interesting criticism; for the statement of what went wrong in the musical is an acknowledgment of what goes right in the book.

A press photograph taken during the supper after the first night shows White between the blissfully exhausted Julie Andrews and Richard Burton opening a bottle of champagne. He is not only almost unrecognizably well barbered and well attired; his expression is totally grave.

December 10th, 1960. To Sydney Cockerell
The reviews of the Musical have been mixed, but it will survive under its own power. I have pretended to everybody that I am perfectly satisfied with this new version of my book, as it is a corporate effort which involves many people, some of whom I love, and it is up to me to put a shoulder to the wheel. Financially, I am indifferent to the profits, as I have no kith or kin to spend them on and no ambitions for myself. But I do have a sort of obstinacy about claiming them and not being robbed by the Income Taxers.

Julie is as always enchanting beyond words and Richard Burton, who plays Arthur, is a great Shakespearian actor from the Old Vic. I have been totally accepted by every member of the cast and every stage hand – even by Lerner and Loewe themselves – and spend every performance crawling over every corner of the theatre to find out how the wheels go round. If I were less miserable in my private life, I would be a very happy man.

If at that point he had done what in 1947 he wrote to Cockerell about doing, and found that log cabin 'near the Columbia river, where I could catch fish and shoot pine grouse and be snowed up in winter and mosquito-bitten in summer' and where the only thing he would miss would be the London Library, he might have cut himself free. But he had not the courage to give up all hope. Before the New Year he was back in his desolate well-appointed house. There he lay alone with his devils, like the red-haired woman whose story he wrote down in his diary on July 18th, 1939 – so fully that it is almost as though some foretelling instinct had warned him that one day her wretchedness would be relevant to his.

March 10th, 1961
Still mostly in bed, with a bottle of brandy a day. In my heart I accuse and excuse alternately.

He had been as bad before, but never for so long. Maisie Allen fetched away the dog and looked after it. Mrs Herivel cleaned the house, her ears pricked for a footfall. 'When Mr White had one of his spasms' was the loyal phrase she used to me about times like these. Fragments of ordinary life, as when he heard the lawn-mower in the garden, emerge in the diary: they are all methodically dated. For the rest, alternately accusing and excusing, he composed letters to be read after his death and posted one or two attempts at a reconciliation with Zed which were rebuffed or ignored.

In May his attentiveness to the calendar reminded him of the deaf/blind. 'These people have to be attended to, however one feels.' He remembered that when he visited Mary Potts in November (it was after this visit that he sent her £200 to repay Potts's anonymous contribution towards sending him to Italy – his accompanying letter was the first she heard of it) she had spoken of coming to help with them. 'Do you still feel the same? You and I could get in quite a lot of our conversation, because you can talk across or about them as if they were pieces of furniture.'

He met her, walking with a limp. When an Admiral went by, also walking with a limp, White's became statelier; but when they went to Burhou it did not prevent him leaping from the boat on to a rock. This was in keeping with the Tim she knew. Not so his appearance. He was sallow and puffy and his nerves were in pieces (he always felt at his worst when he had forced himself back on the waggon). Another thing in keeping with the Tim of the past was that he had asked her to bring Potts's copy of 'Rather Rum'. This much-read book was now read by the Howards. White wrote a foreword to it, and rewrote the foreword, and in the end decided against publication. The time was gone by. But he kept a tenderness for it. 'It might be worth printing as a curio, the year after I die,' he wrote to Pat Howard.

The calendar reminded him of another obligation: the birthday cheque for £5 he was in the habit of sending to his first cousin once removed, Timmy Lane. It was an easy date to remember, since it was his birthday, too. May 29th, 1906, May 29th, 1947.

White was interested in heredity. He traced his own easy standing with animals to his father, who artlessly killed, loved and was loved by them, and could get on with any animal except his wife's dogs. In the spring of 1957 Ruth White – the Aunt Ruth who befriended his childhood – sent him a cutting from a Leicestershire newspaper. It showed her grandson Timmy Lane with the nestful of young hedge-sparrows he had reared by hand. Pleased with this emergence of a family trait in a new generation, White sent the boy a book. His mother recalls that:

> Timmy happened to be in bed at the time, and so wrote quite a long letter telling Tim about all his animals and birds and saying he was hoping to have a Corgi soon. Tim immediately wrote back sending him £5 which he said he hoped would do for the Corgi.

The two naturalists continued to correspond, with Christmas

and birthday cheques reciprocated by presents which were always just what White wanted, invitations to Ambro Mill, Derbyshire, invitations to Alderney. To the invitation of 1961, White replied:

> I will try to fit in a visit, if your mother will let me. As a matter of fact, it's perfectly mad not to come here, as the sea is the right place for the summer, and you could bring your mother or somebody. But perhaps I ought to come on approval first.

A fortnight later, Mrs Charles Lane rang up to ask if he really wanted her son as a visitor. Her proposal showed a magnificent disregard of anything being on approval. Timmy would travel on the plane from Derby and be met in Guernsey by Tim (still Terence to her). After a week in Alderney they were to fly to Orly Airport, where the Lane family, holidaying in France, would meet them.

Peter Lane, the elder brother, was one of the party.

> I think the first thing that struck anybody when meeting Tim was his stature and sloppily dignified appearance. It did not matter how he was dressed, he always looked the part of a rather eccentric, very wise author. The first time I met him was at Orly Airport. He met us there with 'our' Timmy, who had been staying with him, and came on holiday with us. His first words were, 'I have been ordering Timmy about for the past week and now I hand everything over to you.' In actual fact, most of the arranging and the language and the things-to-be-seen were left to him because it became increasingly obvious that his worldly knowledge was far in excess of ours and most things were much better left to him. He also said he had £250 so at least we would eat. We were aghast at this huge sum of money that he mentioned with such nonchalance. But we were to realize later that he thought of money just as a means of getting something else, not as anything in itself.

> He was an extremist and did nearly everything in extremes.

Things he did, and wanted either to do or to learn to do, he did very well and practised very hard at them. Things he did badly, he did very very badly. He was uninterested in mechanical things such as cars and had not the faintest idea how they worked.

I think he was a very lonely man for a lot of his life. Sometimes he completely disregarded everybody else and temporarily had no need of them. Other times he clutched on to something that brought him happiness and the feeling of being wanted and needed.

These are the recollections of someone interested in how things work. The younger brother is objective.

Tim was always good fun to be with as he would always have thrilling ideas, but you would have to be very enthusiastic about them or he would take offence.

He was always very kind, generous and an expert with animals.

If he was going to like or dislike a person he would do so almost at first sight.

He tried to dominate me a bit too much, but even so he broadened my outlook on life greatly. He was very youngish in his ways and I think he would have made a good mod. He approved more of things he suggested rather than good suggestions from other people, which he pretended were no good.

About this date people began to say that White's money had spoiled him, that it had made him overbearing and forgetful of his old friends. But it was his old self he wanted to forget, and the better days of those friendships: to be more remarkable for what he had than for anything he did was a come-down-in-the-world. As for being overbearing, the tendency to take charge of everything, set everybody to rights, impose his judgments and feel a martyr's wounded self-importance when they were rejected, was inherent in his character. His money may have made people more observant of it but it was always there – an inheritance from his mother, as was the vehement possessiveness which had oppressed his childhood and in turn made children find him oppressive.

A great many things changed hands as a result of the meeting at Orly. 'I gave Timmy my watch and my dinghy *Popsie* and an alligator and a Chinese rat and a red squirrel,' he noted in his diary; and later received the reassuring news: 'Your watch is going very well.' To some extent White himself changed hands. 'You can't think how nice it is to have a family to write to at last,' he wrote to Mrs Lane in a letter of October 1961, after he had stayed at Ambro Mill; and in another, 'Can you remember what year my father died in? Where is he buried?' Even if circumstances had not made him a displaced person, he would have become one by choice and temperament; but some part of him had remained homesick for the circle he was born into.

The Lane family included two daughters. 'Girls baffle me,' he explained to their mother, conscious that he had not been much of a cousin to them (and in a letter to John Verney he recalled meeting a Miss Verney, 'who had been ordered by you to go out and catch a pony', and his uneasy surmises 'when she fixed me with her basilisk, pony-club eye').

In the case of the two Miss Lanes, he fell back on a traditional expedient: he wooed them with party frocks from a London modiste; but more practical than most such wooers, added, 'What about shoes, stockings, etc?' He also bought the equivalent of a party frock for himself, to wear when Peter and Timmy Lane spent a play-going week in London with him. From London he wrote to their mother:

> We have been to two first nights. At the second I wore my opera cloak (no, it is white satin inside) with plum-coloured velvet smoking jacket, pumps with bows, white gloves, ebony stick and black Sherlock Holmes hat! Charles won't believe this, but I didn't look *outré*. If you are tall enough and fierce enough and fat enough, you just look impressive.

The ebony stick was grim necessity. If Julie Andrews had not become the daughter-in-law of a surgeon and physiotherapist, White might have gone on putting up with the condition he referred to as 'White's leg' until it gangrened. When Mr Walton visited Alderney in September, White consulted him about his lameness. Mr Walton gave him massage and suggested a course of treatment for White to go on with. The treatment included giving himself injections, touching his toes and rolling on the floor. He did all this, and dieted to get his weight down. But his foot remained numb. On further advice, it was decided he should go to St Thomas's Hospital for an operation. The operation was postponed. The surgeon who was to perform it was not satisfied that White's lameness (intermittent claudication, to name it with respect) was entirely due to arterial blockage. 'He said I could very likely bring it on by worry, unhappiness, etc. I have always maintained this.'

He went back to Alderney, where he was alone, with the broken heart in the calf of his leg for company. 'I have no news,' he wrote to Carol Walton. 'I get up at 7am and touch my toes and live on Limmits and paint all day.' White was usually at a low ebb when he turned to painting (when painting failed, he knitted). He was now engaged in retouching a commissioned portrait of himself which grinned back at him, prosperous and rosy, like a fraudulent Father Christmas. Worse lay in wait. He had to fix a date for the postponed operation; and because if he spent more than three months of a year in England he would be liable to pay Income Tax and because he'd be damned if he did so, he had to look up dates in his diary. The dates in his diary led him to other dates – the pitiable few weeks of Zed's company, the gaunt stretches of time in between. He fell back into the pit.

He was helped out of it by the return to Alderney of the old friend who had seen his arrival there, with Killie straining ahead of him.

March 23rd, 1962. To Carol Walton
I have got a new secretary /gardener/handyman who is doing great wonders with the garden and swimming pool. He was a Lt-Commander in the war, in which he was blown to bits,

one result being that he is now diabetic and I have to keep
lumps of sugar for him. His wife is an old flame of mine
who used to fly Spitfires as a ferry pilot. Now they are broke,
having failed to make good in S Africa, so Harry Griffiths
(his name) is on my payroll.

Harry Griffiths might have been sent in answer to the prayers of
White's friends. He did not attempt to manage White, but he
steered him. He didn't expostulate; he didn't deplore; he didn't
take sides and avoided being swept into the torrent of White's
fate. He got the garden back into order. He drained the morass
of unanswered letters and unpaid bills. He fortified White's self-
respect by making his property a credit to him – for White's
intentions were all towards order and seemliness: it was upkeep
that defeated him – and by being a responsibility, on whose
behalf lumps of sugar must be carried – for White, as Peter
Lane had observed, clutched at the feeling of being wanted and
needed.

It was settled that White should go into St Thomas's Hospital
in May, thus foiling the Inland Revenue. Before then he managed
to spend quite a lot of the money he'd preserved. After Timmy
Lane and the hawk whose education White had supervised
from a distance had spent a week on Alderney, White's mind
returned to the matter of finding a successor to the *Popsie*. He
thought of a catamaran; of a yawl; he went to Salcombe to see
about a cabin cruiser. Finally, he bought a launch (by telephone).
Then, in the same Southampton boatyard as the launch he saw
the lifeboat of Lady Docker's yacht *Shamara*.

May 11th, 1962. To David Garnett
I couldn't resist her. She is fully up to the standards of the
gold-studded Daimler – solid mahogany, all varnish, no
paint, caravel built, 26 ft long, 8 ft beam, 20 ft mast with
new sail, nylon bottom, and I am putting in 2 new diesel
engines. She is unsinkable. It will be something to survive
the operation for.

The operation, the purpose of which was to get an X-ray picture

275

of how much and where the flow of blood was impeded, was performed on May 22nd. Later he wrote to tell Mrs Lane that he had been four hours on the operating table:

> What with drugs and anaesthetics I have put in a delicious amount of sleep and I did have one visitor.

The visitor was David Garnett. A London call was put through to Hilton Hall. White said he had just come round from the anaesthetic and was longing to see him. Date and hour were fixed before White's voice blurred and faded away. When Garnett kept the appointment, White stared at him in amazement and asked, 'How on earth could you possibly know I was here?' All recollection of how he had surfaced and grabbed at the thought of his friend had vanished. But that the friend should appear just then would have been wholly in keeping with his reliance on Garnett's never-failingness.

In June Garnett visited him at 3 Connaught Square. Tony Walton and Julie Andrews were also in Alderney.

> He was a warm and considerate host and obviously devoted to Julie and Tony.
>
> But I was rather shocked at his physical condition. It was warm weather and when he stripped to the waist, Tim was the image of Falstaff. And to sustain the part we banqueted royally and caroused into the night while Tim called for song after song from *Camelot* and Julie good-naturedly obliged.
>
> I had an intimate talk with Tim on Sunday: a talk which arose from my letter of the 10th of January 1956, about our views on women and sexual morals. This had been in his mind, I believe, for several years.
>
> Tim explained to me that he was a sadist and that his imagination was frequently occupied with sadistic fantasies. He explained also that this had been disastrous whenever he was passionately in love. For the sadist longs to prove the love which he has inspired, by acts of cruelty – which naturally enough are misinterpreted by normal people. It

had therefore been his fate to destroy every passionate love he had inspired. In love he was always in a dilemma: if he behaved with sincerity, and instinctively, he alienated his lover and horrified and disgusted himself – if he suppressed his instinctive sadism the falsity of his behaviour became apparent. I was astonished, not by what Tim then told me, for I had suspected something of the sort ever since my visit to Sheskin Lodge in 1939, but that he should have delayed this explanation for twenty-five years.

It was a great pity because I felt the deepest compassion for him and would have behaved very differently if he had confided in me earlier.

In July White and Harry Griffiths brought the *Popsie II* from Southampton. Harry Griffiths had calculated her course assuming a rate of 7 knots. But the device which showed the boat's speed was out of order. This threw out the calculations, so that they no longer matched tides and currents. There was a patchy fog; they could see the Cap de la Hague light – a direction to avoid – but not the Alderney or the Casquets lights. They had to reckon with the Swinge, which might sweep them beyond Alderney, and with the Race which could hurry them on to the rocks of the French coast. And as White had broken the lead of the binnacle light by stumbling over it, the compass had to be consulted by electric torch. He was still flown with excitement when he wrote to Garnett:

> We left Southampton at 9.10 am and did not make Alderney – fog rising suddenly over the great full moon cross swell which drowned six people in Jersey that day – until 2.45 am, by which time the Inner Harbour was too dry for entry.
>
> Eleven people are coming to stay four days hence.
>
> I have bought me three lobster-pots for household use.

Eight of the expected eleven were the Lane party which included his Aunt Ruth and a boy who was a friend of the Lane boys. He had an additional bedroom devised for the occasion —a revision of his earlier view that young visitors could always sleep in the greenhouse.

They came and were gone. The lobster-pots were put by. He settled down and went on reading – for now there was no impulse to write. Reading was the constant element in his life. After attending the funeral service for a drowned fisherman, he wrote in his diary: 'Yesterday, in church, was the first time for years I can remember sitting still without a book in my hands. Even then, I read the burial service.'

On October 12th he began a letter to Garnett: 'I fancy this is not going to be a postcard.' He had been reading *The Familiar Faces*, Garnett's third book of autobiography.

> You hint that the fourth volume may never be completed. This would be UNPARDONABLE. Just as I have nothing to live for, you have nothing to die for, and in the same proportions. I refuse to do without the fourth volume
>
> Now some detailed remarks.

The detailed remarks – each has its page reference – cover five closely-written large foolscap pages. They range from an inquiry why Garnett used the word 'obscene' of a solar eclipse – 'I know it was the right word, but can you explain it?' – to a word-perfect recollection of a conversation reported to him thirty years before, from a comment that 'Oh, let me not be mad, not mad, sweet heaven' is a plain matter-of-fact statement like 'I hope the Joneses won't come to tea on Friday' to an analysis of inhibitions while flying. Some of the remarks stem from the White of Queens' who read for the English Tripos – a comma is lacking, there is no establishing date, an illustration is not accounted for by anything in the text, a reading of Blake's line, 'still as a lady', is open to question. Many of these remarks are self-regarding. He was a self-regarding reader; he searched the scriptures, as no doubt his Scotch forebears did, for what was relevant to his own case. But the overall impression conveyed by this letter is of the long, observant, affectionate, retentive, admiring regard he feels for his friend.

Garnett wrote in reply:

Dearest Tim,

Thank you a thousand times for the most wonderful letter I have ever received. It would have been well worth writing *Familiar Faces* even if you had been the only reader.

On November 5th, he wrote to tell Garnett that he had finally refused to have another operation and was starting for Italy. 'God knows why. Travelling alone is not much fun, but Harry Griffiths seems to think a change would do me good.' He paused in Florence where the Verneys were wintering, then went on to spend Christmas in Rome.

It was Hadrian, the last of his identifications, who took him to Rome – though his fidelity seems to have stretched a little. 'By the way,' he told Harry Griffiths, 'I am writing a book about Hadrian, Lorenzo the Magnificent and Pope Alexander VI.' In the same letter he related a visit to St Peter's, where the font is made from the lid of Hadrian's sarcophagus. A baptism was taking place and when the priest named the child, the name was Adriana. It was clearly an occasion for an extra-liturgical godfather. He had a clean 10,000 lire note in his pocket, so at the close of the ceremony he tucked the note into the baby's shawl, addressed a speech of good wishes to the mother

and vanished before she could answer. The funny thing was that I saw by her eyes that she took this as perfectly natural and just the sort of thing that ought to happen to all new babies.

The book about Hadrian, etc, remained in the air. But a tank of live doomed shellfish in a grand restaurant set him off on writing poetry once more.

GOOD EATING

Lobster living your livid life in the blue tank of the ristorante –
No, you are a crayfish – but there you are calm to be cannibalized –
Alone and aloof and meet to be boiled alive – poco curante –
You waggle complicated legs and arms variously sized.

Some of them look like scillia, if that's the way to spell it,
And two are antennae, and two pink ones have coral fingers
    on each hand.
You hold them out praying like a mantis to water to feel it
    and smell it
And wave them about vaguely in your angular, gauche stand.

An armoured Trojan horse or carapaced colt – your skeleton outside –
With the awkward colt's hocks on barnacle toes –
They must be twin colts, since there are eight in your caparisoned
    stride –
You sea-spider, you oceanic White Knight's horse – in armour
    against your foes –

What are you thinking about, strangeness, with those pebble eyes
    on stalks?
Are you hungry? (We are.) Why do you hold with sweet pleas
Your two pink fingers delicately out, as your mottled robot
    structure walks
In a muddled science-fiction tiptoe of angular knees?

You wipe your armadillo behind with one of those dentist feet.
With another you whisk your Salvator Dali moustachios.
And you are to die, mysterious creature, horribly boiled alive,
    and I shall eat
Those hard, cold, blue, rickety, otherworld gestures of instrument
    toes.

How many aeons are there between you and me?
Are you happy, are you sad, are you afraid,
As we the rich clients of the Roman restaurant
Prepare to boil you to death, whom God made?

Well, that's how it goes, crayfish. Life isn't a bowl of cherry.
I also am subject to Man, brother, so let him eat and be merry.

In Rome, too,

> a gay, clean, girlish gipsy called out to me as we met on the pavement, 'Bel futoro' – then examining the shambling yet noble figure more closely – 'e grande passata.' I said, as I shook my head, 'Passata, si' – which made the younger wayfarers laugh.

Though Rome was 'an eternal, glorious, inexhaustible city' where he did not hear one single Christmas Carol, he didn't like its citizens. 'They seem mean and cold-hearted. Perhaps this was because I was.' He bought a diary for 1963 – equipped with calendar saints and interest tables – and wrote on January 2nd that he was glad to be back in Florence where he liked the beggars who gave him little cards of St Lucy in return for his alms. On the diary's first page he made brief notes of previous sightseeings (among these is a mysterious 'Bones in Coffee Pot'). Of a superlative sightseeing he wrote to Garnett from the Pensione Bandini where he lodged:

> Did I tell you about the Medici villa at Artimino called La Ferdinanda? This I have *got* to rent for two months next summer, if possible. It is quite desolate and the owner obviously seldom goes there, but its views cover half Italy, its approach is through a forest, and it was built as a hunting lodge for Ferdinand the Second (?) Medici. All the beds are canopied, all the out-of-tune pianos or harpsichords have faded silver-framed photographs of the King of Spain, all the vast interior walls (larger than the largest squash-court multiplied by two) are hung with simply terrible portraits of Medicis or Hapsburgs or mythological scenes of the greatest complexity. In the gardens there are loose wild dogs at night for biting trespassers. In the gun room there are two stuffed eagles. The chimneys of its roof look like a sort of mad dovecote. If your family and Michael Howard's family and Verney's family and I were to dwell there for two summer months, it would be difficult to meet indoors except by appointment and map.

The Pensione Bandini was on an upper floor of the Palazzo Guadagni on the Piazza S Spirito (one day when the lift failed White discovered that it was 127 steps up). It was kept by two ageing sisters.

January 10th, 1963
At 1 am Signorina Bandini and I had quite a little adventure with some maniac who was continuously ringing the street door, five floors below. Much rushing up and down in the lift in our night clothes. Eventually, right out in the square and hiding behind a taxi we found a man and our resolute demeanour scared him away.

White had added this much to his diary, when the noise of the lift ascending and descending fetched them out again.

It rose to where we were awaiting it, and there, slowly revealed as it came level, was our own servant Gina – who had gone raving mad. As she rose into view in the lighted lift, she was peering at us through the glass doors and howling Hoo! Hoo!

It is now ten to four in the morning. The police (I thought lazily) and the bold signorina (I thought quixotically) refused to remove poor dear Gina to the madhouse.

As it was obviously impossible to leave the small heroine alone with her maniac, I sat up in the kitchen next door to their room. By then, the signorina had awakened her senior lodger – a charming fellow who has been here for 8 years – and he sat in the kitchen with me. Meanwhile the deaf, crippled elder sister Bandini had tottered into the breach and was taking her turn nobly at calming Gina. In the course of long, long, tired talking in the kitchen – my Italian getting worse and worse from exhaustion – I began to understand the laziness and quixotry (both only apparent). It seems that being put in a loony bin in Italy, which was the only red-tape solution for the police, is a very serious matter. You can seldom get out again. And that was why the sensible policeman and my darling signorina have assumed the burden of not doing so.

It has been a strangely happy evening for me.

He had been of service – the huge, limping, drinking English-man, leaning on his great stick and correcting his *vi* to *Lei*; they would all be friends henceforward.

It was during a second visit to Florence that White said to Harry Griffiths, 'I wish you'd teach me to drink socially.' During this first visit, the English colony came to dread the overwhelming talker whose brio made itinerant musicians shrug their way out of restaurants, who told the same stories, expressed the same opinions over and over again, whose reiterated quip of 'Urinal Bevan' provoked from Harold Acton a quelling 'I didn't know how the name was pronounced.' The Verneys had to watch him being avoided, resented, snubbed by vigorous old ladies. Then something he said or did emitted 'the sort of flash that reminded one (and one needed reminding sometimes) that underneath the drunken bore lay buried a marvellous feeling for language'. Unusual conversational assets also lay buried. After a luncheon at the Consulate he made the note: 'Remember to tell Harcourt that, if he is related to Thomas Harcourt, that martyr's kidney still existed in Aubrey's day – "like an agate polished".'

A recitation of 'In the bleak midwinter' by three Verney daughters was part of the Epiphany Festival at Ognissanti that year. White coached them, and kept a photograph of them, standing erect and doll-like in a diminishing row on a scaffolding above the larger Crib figures. (On the following day they all went to the circus.) Children have unembarrassed eyes. Here is White as seen by Sabrina, Juliet and Angelica Verney.

T H White struck me as being a very lonely pathetic person, however famous he may have been. I remember his joy when he found a copy of *The Age of Scandal* in a dirty Roman bookshop. He smoked Players cork-tipped down to the halfway mark, then stubbed it out and lit another immediately. He filled an ash-tray of half-smoked cigarettes in an hour or less. He got no pleasure from it, he didn't inhale. He also wore a worried faraway expression on his face, which looked rather funny on such a huge chap. He always wore old-fashioned woollen winter clothes and tie, socks, waistcoat, etc.

Mr White lived very near us in Florence so we saw him quite often. I remember him mostly as a huge, gentle, woolly sort of sheepdog; very lazy and fat and extremely fond of his food. He had a rather revolting yellow beard and a red face. Mr White was the sort of person who never admitted himself wrong in anything and he appeared to think that people would respect him however he behaved (often very badly) and whatever he looked like (he made a habit of walking through the town and coming to supper with us in his bedroom slippers).

I think Mr White was quite a nice man, and also funny. He had white hair and a very few times he was cross. I am not glad he died. He helped us with some poems in Italy. He was a very old man.

'I am not glad he died.' This writer was eight years old – an age when it is possible to say exactly what one means, neither more nor less.

January 13th, 1963
Snow, said to be a rarity in Florence. Went for an icy walk by myself, and read and snoozed. Long Italian conversation with senior lodger about fascism and Mafia and Calabria and superstition.

It was the bitterly cold weather of 1963. White lay fully dressed in bed to keep warm, gratefully recording that on January 17th the signorina brought him a hot water bottle (the day before, he had helped her make the beds, since there was no Gina and the waiter was indisposed), that on January 19th his bedroom stove was kindled. He read and wrote, watched little boys snowballing, studied roof-tops and the variety of chimneys and pigeons.

The plate armour of the Florentine pigeons!
Each gunmetal feather fitting over the one beneath!

A mineral oil should be used for them in these regions
To preserve each grey steely slide in its sheath.

Your mail it is Milanese, cap à pied to the tips –
Has its primaries, secondaries, mantles and trains,
Nothing moulted. Every plume intergrips
Like snake scales and pistons of engines of aeroplanes.

Coo-Coo and Ri-Coo you moan for the Medici,
Slanting up and down over the Latin tiles.
And the roofs are red, ramshackle, rust to see,
Old and unpredictable in their styles.

That chimney of small Roman bricks has Venetian arches,
Cracked, smoky, displastered. And those pleasure domes
 Look like broken-down greenhouses shaded in khakis
And the airy acres of architecture make good homes.

There are the TV masts and the Pizzi* and the Uffizzi*
And Santa This and That and the deep-toned bells.
And all the Indian-red which is upside down to me
Is the terra-cotta world where the dove dwells.

Holy Ghosts? The Spring? The Annunciation?
You coo while a skewbald cat stalks with her poker face.
Italian, Roman, perhaps of the Etruscan nation,
You are high high high, wise as old, and you swirl
    like a greystorm in space.

January 21st, 1963
I spent almost the whole day translating my lobster poem
into Italian. I got Sig Borghese to correct my tenses at lunch,
whereupon the waiter, a craggy rather illiterate middle-aged
person, shyly presented himself in my room afterwards, to
recite miles and miles of Tasso. I asked, But why only Tasso?
It seemed that he had been a shepherd (I could not catch the
word) or some other very lonely person who had only one

* Sic

285

book. Consequently he could recite 180 verses of Tasso, but nobody else. We suddenly felt great affection for each other.

White was on demi-pension, dining out, sometimes alone, sometimes with the Verneys and their friends. To go into a warm room from the Gothic cold of the streets and after a day of even moderate tippling beside his stove would have rushed the alcohol to his head: perhaps it was after the cold weather began that he became so manifestly a drunken bore. Drinking did not blunt White's irascible sensibility; his insecurity made him as quickly aware of being disliked as it made him aware of being liked and his resentment of the one was as exaggerated as his gratitude for the other. Finding that the English colony viewed him with reservations, he retorted on society.

February 3rd, 1963
Here goes another sudden burst of verses. My trouble as a poet is that I am not lyrical enough.

DID HE WHO MADE THE LAMB MAKE THEE?

(Yes)

Convict's clothes are striped like tigers.
Hangman's hands are crooked like claws.
Judge's jocks are black as niggers'.
Bishop's blood is bright as whores'.

Tiger-convict, crooked hangman,
Frigging judge and fiery bish
Hail the haggard haunts of gangmen,
Saying That is right or This.

Each of you procures the other,
Tiger bite and bishop bless.
In the jungle, twin to brother,
Howl your hymns of happiness.

Gobble bishop, gabble jury,
Hangman hanker, convict curse,

Knowing nothing in your fury,
No, not even what is worse.

He left Florence on February 10th. Much of his stay had been a disappointment – but not Italy. He had returned to it like a fish to water, his greatest pleasure to find himself talking Italian again, topping-off the christening in St Peter's, making up the beds with Signorina Elena, conversing with beggars and news-vendors, having his tenses corrected by Signor Borghese, able to read anything that came his way and to follow a film pretty well on a second hearing, finally able to judge that he spoke Italian 'about as well as the lowest waiter in Soho speaks English'.

When he was expecting to be operated on he made a new will. This may have reminded him of some unprovided-for dependents, for in February 1962 he wrote to Michael Howard about a printing of his poems. It was to be a limited edition, which he would pay for, and only for distribution among his friends.

On his return he found the hundred copies of his privately printed *Verses* waiting to be inscribed. He took pains to individualize inscriptions, or embellish them. Mrs Herivel's copy has a heart with an arrow through it. So has the copy he sent to his old pupil, then Provost of King's College, Cambridge, Noël Annan.

Thirty-four years elapsed between *Loved Helen* and the privately printed *Verses*. The creative interval was not so long. Most of the poems in the later volume were written during his first winter in Ireland. In both volumes it is the personality behind the poetry which impresses the reader, but in the second the personality is disengaging itself from the advantages that beset it at the time of *Loved Helen*: the accomplishment, the arrestingness, the knack of swivelling from eloquence to wit. The personality has matured and admits uncertainty; it is at the mercy of enthusiasms and expresses them in pastiche. But the best Irish poems reflect nothing but his own mind. 'The marvellous feeling for language' which John Verney saw in flashes was at the disposal of plain statements, strong feelings and an argumentative disposition. 'This will be no good poem, but it will be truth' – so one begins.

Freed from his advantages, he was also freed from the obligation of authorship which subjected everything he wrote in prose to being potential book-fodder. His poetry led a private life. When the impulse left off, he left off.

The Irish impulse left off in 1941. In Alderney he wrote again, but too many people and too many irons in the fire got between him and his own mind. Two poems, 'The Tower of Siloam' and 'After Seven Years', have the same rationalizing melancholy which makes the Irish 'A Joy Proposed' so impressive and so indisputably personal. Apart from these, he had to wait for Italy before he found something to say and a way of saying it.

Three days before he left Florence he had talked to Signor Borghese about the Pensione Bandini's finances. Learning that they were precarious, he decided to come back for April, bringing Harry and Daphne Griffiths with him. At the beginning of May, the Griffithses having left for Venice, he went on to Naples.

May 20th, 1963. To John Verney
I am having a comical, touching, rather impendent* adventure here, as I have been adopted by a family of coster-mongers about the same size as yours. There are Mamma and Papa and five sons and one daughter, all as poor as church mice, to whom I am a godsend for purposes of exploitation. The two who have particularly adopted me are Gianpaulo and Alfredo. What can you do when a boy of 19 says, Please, I would rather not be buggered, but I *would* like a new pair of shoes? The next moment he takes you confidently by the hand, leads you to the nearest jewellers and asks for a pair of cuff-links at £60 sterling. I can't *resist* their greed,

* Overhanging, threatening.

gaiety, childishness and essential goodness, but I can resist £60. (Anyway it has cost much more than this to reclothe them both with normal elegance.) They arrive at the hotel every morning long before I want to get up, bearing a rose which they claim to have bought for me (pinched). They have stopped me drinking too much – in fact, drinking at all – by the unusual expedient of bursting into tears! They dash into my room at all hours of the day, rummage in my clothes with cries of delight, polish my shoes, dress me (gentle and melancholy Gianpaulo pulls on my socks) and off we go for another day on sea or land, generally ending at a cinema or night restaurant high above this starry bay. (I also have a private orchestra of 2 violins, 1 guitar, 1 mandolin and 3 irresistibly comic singers.)

They call me Il Professore and treat me as tenderly as a baby, leading me like one. 'This way, Professore. Don't fall down just here. We will be there in a minute. Don't forget the *bastone*.' Sometimes it is Papa Zeem. The amused old Silenus is gently hustled along with help and exhortation.

At other times, they draw me aside, explain that their Daddy has asthma and that it would be very nice if I gave him half a million sterling to make it better. Or Alfredo, who is the more dashing of the two, says hopefully, 'Professore, will you give me an MG?' They *implore* me to take them away, to France, to England, to America, to Alderney, to anywhere. I blush to say I am going to. At least I can give them 3 summer months in Alderney, teach them English, show them that little bit of the world's journey and return them with a wider equipment for life. When I said I would, they threw their arms round me and kissed me – no unusual occurrence if pleased, like babies. They rob me a good deal, but not surreptitiously or out of proportion.

Here are some pictures of my orchestra, with which we hope to tour the islands of the bay.

The strains of the orchestra must have attracted some prowling photographer, for the pictures are flash-lit, hard and sharp as a tin edge. In order to get everyone in, the players and comic singers are grouped closely around the table; they look like a pack. Silenus sits between Alfredo and Gianpaulo; his hands rest on his stick, he is wearing a terrible tie. The Neapolitan barber has close-trimmed his beard and plastered down his hair with oil and it does not suit him. Gianpaulo and Alfredo are wearing their identical new checked jackets. The jackets do not suit them, but they think they do. Everyone is devoting himself to Silenus. The singer, singing a dirty song of great simplicity, postures and narrows his eyes at him. The mandolin player thrums at his ear, the violin is being played immediately above his head. Even the waiter in the background keeps an eye on him. On the table are bottles, glasses, paper napkins, lottery tickets and a very expensive camera. Silenus smiles, approves, tilts his head alertly, has made a joke. If one feels a certain sadness about him, it is not because he is old – the violin-player is probably much older – nor because the barber has trimmed his beard so unbecomingly, exposing several double chins, nor because of the headache he will have in the morning. One's sadness is protective. He looks so much out of place, heavy and lumbering, like a bear out of a northern forest, turning his massive head, clutching his staff and wearing spectacles, alone among these sinuous Mediterraneans with their beady eyes and their amiable vulpine grins.

On the other hand, he is the only person in the group who is not conscious that he is being photographed.

May 22nd, 1963. To John Verney
One of the best things about my costermongers has been that it has given me a safe-conduct all over Naples. There isn't any murderous street anywhere they can't take me, and they are related to everybody else. I can go to any cinemas in the roughest quarters and be accepted there because of my friends. It seems as if I had become Il Professore to half the city. The banks, the cinemas, the restaurants, the terrace cafés treat me as such, and really I have *not* been swindled very severely. The more the family realize that I really have

adopted them, or they me, the more anxious they are to give and get me justice. Alfredo has become positively miserly on my behalf. The only place they won't let me go to is the Galleria Umberto. This is the famous gallery where one used to have to go to be solicited to see the girl copulate with the donkey. The family are strict moralists (I have to go to Mass) and will not allow me the pleasure of this spectacle.

I not only have a private orchestra, private taxi, and two private secretaries, but also a private *magician*! I have never had one before. He is a timid, hopeful, oppressed little man, who believes his own horoscopes, so it would be unkind not to believe them too. He assures me that I am a widower who used to own an important factory. Then he looks at me hopefully, so I have to say, Yes I am. He has a visiting card, very faded and ill-printed, on which he describes himself with simplicity with the one word **MAGO**.

Yes, and now we are going to Faust on Saturday – Gounod's of course – and you can bet your bottom dollar Mephistopheles will have proper horns, eyebrows, waxed moustache, short cape with red-and-green spangles and scarlet trunk hose with rapier. I can't wait for his devilish laugh. We take the private taxi-driver but can't afford to take the private orchestra as well. This, this is the way to end an ill-spent life! I feel as wicked as when I was 20 (in Naples, incidentally).

It was for this occasion he dressed the whole family. It cost him over £500.

There is a photograph which shows a similar, perhaps even the same outing. Gianpaulo, Alfredo, the private taxi-driver and White are sitting in a row in a foyer. Three pairs of eyes are directed to the photographer. White is composedly reading – reading a programme, as he read the Burial Service at the fisherman's funeral.

At that moment – but his guests did not know it – he was exposed to a more powerful spell than he would have been in the Galleria Umberto.

But they did not lose him. Except that he went to six music shops for a copy of the dirty song of great simplicity (and could not find one and eventually wrote to his literary agent to continue the search in London) he had no dalliance with the printed word while he was in Naples. He carried on his study of public fig leaves (vine leaves in Rome, in Naples they were positive sporrans); he gained the customary access to the locked room of the Naples Museum; he went to Mass on Sundays, for the family insisted on it. For the rest, the private taxi drove him, and the private orchestra played for him, and the rose was brought every morning, and he was recognized by more and more people, and the magician reflected that it must indeed have been a very important factory. Even with Alfredo's hand on the purse-strings, countless people must have been the better for him. His wealth spouted from him like wine from a fountain on a royal birthday. He enjoyed himself, he gave enormous satisfaction. There was no need to feel that Consular sadness about him. He could easily have spent less and had much less pleasure from it.

By June 18th he was back in Alderney, with three months to go before he sailed (he refused to fly) for the United States and the lecture tour arranged by Colston Leigh, Inc. He had promised four lectures: 'The Pleasures of Learning', 'Luck in Literature', 'Poets Unfashionable', 'In Search of an Emperor'. This last (the Emperor was Hadrian) replaced an earlier choice: Shakespeare as a Ham. It seems a pity. Ham would have called to Ham; and though White could not write a play, he had wanted to, and felt such admiration for Shakespeare's plays that he tried to give them to Sir Walter Raleigh. But he had already 'got up' Hadrian and had quantities of pertaining photographs, including photographs of the most recent temple, in the garden of 3 Connaught Square. It shows what the last seven years had done to him that the lecture on Hadrian was the only one to record a new interest. 'Poets Unfashionable' attempts to recall attention to the poems he read at Stowe, 'Luck in Literature' is a chivalrous attempt to revive books he had admired as a young man, 'The Pleasures of Learning' has no speculations about new learnings. He depended on the already known and on the brilliant young man at Stowe.

In some ways, he was better equipped than before. By hanging round *Camelot* he had learned about pacing and delivery; and since the December of 1944 Carol Walton had been born, and gone to school, and taken a secretarial course with shorthand and was there, ready to take down the lectures from dictation and to accompany him on his tour as secretary.

This came as a surprise to them both. She was in Alderney, convalescing from an appendix operation.

> We were sitting at the bar at the Connaught Hotel with a crowd of friends and Tim remarked that if he went on the lecture tour alone he would never come back alive. I jokingly said I'd go along and take care of him and then one of the group said, 'Why don't you take Carol as your secretary?' Tim said he thought this a splendid idea and would I go. I – still jokingly – said, 'Certainly'. After lunch it became apparent that he really meant it. We called Colston Leigh, Inc. in New York and suddenly there were a thousand and one things to be organized.

She was still in Alderney when Alfredo arrived. Surroundings are a kind of orchestration. Transferred from Naples where they blended to Alderney where they didn't Alfredo's artless demands sounded extremely raucous. They were not restricted to his patron either. White's design to return him with 'a wider equipment for life' rapidly took the simpler form of wanting to return him.

July 27th, 1963. To Carol Walton
I am managing to keep my head above water and Harry has

banished Alfredo as from this Monday. We shall have to bribe him a little to go away. But the other one called Vito arrives on the 1st of August. So far as I know, he will be less trouble.

It was a pity it ended so, when there had been so much acceptance and obligation on both sides. White came as a godsend into that large impecunious family, but they were hospitable to Silenus. They kept him tidy, they tried to keep him sober, they were his safe-conduct through murderous streets, they saw to it that he went to Mass. If Alfredo in Alderney was a disillusionment to White, Alfredo must have felt a reciprocal disillusionment.

Vito Moriconi (his father was the private taxi-driver) was gentle and well-behaved and made no demands except to be taught. But White's temper had been shaken and he was temporarily pettish with his secretary.

(August) To Carol Walton.

I am sorry I have not written often enough. I have had my hands full of Alfredo and now Vito (who is a dear) and it is Alderney Week into the bargain and Harry has cracked his ribs and everybody is having parties. Forms and things keep arriving, none of which I can make head or tail of, and some of which are nonsense.

Can't all this stuff which you keep sending me wait till I get to Walton-on-Thames on the 8th? I really can't cope with it – it is what you are for. For instance, today's programme so far has been (1) after breakfast go to Packe's to interpret to his Italian gardener about conditions of employment, (2) go shopping with Vito who wanted dress lengths for his sister, films, dark glasses, post-office business and food to eat, (3) feed us and Jennie, (4) read letters from you and Richard* with dismay, (5) drive around town looking for Mr McQueen because the colonel has burst the self-starter on one of my boat's engines, (6) take a fishing party when engine is mended, (7) drive round organizing a party of seven to

* Richard Walton, Carol's brother.

take to France on Monday. It is now 5.30 and I am due to go to the opening of the Art Exhibition at 6.00. Other guests arrive at 7. In between times I am supposed to be teaching Vito to drive the car.

I CAN'T and WON'T write to Richard about whether I am suffering from actinomycosis.

By the second week of September he was staying with the Waltons at Walton-on-Thames. His affairs were taken in hand, he was calmed and got ready for his departure on September 19th. On the eve of departure he wrote to Harry Griffiths:

I have bought some very chaste clothes and we have to be on the Elizabeth by about 10 am on Thursday. I suppose we shall pass Alderney some time in the afternoon or evening. My dear Carol sends you her love.

Before then, Carol's father had told her in confidence that White 'could very possibly have a stroke – a coronary – and die suddenly. I felt I had to warn her of this.'

XIV USA: 1963–64

'The good part is seeing America, the bad part is being seen.' So he wrote in his diary on the eve of departure. What he had not reckoned with was that he was going among people who had not seen him before – nor anything quite like him.

> First the size of the man, then the brilliant blue, rather bloodshot, unhappy eyes, and the patient voice which usually sounded as though he were very carefully explaining something to a child and which would then split with the sudden realization of an absurdity, or a shared joke. Tim was usually intensely serious when he made a remark; the comic became apparent as he gave it a second look.

This was the 'immediate and unforgettable impression' he made on Garnett in 1936. In 1963 the size of the man, a much bulkier man, was compromised by a lame leg and the eyes were behind spectacles and the unhappiness had spread over the whole countenance. He was the worse for a great deal of wear. But the patient voice – the 'rather Ophelia-like register' a Stowe pupil remembered – splitting with the sudden realization of an absurdity, and the gravity capitulating to the ridiculous, remained; they were part of him, a Will-o'-the-Wisp exhalation from his mistrust and melancholy; they gave him the charm of incalculability. It was a private person appearing on public platforms.

On the boat and in New York, he worked and fretted. 'I spent a wretched morning trying to get these futile lectures into my head and to memorize great blocks of Georgian poetry. My poor old head, once a serviceable one, is full of cotton-wool.' Here is Carol Walton:

> Our first engagement was at Williams College in Williamstown, Massachusetts. The lecture was 'The Pleasures of Learning' and Tim was visibly nervous and his hands were shaking for the first ten minutes or so – then he suddenly realized that the audience was with him and

willing him to do well and from then on he was fine and decided he was really going to enjoy lecturing.

At his next lecture at Boston College, he let himself go and recited the great blocks of Georgian poetry – Housman and Owen and Thomas and Flecker's long speech of Don Juan which he had repeated when the drunken party drove back to Trim with the tiercel – with such fire that he was given a standing ovation. He was as thrilled as a small boy would have been at a particular word of praise.

When we got back to the hotel he kept asking me what the students had said about him and what I thought of the lecture.

There is a chalk and cheese difference between readers' and hearers' appreciation. When White left Stowe he renounced an irreplaceable thrill – the sensation of exciting a young audience (even though boys in the mass were like haddocks). Twenty-one years later his passion to teach, to inspire, to master, came back in force, to be concentrated on an occasional Zed. Now he had young audiences again. As the tour continued the lectures became increasingly the clothes-horses on which he hung new impressions and enthusiasms, and it was the questions at the end he lived for and the opportunities they gave for impromptu post-lecture lecturing. 'Mr White is a full well', said one of his chairmen. He was a winterbourne stream in full rush.

Not all the lectures went well.

Sometimes during the tour he was very difficult. At one college he was supposed to be doing 'The Pleasures of Learning'. When he arrived he discovered that it was a girls' college and announced that 'The Pleasures of Learning' had been written for boys so he'd have to rewrite it, so instead could he do 'In Search of an Emperor'. (He had been longing to give this lecture on Hadrian which was illustrated by slides.) This change of plan led to an eventual complaint by the school to the lecture bureau and by the lecture bureau to Tim, who was furious and informed me that he refused to speak to anyone at the Colston Leigh office and proceeded to write them a rude letter.

When the same lecture was chosen by the University of Pennsylvania, an Inter-Office Communication from the Bureau pointed out:

> They would like a few slides but certainly not all of the sixty listed, and they want to be sure that Mr White is aware that this audience will be made up of mostly History and English Department professors and other people of very erudite and sophisticated mentalities.

Recording this lecture he wrote, 'It was fine to sink back into the academic atmosphere.'

Among those who heard the lecture was Mr Alan Warren:

> White spoke at great length of his travels in search of Hadrian. He told of his having bought a small estate in one of the Channel Islands and deciding, while repairing the two cottages on the property which had been bombed during the war, to make one into a Temple for Hadrian. In addition to the various artifacts and busts of the emperor which decorate the building, he described how he placed 'Britannia' coins into the concrete floor to form Hadrian's name.
>
> But perhaps his most absorbing tale, which grew out of his travels for the purpose of seeking and photographing statues of his idol, was his description of his search after his coffin.

This narrative – somewhat ennobled, like the Britannia pennies – culminated in the baby. It must have been a queer farrago; but one listener at any rate was mastered by White's spell.

> He struck me as not being a very effective speaker in the sense of oratory, but the genuine warmth which he generated with the pleasant sound of his quiet voice (coupled with the visual effect of seeing his brilliant white hair and beard) all blended into an aura of compelling fascination. His enthusiasm for his subject was clearly communicated through his personality, rather than by his ability as a public speaker.

Another thing which did not go well was a conducted tour in Washington which he and Carol Walton attended.

All was fine till we entered the Bureau of Printing and Engraving – we had queued for some time to get in. We were watching dollar bills being printed when Tim suddenly declared that the whole thing was fatuous and that you might as well watch the production of lavatory paper. He announced that he was leaving the building immediately (which he did, causing great confusion as he and the guide had to fight their way back through the crowds which were following on and arrange for one of the elevators – which supposedly only went Up – to go Down), and if I wanted to bore myself going on he would meet me outside.

She went on, and photographed him, still fuming, when they re-met.

White had the hallmark of the English eccentric – the mild, unprotesting acceptance of a destiny to be conspicuous. She had already noticed this during a jaunt to Cherbourg *en fête*.

Everyone stuck feathers on to everyone else (they were the kind that would catch on to clothes and stick upwards and outwards). Most of the party spent the whole time being embarrassed and hurriedly picking off the feathers. Tim walked round Cherbourg with feathers sticking out everywhere.

Her photograph caught him wearing his own ruffled plumes with the same unconcern. Of the guide's sufferings there is no record.

One free day (every free moment was filled with seeing or doing something) we took a bus which drove the three hours from Washington to Charlottesville and saw Monticello. We asked endless questions about Jefferson and Tim got extremely excited as more and more about Jefferson came to light that was comparable with the Emperor Hadrian, and decided that when he got home he might use the similarity between the two men as a basis for a new book. All through the tour he was filled with ideas about what he was going to do when he got home.

When the tour took them west another book beckoned – the epic of the pioneers.

He wrote in his diary:

> We must have flown near Lake Tahoe and the ghost towns of the Forty-niners. Imagine the tribulations of the original covered-waggoners who once plodded the sierras thirty thousand feet below our whistling wings – the snows, the waterless deserts of Nevada and Utah, the immense Rockies, the enemy Indians of the Great Plains. Above all imagine their distances. It took four months to come from Missouri to California. At the Donner Pass a party under the leadership of a man called Donner got badly organized and caught in the snow. 'After terrible privations they descended to cannibalism and murder.' We were eating Homard Americaine above their glaring phantoms.

White's imagination was moral, like a child's. It caught fire from facts.

San Francisco, Los Angeles, Las Vegas, Portland, Pasco, Seattle (where they felt their first rain since leaving England); then back to San Francisco and thence to Salt Lake City.

Carol Walton continues:

> While we were travelling so much – plane journeys most days and sometimes several in one day – airports became havens of rest; the only places where we did not have to be charming and polite to strangers. There was less to look at and fewer questions to ask. We would sit in silence or read or discuss what we had seen and the people we had met and what we wanted to do next.

In Salt Lake City, where he lectured to an audience of nine or ten thousand and discovered that the extra zero made little difference, White realized that the new book must tell the story of the Latter Day Saints. For there he talked to people whose fathers' fathers remembered the day when Brigham Young's party outspanned at noon and got the potatoes in before any meal was eaten, so desperate was the need to secure one food-crop before the winter struck. There was so much to ask and learn 'that we decided to stay on an extra twenty-four hours'.

Chicago, Springfield, Pittsburgh, Delaware, New Orleans.

In New Orleans we stayed with my godmother. Her husband is a doctor. The lecture at Tulane University didn't go very well. Tim looked tired and ill. After the lecture he spent a long time talking to students and refused to leave. When we did get home we watched a television programme that we had recorded that afternoon, so it was late when we went to bed. Early next morning Dr Unkauf woke me to tell me that Tim had woken him much earlier in dreadful pain – another doctor had been called who had given Tim a shot and an ambulance was on its way.

It was another of his psychosomatic attacks, due to extreme exhaustion. Lying in hospital, he heard of President Kennedy's assassination. American history, so movingly recent, now stood at his bedside.

He was in hospital for a fortnight, and left too soon. But he was booked to give a talk in the Library of Congress and saw it as an appointment with Jefferson, whose books are on the shelves. There was still another fortnight of lecturing and travelling. It began well with a second standing ovation, this time at St Andrew's School, Wilmington.

My reading desk was on the floor of a slanting auditorium so that the audience was higher than I was. They towered over and crushed me with enthusiasm as they stood. They were like a wave.

But from now on the distances were less and the journeys took longer, for they were mostly travelling by train – trains that ran too early in the day to have restaurant cars, trains that did not arrive till after midnight, trains starting before sunrise for which they waited in cold dirty stations, sitting 'on a narrow, old, hard bench'. Summing up a week of such travelling, he wrote, 'It was agony. It was worth it.'

It was worth it for her too, though she had the harder part, writing, planning, telephoning, laundering and packing, continually on the alert. 'Tim was the most interesting person I've ever known to go places with,' says the remarkable young person, so small and slender that if she had been a few sizes smaller he could have carried her on his wrist like a falcon;

he always noticed the unusual aspects of anything he saw and would go to endless pains to find out more about something that interested him. He and I had marvellous conversations that I shall always remember. He always made me feel that I interested him too. When he was talking to people during the tour or even in the lectures, it was never 'I have been to' or 'I have noticed' it was always we. He included me in everything and I appreciated that. He seemed really happy and alive and vital on the tour and didn't want it to finish at all. He said he had been happy teaching and learning and loved America and didn't want to leave. I had promised my family I would be home for Christmas, but Tim decided to stay.

At the end of the tour he wrote:

The students of La Salle College gave me for the last time I shall get it the stunning applause and affection which makes my heart turn over, and I am miserable that the tour is finished, and I don't want to stop ever ever ever. How will I do now, without the generosity and enthusiasm of youth, and the hospitality of my beloved continent, and the excitement of aeroplanes and trains and cabs and automobiles and even ferry boats? We have not missed a single connection, except through being in hospital, and we have gathered a sort of momentum of travel which does not know how to stop, and all the mountains, deserts, rivers, forests, homes, people, kindnesses, warmth, love ... yes, love, novelty, discovery, beauty, grandeur, simplicity, seriousness, youth, vigour, enormousness of the United States combine to look over our shoulders and say, Don't go. In spite of the killing struggle, perhaps because of it, I have never been happier in my life.

He was not a man to take the name of happiness in vain since it was not a state he could take for granted. He had been unlucky with his happinesses; except for the fishing on Beldorney Water, they never died a natural death. He was happy at Cambridge – till the diagnosis of tuberculosis. He was happy in his gamekeeper's cottage – till the threat of war came and the gas-mask was pulled over his face. From the disappointment of Sheskin onward, his assertions of happiness in Eire were at the mercy of conscience or circumstance. He downed conscience and completed his Arthur – and circumstances in England prevented its publication. Clambering back into a serenity of creation he wrote *The Elephant and the Kangaroo* and then *Mistress Masham's Repose* and returned from dispatching the former to the USA to learn that Brownie, the only unhaunted love possible to him, was dead.

God's most deep decree

Bitter would have me taste.

The line from Hopkins he used to quote with such ready petulance when he was a young man became too real for quotation. In his diary for 1959 he analysed his inability for happiness. 'My trouble is that my intelligence is materialistic, agnostic, pessimistic and solitary, while my heart is incurably tender, romantic, loving and gregarious.' The lecture tour, which he set out on supposing merely that the good part would be seeing America, resolved the contradiction. New things to learn aerated his intelligence, his gregarious heart was appeased by meeting a succession of friendly strangers – who being successive, left it uninvolved. But it was more than the surprise of feeling happy and the stimulus of having so many young audiences that enabled him to say, 'I have never been happier in my life.' In the Western States he found a whole new aspect of youth to love: the impersonal youthfulness of a young country. Here at last was something he wanted to write about. He had never been happier. 'In spite of the killing struggle, perhaps because of it …' If because of it, then because he was companioned, and by a companion so young that he could feel protective, so protecting and providing that she restored to the ageing man who might drop dead at any moment something of the security the child had lost when he lost the ayah in whose care he felt safe, and was good.

He had promised me that during the tour he wouldn't drink at all (he had said that first day in Alderney that he thought it would be unfair to me if he was drinking). He kept this promise rigidly – only broke it that morning when he was in such pain before going to hospital. But after the tour was over I think he was miserable and I heard from a friend that he began again in no uncertain manner.

My last few days in New York were hectic, getting things tied up with the Lecture Bureau, sorting out Tim's tax, getting his washing up to date and so on. He came with me to the airport and we sat for a good deal of the time there in silence. I had enjoyed the tour and didn't really want to leave and I think he wished that I would stay too. As I went to go out to the aircraft Tim wept and turned and stomped off into the New York night looking so sad and lonely that, had I stood there a moment longer, I think I would have stayed.

Before the New Year he sailed for Europe on the *SS Exeter*.

January 2nd, 1964. To Harry Griffiths
This disorderly letter is written a day past the Azores in a semi-cargo vessel and the same sort of weather you first saw me in. We have had a choppy swelling beam sea trip of it so far and it is getting worse. It makes me think of your convoy days (couldn't sleep much last night through difficulty of keeping in bunk) and how your main feeling apart from

tiredness and fear must have been exasperation. Why won't anything stay anywhere? (There goes the coffee.) Things are always getting out of control even at the best of times, but in an Atlantic winter, as you remember, they take on a silly life of their own.

I keep a sort of lion-tamer's eye on all the great cats in my cabin, in case the suitcase pounces out on me from behind, or all the drawers take over and pour out on my feet (There go the hair-brushes.)

I *may* pick up Vito in Naples – it depends on his college vacations I suppose – but in any case I will go on myself to Egypt, Lebanon and Greece. It is just a sort of tourist ship (plus cargo) so I may as well complete the circle while I'm on it – particularly as it will give me a chance to photograph some Hadrian buildings.

I feel a bit out of touch, but it can't be helped, Perhaps I might be back in Alderney in February.

Love to all from Tim.

This was posted from Barcelona, where he added:

My God, how shabby poor Spain looks after America! But, as usual, it is nobly shabby. Everybody is a proud, masculine gentleman. Our kind and beautiful old guide in Cadiz was living on about tuppence a day, but he was a lovely courtly old stick.

In Naples he picked up Vito.
Egypt, Lebanon …
By the morning of January 17th the *SS Exeter* was in the port of Piraeus. At midday this entry was made in her Log Book:

On this day at 1037 Hours Master was informed that a passenger in Room 109 was found dead. The deceased was a Mr Terence Hanbury WHITE, British Subject, Passport 7236, Age 57 years, Residence British Channel Island of Alderney. Upon investigation it became known that the deceased had been discovered by a Mr Vito MORICONI, secretary to

Mr White, who was travelling with him but in a different room. Vito Moriconi stated that he had knocked on the door of Mr White's room and upon receiving no answer obtained a key from Mr J J Barrett, Assistant Purser. Upon finding Mr White lying on the floor of his room he summoned the Assistant Purser who immediately sent for Dr James S Taylor, ship's surgeon, and the Master.

AFFIDAVIT OF SHIP'S SURGEON, JAMES A TAYLOR, MD FACs

At 1030 local time on Jan 17th, 1964, I was summoned to SR 109 occupied by Mr Terence Hanbury White, by Asst Purser Mr Joseph J Barrett.

I found Mr White partially lying on the floor with his chin resting against a table top where he had fallen (forward). I pronounced him dead at 1035.

It is in my opinion that the likely cause of death was acute coronary heart disease.

The British Consul was informed and White's body taken ashore. Harry Griffiths was telegraphed to, and flew to Athens. White left no directions as to where he wished to be buried; after consulting a couple of White's relations, who had no views about it, Harry Griffiths had to make the decision himself. A member of the British Consulate staff in Athens took him to the Protestant Cemetery. He pointed out two monuments within view: one was the Temple of Zeus; the other, Hadrian's Arch. This settled it; on January 20th, White was buried in Athens.

Writing to Garnett from Florence in November 1962, he had said: 'I think I will go on to Venice and Naples and perhaps do a Byron and never come back any more.' Two years earlier he had written in his diary: 'I expect to make rather a good death. The essence of death is loneliness, and I have had plenty of practice at this.'

Appendix: The Works of T H White

This Appendix is based on the bibliography first prepared by Sylvia Townsend Warner for the 1967 edition of her biography. It has been updated to list works by T H White that had been missed, and to include titles published after 1967.

Published

Loved Helen, And Other Poems (London: Chatto & Windus, 1929; New York: Viking Press, 1929).

The Green Bay Tree, Or, The Wicked Man Touches Wood (Songs for Sixpence, No 3, Cambridge: Heffer, 1929).

Dead Mr Nixon (with R McNair Scott. London: Cassell, 1931).

Darkness at Pemberley (London: Gollancz, 1932; New York: G P Putnam's Sons, 1933).

Song Through Space, And Other Poems (London: Lincoln Williams, 1935).

They Winter Abroad. A novel (under the name of James Aston. London: Chatto & Windus, 1952; New York: Viking Press, 1932).

First Lesson. A novel (under the name of James Aston. London: Chatto & Windus, 1932; New York: Alfred A Knopf, 1933).

Farewell Victoria (London: Collins, 1933; New York: G P Putnam's Sons, 1934).

Earth Stopped, Or, Mr Marx's sporting tour (London: Collins, 1934; New York: G P Putnam's Sons, 1935).

Gone to Ground. A novel (London: Collins, 1935; New York: G P Putnam's Sons, 1955).

England Have My Bones (London: Collins, 1936; New York: G P Putnam's Sons, 1936).

Burke's Steerage, Or, The amateur gentleman's introduction to noble sports and pastimes (London: Collins, 1938; New York: G P Putnam's Sons, 1939).

The Sword in the Stone (London: Collins, 1938; New York: G P Putnam's Sons, 1939).

The Witch in the Wood (London: Collins, 1940; New York: G P Putnam's Sons, 1939).

The Ill-Made Knight (London: Collins, 1941; New York: G P Putnam's Sons, 1940).

Mistress Masham's Repose (London: Cape, 1947; New York: G P Putnam's Sons, 1946).

The Elephant and the Kangaroo (London: Cape, 1948; New York: G P Putnam's Sons, 1947).

The Age of Scandal (London: Cape, 1950; New York: G P Putnam's Sons, 1950).

The Goshawk (London: Cape, 1951; New York: G P Putnam's Sons, 1952).

The Scandalmonger (London: Cape, 1952; New York: G P Putnam's Sons, 1952).

The Book of Beasts. Being a translation of a Latin bestiary of the twelfth century (London: Cape, 1954; New York: G P Putnam's Sons, 1955).

The Master. An adventure story (London: Cape, 1957; New York: G P Putnam's Sons, 1957).

The Once and Future King (comprising *The Sword in the Stone*; *The Queen of Air and Darkness*, first published as *The Witch in the Wood*; *The Ill-Made Knight*; and *The Candle in the Wind*. London: Collins, 1958; New York: G P Putnam's Sons, 1958).

The Godstone and the Blackymor (London: Cape, 1959; as *A Western Wind*, New York: G P Putnam's Sons, 1959).

Verses (privately printed at The Shenval Press, 1962).

America at Last. The American Journal of T H White (New York: G P Putnam's Sons, 1965).

The White/Garnett Letters, edited with a preface by David Garnett (London: Jonathan Cape, 1968).

The Book of Merlyn (the final book of *The Once and Future King*, completed in 1941. Published with an introduction by Sylvia Townsend Warner. Austin: University of Texas Press, 1977; London: William Collins, 1978).

A Joy Proposed. Poems (London: Bertram Rota Publishing, 1980).

The Maharajah and Other Stories (London: Macdonald, 1981).

Letters to A Friend. The Correspondence between T H White and L J Potts (New York: G P Putnams, 1982).

Contés étranges et histoires fantastiques de T H White. Traduction et préface de François Gallix (Paris: Publications de la Sorbonne, 1987).

Unpublished

'Three Lives' (Joanna Southcott, Admiral Byng, Sir Jeffrey Hudson. Complete. 1929).

'Rather Rum' (A novel. Complete. c. 1931).

'You Can't Keep a Good Man Down' (A novel. Complete. 1936).

'Grief for the Grey Geese' (A novel. Unfinished. 1938).

'The Insolence of Man' (A treatise. Complete. 1942).

'Beware of the Dogs' (A novel. Unfinished. 1943).

'Biography of Brownie' (A private memoir for William Potts. 1943).

'Ants' (A play. First Act only. 1944).

'Troilus and Cressid' (Beginning of a novel. 1946).

'Dry Blood and Distant Thunder' (Film script. Unfinished. c 1949–51).

'The Merlins' (Projected follow-on to *The Goshawk*. Based on diaries of 1958. Abandoned. c 1952).

'Macbeth the Knife' (Play. Adapted and condensed from W S for private theatricals. 1960).

Short stories

Those with an asterisk* are published in *The Maharajah and Other Stories* (1981).

'No Gratuities'*

'The Maharajah'*

'Soft Voices at Passenham'*

'Success or Failure'*

'Kin to Love'*

'A Rosy Future'*

'The Man'*

'A Sharp Attack of Something or Other'*

'Jostling the Constable'

'The Black Rabbit'*

'The Perfect Plot'

'Christmas Eve in the Schoolhouse'

'Nostradamus'*

There is also a considerable body of fragments [in White's papers] about his two setters and the training of gun-dogs. He may have had in mind a book on the lines of *The Goshawk*.

Notes on the text

BY KATE MACDONALD, WITH THANKS TO EMER O'HANLON

Davies Introduction

in petto: Italian, literally 'in the chest', from the Latin *in pectore*, referring to matters that in the Catholic Church must be kept secret, in the heart alone.

in medias res: Latin, in the middle of things. A writing technique of going straight to the heart of the matter and avoiding preliminary exposition that can wait until later.

Morte d'Arthur: the sequence of chivalric tales assembled and rewritten by the English knight (though not of a spotless character) Sir Thomas Malory in the fifteenth century, collecting together in English for the first time the early medieval 'Matter of Britain', stories of King Arthur, Queen Guinevere and Sir Lancelot, the Holy Grail, the Round Table, and the tragedy brought about by Mordred, Arthur's son by his half-sister Morgause.

solipsism: a philosophical position that only one's own mind can be said to exist; everything else is debateable. Can also be used as a synonym for selfish or self-absorbed.

Erratum slip

p52: in this edition the reference is on p 37. It has not been corrected.

Verney Foreword

[Sir] John Verney: distinguished painter, author, illustrator and former soldier.

Michael Howard: Michael Spencer Howard worked for Jonathan Cape and became that eponymous publishing house's chairman. He was T H White's publisher and literary executor.

pensione: boarding house or guest house, where meals may be included in the rates.

Ernest Hemingway: in his later years White did look remarkably like Hemingway at the same age.

lionizing: treating him with exaggerated deference because of his celebrity.

'**Farewell State**': a spoonerism on the British form of government called the Welfare State, which aimed to give all citizens the same access to health and economic benefits. It was brought in by the Labour government of 1945, and was sneered at by conservatives, evidently until well after twenty years later.

Salinger: J D Salinger, American author best known for his 1951 novel *The Catcher in the Rye*.

Ray Bradbury: American author, best-known for his science fiction and fantasy writing.

Waugh, Greene and Ackerley: Evelyn Waugh, right-wing contrarian and brilliant English novelist; Graham Greene, also one of the great English novelists of the twentieth century, and also, like Waugh, a passionate Roman Catholic; J R Ackerley, playwright and author, and long-time editor of the BBC magazine *The Listener*, which enabled him to launch the careers of many British writers. He lived an openly homosexual life, which was rare and brave for the period, and like White was devoted to his dog. All three men were White's contemporaries.

The Midnight Folk: children's fantasy novel from 1927 by John Masefield, who served as the British Poet Laureate from 1930 to his death in 1967.

His Monkey Wife: a fantasy novel from 1930 by the British author John Collier, with a cult following.

Mr Fortune's Maggot: Sylvia Townsend Warner's second novel from 1927, about an English Christian missionary who fails to convert the South Sea Islanders and falls in love with a lissom but indifferent youth.

T H White

L J Potts: Leonard James Potts was a Cambridge scholar, most known in his field for his writing on classical literary theory. He became a close friend of White's and was his former tutor (see 21).

Warner Introduction

Book of the Month Club: this subscription book club was an important buyer of large quantities of new books for its subscriber members, in the US and also in the UK through the British version. Authors of the Club's selections for the Book of the Month were guaranteed large sales and consequent excellent publicity.

Radnorshire: one of the thirteen counties of Wales, halfway up the English-Welsh border.

Siegfried Sassoon: one of the few surviving Great War poets and a famous resister of military bungling. He was also homosexual, and a leading British cultural authority.

Major Allen: Major Stanley Allen was then one of the leading British authorities on falconry.

Sir Sidney Cockerell: an eminent English museum curator and collector. He was Director of the Fitzwilliam Museum, Cambridge, from 1908 to 1937, and became a close friend and correspondent to White.

Balin and Balan: the merlins, the smallest of the hawk family, were named after two knights from Malory's *Morte d'Arthur*, who have tragic ends.

Munich crisis: in 1938 the British Prime Minister Neville Chamberlain managed to appease Hitler by agreeing to Germany receiving the Sudetenland in Czechoslovakia, thus postponing war between Nazi Germany and the rest of Europe. While Chamberlain was condemned for this political betrayal of a 1924 treaty designed to prevent such an invasion, his action gained Britain and its allies one more year to arm for the inevitable war.

David Garnett and Ray: the author, bookseller and publisher David Garnett, also part of the Bloomsbury coterie, was one of White's long-standing correspondents and would be an important literary advisor and friend. His wife Rachel ('Ray'), a well-known book illustrator, was an affectionate and wise friend to White as well; she would die young from breast cancer in 1940.

Humbert Wolfe: a prominent Italian-British poet, translator and critic, with Jewish and German ancestry, who would die in 1940. He was a high-ranking civil servant in the Ministry of Labour.

Pamela Frankau: prolific and very popular British novelist, estranged daughter of the novelist Gilbert Frankau. She had long-standing love affairs with Humbert Wolfe and a number of women.

Wilfrid Scawen Blunt: a British poet and an anti-Imperialist activist, married to the Arabian horse-breeder Lady Anne Blunt, who was Lord Byron's granddaughter. He maintained complex extra-marital relationships and had a difficult relationship with his single surviving child over money. He had died suddenly in 1922.

Thomas Hardy: the great English novelist's body was buried in Westminster Abbey in 1928 but his heart, according to his widow's wishes, was buried in Stinsford where Hardy's parents were buried. A persistent story also relates that after the heart had been removed from Hardy's body, a house cat was discovered eating it. The cat was killed quickly by the undertaker and was buried with the heart.

Lang: Archbishop Lang was not sympathetic to Edward VIII during the Abdication Crisis, and at least one popular rhyme was circulated mocking him. This one is by the popular novelist Gerald Bullett. 'Cantuar' is the formal signature for the Archbishop of Canterbury, and is also a neat pun on 'cant you are'. 'Cant' can mean thieves' slang, or sanctimonious verbiage.

My Lord Archbishop, what a scold you are!
And when your man is down, how bold you are!
Of charity how oddly scant you are!
How Lang O Lord, how full of Cantuar!

I India, Cheltenham, 1908–1924

The bedding: her first experience of sex.

tongas: a small canopied carriage for two drawn by a single horse, with some room for baggage behind.

ayah: an Indian nursemaid or nanny, who would normally be expected to stay with the child's household until the child was an adult.

watered the decanters: diluted the sherry and whisky in decanters from which the gentlemen would serve themselves, so Garrick would not get so drunk.

perquisite: an extra gift or service that accompanies the job, now better known as a 'perk'.

preparatory to a public school: normal for the upper middle and upper classes in Britain, boys were sent to school at age eight or so, sometimes to board weekly or termly, or to attend as a day boy, where they began to study Latin, Greek and other subjects thought necessary. At age eleven or so they moved to public school, a fee-paying private boarding school for boys which might have a particular 'side' or stream destined for future military service, or the civil service. Classics would again be the principal focus of study, with mathematics, English and practical skills.

education must be harassing: Warner writes here sardonically as the daughter of an enlightened and much-loved housemaster at Harrow School, one of the leading English public schools, who supervised her education at home and later with his pupils.

OTC: Officer Training Corps, the cadet force of the Army run by schools to prepare boys for later military service. Public-school boys were expected to become officers as a matter of course.

Guards' standard: the Grenadier Guards are renowned for their precision and high standards in public ceremonial duties and turnout.

flagellant: one who beats or whips oneself for sexual pleasure, or for religious devotion.

The Song of Roland: *Le Chanson de Roland* is the earliest work in French literature, an epic poem of military adventure from the eleventh century.

II Cambridge, 1925–1929

Michaelmas Term: in October, at the normal beginning of the academic year.

English Tripos: the Cambridge University course of study for English literature and associated subjects.

T R Henn: Thomas Rice Henn was a Fellow and later Senior Tutor and President of St Catharine's College, Cambridge, and would become a distinguished literary critic.

épater la bourgeoisie: French, to impress the middle classes, to show off.

College Exhibition: a small grant to reward excellence in study or to help with financial hardship.

hatless young men: in the 1920s young men without hats in public suggested a degree of informality, impatience with convention and a modern attitude.

E M W Tillyard: a central figure in the new English School at Cambridge University, who would become one of its leading theoreticians. He would support White in his early writing career.

Speriamo: Italian, 'Hopefully', 'Let's hope so', an expression of optimism.

Lux: a brand of soap flakes, making a froth.

quadrilling: performing the steps of a formal dance.

I A Richards: Cambridge scholar whose work in the New Criticism made 'close reading' an important part of the teaching of English and other literatures.

the *Granta* and the *Cambridge Review*: the leading Cambridge undergraduate periodicals.

Saturday Review: the leading British literary weekly of the 1920s and 1930s.

Fitzwilliam Extension: the first extension to the Fitzwilliam Museum, Trumpington Street, Cambridge, which was being overseen by Sir Sydney Cockerell (see above and 32). When White was critiquing the extension it was still being built.

J C Squire: editor of the *Saturday Review* and one of the most influential British reviewers and literary critics of the day.

styptic: a remedy to stop bleeding.

III Prep School, 1930–1932

Joanna Southcott: eighteenth-century prophetess celebrated for her visions and leadership of a religious cult, and her belief that at the age of 64 she was pregnant with a new Messiah.

Admiral Byng: John Byng, the vice-admiral and member of Parliament who was court-martialled and shot for allowing the island of Minorca to fall to the French.

Sir Jeffrey Hudson: a courtier of Queen Henrietta Maria, notable for his condition of dwarfism. He fought with the Royalists in the English Civil War, was exiled to France with the Queen, and was later captured by pirates and spent twenty-five years as a slave.

usher: an archaic term from the sixteenth century for a lesser schoolmaster's assistant, usually regarded as being at the same level as the most senior scholars.

q v supra: abbreviation for Latin, *quod vide supra*, 'see above'.

one's rosebuds: from the seventeenth-century poem 'To the Virgins, to Make Much of Time' by Robert Herrick, which begins 'Gather ye rosebuds while ye may', or, make the best of your youth while you have it.

roué: an elderly libertine, one who has led a debauched life but has not yet died of it.

casuistry: a way of resolving a difficult ethical situation with one's conscience.

let Nelly starve: 'Let not poor Nelly starve' were reputed to be the last words of Charles II on his deathbed, referring to his celebrated and lowborn mistress Nell Gwynne.

IV Stowe, 1932–36

the Grafton: the Grafton Hunt was and is a fashionable pack for fox-hunting, active in Northamptonshire and Buckinghamshire.

Chiron: the Centaur who taught Alexander of Macedonia, among other boys in Greek myth.

hunting-tops: distinctive riding-boots with a contrasting coloured band of leather at the top.

South Wind: this 1917 novel by the scandalous novelist Norman Douglas, who later felt obliged to remove to Capri to avoid prosecution by the British authorities, concerns the affairs of tourists and residents of Capri.

Beverley Nichols: originally a fashionable magazine columnist and novelist, his later semi-autobiographical books about gardening and the home, exemplified by *Down the Garden Path* (1932), attracted a cult following.

'lists: archaic term for enlisting in the army.

screw of a horse: a poor specimen, in ill-health through being overworked.

Piers, Hodge, the homeward ploughman, the Lincolnshire Poacher: all exemplars from English folksong and early literature of the English country labourer.

Isandula: now known as Isandlwana, this was the site of a battle in 1879, at the beginning of the Anglo-Zulu War, in which the Zulu army inflicted the worst defeat upon the British Army that it would experience in the Victorian era.

Sapphics: Sapphic stanzas, four lines of unrhymed verse that depend on the weight of their syllables to form the lines rather than a metrical pattern.

Miracle at Verdun: a play of eight scenes by the Austrian playwright Hans Chlumberg (1930), with a modernist structure requiring experimental production.

pro tem: Latin, abbreviation for pro tempore, for the time being, usually referring to a person in a temporary role.

frondeur: a participant in the French seventeenth-century civil wars, with a reputation for committing violence only when the authorities were not looking.

Surtees: Robert Smith Surtees, Victorian editor and sporting writer whose novels recreated a world of riotous hunts and hard-riding squires. White's subtitle refers to *Mr Sponge's Sporting Tour* (1853).

materia medica: a term from the history of pharmacy, the knowledge of the qualities and properties of substances used in therapeutic healing.

V Stowe Ridings, 1936–38

Edward Garnett: Victorian and Edwardian literary editor and critic, who was instrumental in promoting the writing of D H Lawrence, Joseph Conrad, Robert Frost and T E Lawrence, among others.

James Agate: one of the most prominent literary reviewers of the 1930s, of films, plays and novels.

billet de digestion: the context suggests a thank-you note, and its name may be a private or period joke.

Scythrop Glowrie: the protagonist of Thomas Love Peacock's novella *Nightmare Abbey* (1818), which is a parody of the literary conventions of Gothic excess.

jesses: thin leather straps used to tether birds while in training.

John Mytton: a nineteenth-century Shropshire squire with a spectacularly eccentric career, nicknamed 'Mad Jack'.

Te Deum: a sung prayer in the Catholic and Anglican churches, giving thanks and praise.

Lonsdale Library: a series of books on sports, pastimes and games, published from 1929 by the publisher Seeley, Service. Several of these became authoritative commentaries on the game or sport in question.

Wen: the Great Wen had been an archaic name for London, so named for its (then) stinking river and general unhealthiness. A wen is a kind of boil or tumour under the skin.

Microcosmographia Academica: a satire on academic politics by the classicist F M Cornford, published in 1908.

swinish Milne-ish parts: White had been rude about the writing of A A Milne before; here he is uncomfortable with the anthromorphism in *The Sword in the Stone* which might be read as an endorsement of *Winnie-the-Pooh* (1926) and other animal fables by Milne.

Kingdom of Grammarie: 'grammarye' has two meanings, an old name for grammar, and an archaic term for mystical learning.

all befurred: from Chapter XVII of Malory's *Morte d'Arthur*.

Silvia Daisy Pouncer: the name of the witch, and governess, in John Masefield's *The Midnight Folk*.

twenty pole: an archaic unit of measurement, equivalent to about a fifth of a metre in length. Twenty pole is nearly four metres.

my Pocahontas, my nonpareil: this could refer to George Frederick Viett's work of 1906, *Pocahontas, the Virginia nonpareil. A drama of the 17th century,* but is more likely to be a reference to David Garnett's novel *Pocahontas, Or, The nonpareil of Virginia* (1933).

stoop: the downward plunge of the raptor, sometimes over hundreds of feet at high speed, to seize its prey.

Roxburgh Society: the Roxburghe Club is an English society of eminent bibliophiles, librarians and scholars, limited to forty members, who, among other activities, produce facsimile editions of rare books.

bestiary: a book collecting and collating fabulous beasts, most famously from the medieval period.

Miss Shirley Temple: the celebrated child star of Hollywood films, whose hair was routinely arranged in curls or ringlets.

When Hayley finds out what you cannot do: from William Blake's verse grumbling about the demands of his patron, the successful author William Hayley.

Seven Pillars, *The Mint*: both works by T E Lawrence, who had been killed in 1935.

drain: a wide drainage ditch dug in flooded and low-lying grazing areas with high water tables.

sobrius et castus et spiritualitus: Latin, sober and chaste and spiritual.

Tunc congaudunt mihi angeli et omnes virtutes celorum: Latin, then the angels and all the powers of heaven rejoice with me.

VI Doolistown, 1939

Infant of Prague: a seventeenth-century Spanish image of Jesus as a child, now venerated in the Carmelite Church of Our Lady of Victories in Prague, Czech Republic. It has a particular devotion in Ireland.

Rupert Brooke, Edward Thomas, Wilfrid Owen: three of the most important British male poets of the First World War, which also killed them. Brooke died in 1915; his first and posthumous collection of poetry received wide praise for its evocation of the 'Georgian' school of poetry, valorising war with euphemisms and high-flown imagery that avoided details of slaughter. While the poetry of Thomas was much admired during the war, and Owen's poetry received strong appreciation on its first publication in the 1920s, when White was writing in the 1930s Brooke's ideology of poetry and war was still dominant.

Blest Shepherds: from a song in John Dryden's libretto for the opera *King Arthur* by Henry Purcell, first performed in 1691.

AA: not Alcoholics Anonymous, but the British car-drivers' Automobile Association, for breakdown help and insurance.

Compton Mackenzie: prolific and respected Scottish novelist, most famous now for his satire *Whisky Galore* (1947).

Feathers, Ludlow: one of the most famous hotels in Britain, packed with half-timbering and Jacobean architecture, it was converted to an inn from a private house in 1670.

Walcot Hall: extensive Georgian mansion in Shropshire with fine grounds, privately owned.

Holyhead: the port on Anglesey where one takes the ferry to Dublin.

Tara: the Iron Age hillfort called the Hill of Tara is about half an hour's drive from Doolistown. It was recorded as the seat of the High King of Ireland in early medieval times, and is still culturally significant.

Bradman: the Australian cricketer Sir Don Bradman, one of the greatest batsmen of all time.

eyas, falcon, tiercel: hawks taken from their nests as chicks and reared for falconry. The female is the falcon and the male is the tiercel.

Kill Harriers: a hunt based in County Waterford. If White had accepted the mastership he would have moved to the south coast of Ireland.

Trim: the local town to Doolistown.

Sandow: Eugen Sandow, the German father of international bodybuilding, who began developing the practice into a disciplined sport in the early 1900s.

granny: the granny knot is notoriously easy to tie by mistake when attempting the more reliable reef knot. Both knots involve the rope ends moving over and under each other in a specific pattern.

Proprietates ebrii: Latin, The qualities of the drunken man

Firstly, delighted and joyful,
Secondly, serene and wise,
Thirdly, miserable and demented,
Fourthly, helpless. In the end, stupid
and dying, and lacking all sense
and all goodness.

Childe Roland: the title of a poem by the narrative poet Robert Browning, published in 1855. See also The Song of Roland, above, which may have been one of Browning's sources.

volcano: Warner refers to the year of suppressed international tension in Europe between the Munich Crisis in 1938 and the German invasion of Poland on 1 September 1939.

mantling: after a hawk or predatory bird has killed it may spread out its wings over the corpse to hide it from competing birds.

Dun Laoghaire: the port of Dublin.

Flecker: *Don Juan. A Play in Three Acts*, by James Elroy Flecker (1926).

atrabilious: an archaic alternative for 'melancholy' deriving from the Latin for 'black bile'.

Lord Dunsany: an Anglo-Irish novelist and playwright, most admired for his early fantasy writing.

laidly worm: Warner refers to a traditional ballad name for a dragon.

VII Belmullet 1939–40

qua: Latin, where, of its.

Mrs Be-Done-By-As-You-Did: a character in Charles Kingsley's children's novel *The Water Babies* (1863), who was the sister of Mrs Do-As-You-Would-Be-Done-By. Both represent moral positions.

Gesta Romanorum: a Latin anthology of scraps of tales and legends compiled at around 1400, very popular in its day and an important sourcebook for many British poets and authors since.

blued: slang for to spend recklessly.

Henry Hall: English musician and conductor who with his band was a fixture on the BBC during the war years and up to 1960.

Anser albifrons: the white-fronted goose.

Ite, missa est: Latin, Go, the Mass is ended; the concluding phrase of the Latin Mass. White may have intended a more literal translation 'Go, it is dismissed', which would make sense in the context.

Douai Testament: part of the Bible for Catholic devotions as translated from the Latin Vulgate by members of the English College, Douai, in the sixteenth century.

Croagh Patrick: a mountain of 2,500 feet high in County Mayo, which has been the site of veneration and pilgrimage since prehistoric times. It is a site of special devotion to Saint Patrick, which reaches its annual peak on the last Sunday in July.

Knock: the Knock Shrine in County Mayo is a site of special devotion to the Virgin Mary.

spatterdashes: spats, a covering for the foot that buckles or buttons at the side or back, intended for human wear.

VIII Doolistown 1940–41

vatic: of a prophet or an oracle.

DV: abbreviation for the Latin deo volente, God willing.

Sam Butlerish: after Samuel Butler, the English novelist of utopia, who had a lifelong interest in the new Darwinian thinking about evolution.

exeat: Latin, a formal permission from school or college to be absent from class.

IX Doolistown, 1942–45

DNB: *Dictionary of National Biography*, then the standard collection of short biographies of eminent people.

Julian Huxley: Oxford evolutionary biologist and then secretary of the Zoological Society in London.

ex cathedra: Latin, from the chair, meaning a statement from the ultimate authority.

disguise: eighteenth-century term for being drunk.

Sir James Frazer: anthropologist and ethnologist and author of the *The Golden Bough. A Study in Comparative Religion* (1890), which had an immense effect on European thought on myth, story, culture and identity.

the nettle reputation in the bubble's mouth: an adaptation of the phrase 'to seek the bubble reputation in the cannon's mouth', from Shakespeare's *As You Like It*.

nihil obstat: Latin, nothing prevents or hinders, used as a formal assent in the Catholic Church and elsewhere.

sciant presentes et futuri: Latin, let them know the present and the future.

excommunico: Latin, excommunicate, to cast out from the communion of the church.

nolle prosequi: Latin, to be unwilling to pursue, used when prosecutors wish to halt proceedings before a trial has reached its conclusion. These all signify formal decision-making powers that White is teasing Potts about.

mumness: the quality of keeping silent.

Field or *Country Life*: at the time these were two of the leading English periodicals with an interest in rural living and country pursuits as lived by the classes who could afford them.

fortunate and unconcerned: Warner had personal experience of this: while she was writing this biography the health of her lifetime companion Valentine Ackland was deteriorating, and she would die in 1969.

X Duke Mary's, 1945–46

trailed his petticoat: a variant of trailing one's coat, to be provocative with the intent of picking a fight.

smore: the more usual spelling is smoor, to cover a fire with peats to keep the embers alive till the next morning but prevent it from throwing sparks.

Aldrovandus' *Historia*: the *Monstrorum historia cum Paralipomenis historiae omnium animalium* (1642), *History of Monsters with Chronicles of all the Animals*, by Ulisse Aldrovandi, an Italian naturalist.

Lucie's: St Lucy's Day is 13 December.

Quaritch: a well-known and much respected London antiquarian bookseller's.

Diomed: in the story of Troilus and Cressida in medieval versions of episodes from the *Iliad*, the Trojan maiden Cressida's love for the Trojan prince Troilus depicts her as a faithful lover, but when she turns to the Greek warrior Diomedes her character suffers a fall.

surtax: an extra tax on very large incomes.

Ellen Wilkinson: a prominent Labour Party MP, and at this time Minister of State for Education in the Labour government, a combination that enraged White, though he was not particularly anti-feminist.

XI Alderney 1946–57

2s: two shillings.

fiat mihi: Latin, be it done to me, most famously ascribed to the Virgin Mary at the Annunciation.

Woodforde: James Woodforde kept a daily diary for forty-five years, almost all of his life as a country curate in Somerset and a vicar in Norfolk in the eighteenth century. *The Diary of a Country Parson* was first published in the 1920s as a five-volume abridged version.

nil admirari: Latin, to be surprised at nothing.

Lord Camelford: a naval officer and a peer, whose violent and prideful life made him a vengeful character. White writes about him in chapter two of *The Scandalmonger*.

de haut en bas: French, from top to bottom, with no detail spared us.

piano nobile: Italian, literally the noble floor, or the principal floor for the public rooms.

Ylla: the Austrian Camilla 'Ylla' Koffler was one of the most admired and proficient photographers of animals in this period; she died in 1955.

capeline: a bandage designed to cover the head or the stump of an amputated limb, with many strips of cloth covering the hemispherical surface.

compos: Latin, compos mentis, in control of the mind, of sound mind.

left undone: this paraphrases the General Confession in the Anglican *Book of Common Prayer*: we have left undone those things which we ought to have done.

Society of Friends: the Quakers, who have a long record of reforming in the interests of social justice.

XII Alderney, 1957–60

Planglosses: Dr Pangloss is tutor of Candide, in the eponymous satire by Voltaire (1759), who teaches his pupil that they live in the best of all possible worlds and that everything that happens is for the best.

Under Milk Wood: a radio drama in verse by Dylan Thomas from 1954.

the comet: Halley's Comet appeared in White's lifetime in 1910, when he was four. The 1957 comet was probably the non-periodic comet C/1956 R1 (Arend–Roland), discovered in late 1956.

gear and tackle and trim: from the poem 'Pied Beauty' by Gerard Manley Hopkins, published in 1918.

fox to my bosom: the myth of the Spartan boy and the fox is an allusion to secret suffering. In Plutarch's *Moralia* (c 100 CE), a Spartan boy stole a fox, sheltering it under his cloak, and endured the fox gnawing at his flesh rather than reveal his crime and be dishonoured.

C Northcote Parkinson: historian, later a novelist, and the creator of the satire on bureaucracy, *Parkinson's Law* (1957), which would have appealed to White. He lived in Guernsey from 1961.

wrongs shall repent to diadems: Warner quotes from Richard Crashaw's long poem from the seventeenth century, 'A Hymn to the Name and Honour of the Admirable Saint Theresa', in which when the saint ascends to heaven, 'Tears shall take comfort and turn gems, / And wrongs repent to diadems.'

holde Leichtsinn: German, lovely carelessness.

surprised by joy: the title of a sonnet by William Wordsworth from 1815, in which the speaker realises that in his joy he has forgotten that his dearest friend is dead. The title was also used by C S Lewis in his account of the surprise of his marriage late in life, published in 1955.

Josephus: Flavius Josephus was a Roman-Jewish historian who recorded histories of the first century CE in Palestine.

Hadrian: the Emperor Hadrian (76–138) was one of Gibbon's 'Five Good Emperors', and was passionately in love with a Greek called Antinous, after whose death he had deified. Affinity with Hadrian has long been a code for male homosexuality.

ΑΔΡΙΑΝΟ: Greek, to Hadrian.

τωι θηωι αδριανωι αγαπητωι και αειμνηστωι: Greek, to the never-forgotten and beloved divine Hadrian, a temple dedication written by White.

tic douloureux: neuralgia, an agonising and intermittent pain in the face caused by damage to the trigeminal nerve.

XIII Alderney, Florence, Naples, 1961–63

mod: Timmy Lane was writing between 1964 and 1967, when the British youth culture of mods and their music was at its peak.

Limmits: a meal replacement brand of biscuits sold as a weight-reducing diet.

Lady Docker: an English socialite and serial wife. As well as making public appearances with a gold-studded Daimler to boost her husband's business she and her third husband owned a large yacht called the *Shemara*.

poco curante: Italian, careless. Laurence Sterne used the phrase in *Tristram Shandy* to mean a careless fellow.

White Knight's horse: in Lewis Carroll's *Through the Looking-Glass* (1871) the White Knight rides a horse which wears protective spikes around its hocks, or ankles, to guard against sharks.

Dali: the Spanish Surrealist artist Salvador Dali wore extremely long waxed moustaches.

bel futoro e grande passata: Italian, a good future and a great past.

vi, lei: Italian, you, and she: White was mixing his pronouns.

Urinal Bevan: White is wilfully mispronouncing the name of the Welsh Labour politician Aneurin Bevan, who brought the National Health Service and Welfare State into being in 1945 (see 'Farewell State' above).

bastone: Italian, stick or cane. White's leg was still troubling him.

Silenus: an agéd but vigorous satyr in the company of Dionysius, given to mild debauchery and drunken extravagance.

Consular: possibly in the sense of the sadness of the law seeing robbery being done, but not seeing the human good that the robbery achieved.

XIV USA, 1963–64

winterbourne: a stream that only flows in the winter when the water table is high.

God's most deep decree: from the unnamed poem by Gerard Manley Hopkins beginning 'I wake and feel the fell of dark, not day' (1918).

Index

M

N

O–P